ESSAYS IN

MW01244284

⌣⌡

JAMES WARD

Late Professor of Mental Philosophy at Cambridge
Fellow of the British Academy and Corresponding
Member of the Institute of France

With a Memoir of the Author

by

OLWEN WARD CAMPBELL

CAMBRIDGE
AT THE UNIVERSITY PRESS
1927

James Ward

1911

1843-1925

PREFACE

IN recent years Professor Ward sometimes spoke of publishing a volume of essays and even jotted down a provisional list of titles; but he took no further steps in the matter, beyond leaving directions in his will that none of his writings should be published without our approval. In accordance with this provision, a book on *Psychology applied to Education* has already appeared under the editorship of Professor Dawes Hicks, to whom the bulk of the material for it had been entrusted by the author shortly before his death. From his occasional writings, whether in manuscript or printed in journals, it has fallen to us to make the selection; and for this selection we are alone responsible, though it follows in the main the list drawn up by the author.

We have not included any of the psychological papers which he contributed from time to time to *Mind* and other journals, for it became apparent on examination that these important discussions had been pretty completely incorporated in his *Psychological Principles*. He left behind him great masses of notes for courses of lectures, which shew the thoroughness of his preparation and contain many pregnant suggestions; but they were only material for his own use, and, even when the spoken word was taken down by students, it is doubtful whether any one but the author himself could have worked up the result into a book which would have satisfied him. There are also one or two technical papers, such as that on "Bradley's Doctrine of Experience," published in *Mind* for January 1925; but these are already easily accessible to readers interested in the subject, and their character differentiates them from the contents of the present volume.

This volume of essays is not severely technical; it is in fact 'popular'—as the author would have used that word; it has also, we believe, a certain characteristic unity. It is a series of attempts—of 'essays' strictly so called—to approach the problems of philosophy, to understand their conditions, and to contribute to the solution of some of them. Besides their intrinsic value, the essays form part of the author's philosophical biography. Their composition was spread over the period from 1879 to 1924, and the continuity of the author's thought may be illustrated by comparing the first essay with the last. The former differs somewhat in style from the remaining essays: it is more familiar, perhaps less guarded; but it is the first statement of a line of thought to which he frequently recurred. It was read originally to the Cambridge society known as "the Apostles"; its leading ideas re-appeared in a paper on Faith and Science read to the Synthetic Society and privately printed in the records of the Society, were more fully elaborated in a lecture with the same title given at San Francisco in 1904, and received their most significant expression in the concluding lectures of *The Realm of Ends*.

The following is a record of the provenance of the other papers in the volume. The second essay is an address to the Philosophical Society of the University of Glasgow in 1889, and was published in *Mind* for April 1890. The third is an address to similar societies in Edinburgh and St Andrews in March 1892. It was described by the author as a pendant to the preceding essay but has not hitherto been published. The fourth was written in 1903 and given as a lecture at University College, Cardiff, and afterwards in America. It also has not been published previously. The fifth is an address to the Philosophical Union of the University of California and was published by the University

Press, Berkeley, U.S.A., in 1904. The sixth was written, or at any rate begun, in 1918 and was published after the author's death in *The Monist* for January 1926. The seventh is the Adamson Lecture given in the University of Manchester and published in *The Hibbert Journal* for October 1905. The eighth is the Henry Sidgwick Memorial Lecture given at Newnham College on 9 November 1912; it was published in book form by the University Press and is now out of print. The ninth is a Presidential Address read to the Aristotelian Society on 3 November 1919 and published in the *Proceedings* of the Society. The tenth was read to a discussion society in Cambridge and is now published for the first time. The eleventh is the Annual Philosophical Lecture read to the British Academy on 29 November 1922 and published in the *Proceedings* of the Academy. The last paper was read to the Cambridge Theological Society in 1924 and published in *The Hibbert Journal* for January 1925. To the editors or proprietors under whose auspices the papers appeared which have been already published, thanks are due for permission to reprint them here.

The author's copies of his published papers were in some cases revised and corrected by himself, and the changes he made have been incorporated in the present text. The few editorial footnotes in the volume are distinguished from the author's own footnotes by the signature 'Ed.'

The Memoir with which the volume opens has been written by Professor Ward's younger daughter.

W. R. SORLEY

G. F. STOUT

March 1927

CONTENTS

ILLUSTRATIONS

In their Cambridge Garden during the War

MEMOIR

Aetat. 21

MEMOIR

I

THE life of Professor James Ward is perhaps for several reasons of considerable general interest. Its appeal is not only for those who came under the direct influence of his very unusual personality; it reaches beyond that wider public who are stimulated by his books. It is one of those lives which are of interest to every adventurous spirit because they are in essence a voyage of discovery, where the traveller sets out with no other guide than the pointing compass of his own soul, for an unknown land, and after many conflicts, obstacles and inevitable losses, arrives at his goal. This may seem a highly coloured description of a life which was for more than forty years entirely academic, but forty years was less than half that life. From the dismal back-woods of a narrow Congregationalism, uncultured and Calvinistic, to regions of unlimited speculation, of wide vistas in science and philosophy, and equally wide outlook upon political and social movements, in fact to a quite unusual liberality of thought, opinions and sympathies, is after all a long journey; and it was not an easy one to make. It is true that such journeys were not uncommon in the generation to which he belonged: but they are none the less

instructive and interesting to our own. And Ward had
to contend with two serious handicaps—lack of health
and lack of means.

James Ward, Senior, was an interesting character,
and resembled his son in a good many ways: but he did
not arrive. His life was filled with failures, practical
and to some degree also moral, the consequences of
which were felt perhaps most keenly by others than
himself. Commenting upon a portrait of his parents,
taken in the year 1886, Professor Ward wrote to his
sister: "It is characteristic of the two that in her fore-
head the deepest wrinkles are perpendicular, and in
the father's horizontal: he has *made* the trouble, and
she has *felt* it." Perhaps their son had felt it even more.

This James Ward was a merchant. Son of an idle
and self-indulgent father, he had been well educated
by the special foresight of his grandfather (who came of
a prosperous land-owning stock, in the neighbourhood
of Birmingham) but finding himself without a profession, and being too impatient perhaps to set himself
to acquire one, he rushed into business while very
young, on the strength of five hundred pounds realised
by selling his interest in his grandfather's will. The nail
factory started in this rash manner soon came to an end;
it was his first failure, and it was some time after
followed by his second. After some years of poverty he
entered the glass business, and was soon running a
prosperous trade with India: he married and settled
down in Liverpool. His wife was lacking in education,
but was a woman of high character, deeply religious,
and with a certain energy and fire. Throughout her
long life and his frequent calamities, her loyalty to her
husband was never shaken.

Their eldest child, James, was born at Hull on
January 27th, 1843. In the following twelve years or
so six daughters were born, a son who died, and lastly

another son, Arthur—eventually a Wrangler at Cambridge and Professor at the Canning College at Lucknow.

James Ward, Senior, was a very good father in many respects. He was sincerely devoted to his family, and had every intention of giving them, boys and girls alike, a sound education. But he was also determined himself to make a splash—to be, as he is reported to have said, "a man or a mouse," and though clever, he was devoid of judgment, and quite lacking in self-criticism. He inclined to the speculative. He speculated in scientific inventions—for dredging the Mersey, for searching the sea bottom: he speculated also in religion: and he speculated with money. His religious speculations, unlike the business ones, were not at all dangerous; as in business he assumed the successes he had yet to win, so in theological discussion he naïvely postulated the positions he was setting out to prove. He had a liking for science and a certain gift for it, and he wished to believe in natural laws—but miracles he found easy to reconcile with them. He had certainly the seeds of philosophy: but he philosophised with too much ease. There was nothing very incredible in Jonah's remaining alive for two days in the belly of the whale: for—as he once wrote in a letter intended to allay his son's growing doubts—"the laws of digestion would not be interfered with, for while Jonah was alive no action would be produced on him; the natural effect on the fish would be to turn Jonah out again. There is nothing very hard to believe...." God, in fact, "with amazing condescension" was prepared to do anything according to his own natural laws: what an impressive testimony therefore are the ways of nature to the existence of God!

When his business speculations, which were so much more subversive, had reduced him pretty much to being, unwillingly, "a mouse," he published a book entitled *God, Man and the Bible*, in which his scientific talent and scraps of scientific knowledge led to an intriguing explanation of the Flood.

"The diurnal motion," he writes, "which God gave to the earth, to gather the waters about the equator so that dry land should appear, had only to be suspended, and the waters would return by their gravity to cover the land, the centrifugal force being taken away. A sudden stoppage of the rotation of the earth would have been very disastrous to all things on the surface of the earth, therefore it appears that God brought about the stoppage gradually."

The earth being still, and one side sunless, the Ice Age is also easily explained—"it endured for the 150 days that Noah was in the Ark." When God again set the earth moving there would be of course, what Noah felt, "a wind passing over the earth."

His inventions were not without a certain brilliance. His son had a high opinion of their possibilities, but nothing ever came of them. Trusting to God perhaps for some minor adjustment[1], their inventor failed to perfect them himself.

However, for a good many years all went prosperously. The eldest son was soon recognised as having unusual promise. He was a difficult child, at once hypersensitive and masterful, but adored by the whole family, including an aunt often resident with them. The feminine worship and dependence of six sisters, a mother and an aunt, may have had some undesirable effects upon his naturally dominating character, but he certainly repaid it by a very sincere affection for them all. He was sent for a short time to the Liverpool Institute, and afterwards as a boarder, at the age of eleven, to Mostyn House, Parkgate, a preparatory school

[1] *God, Man and the Bible*, p. 88, *re* gravitation and matter, reads, "These two forces are opposed to each other, and their exact equilibrium, which only God could adjust, is the basis of stability."

for Rugby. At this time his father was very well off, and in addition to his business premises in Bold Street, Liverpool, owned a country house at Crosby. When James wrote home from school for money, he got it. Two years of school life were passed happily and profitably. James was plainly devoted to his father, from whom he often implored a letter. "I arn't very well here without a letter, I think I might have one. Come, now, it is wrong to write on Sunday, but tomorrow write to me."

In June 1856, when James was thirteen and a half, he was suddenly summoned home. He did not know the reason, but on calling at his father's office found the shop full of strangers and his father nowhere to be seen. The business had failed. The conditions of the failure were possibly not of the most excusable, and though the boy did not understand much about the details, the shock of this event ate into his proud and sensitive nature. For himself it meant the end of school life and separation from his companions there. The creditors behaved leniently, and the family managed to get along somehow in a small house at Waterloo near Liverpool. The father got gradually back into some sort of business. James, for two years, had neither schooling nor occupation but what he made for himself. The best his parents could do for him was to give him freedom, and this they certainly did. Waterloo was only a village in those days, and wild stretches of sandhills lay beyond it for many miles. Here he used to wander for hours on end, alone with his own thoughts and the sea birds, in whom he soon began to take a lively interest. His only obligation was to watch for the towel which was hung from the windows of his house when it was wished to summon him back. A very keen delight in nature was his from this time on; solitude bred it in him, for he had been by birth a thorough town child. "I do not like the church here," he had written from Parkgate, "it is so country like with birds flying about." A year or two later, and the birds were his favourite companions. He soon became, without any assistance but his own piercing eyes and keen powers of observation, quite a good ornithologist; he took notes of what he saw, and was planning to write a book on birds, under the impression that none had ever been written! He often spoke in later life of the surprise—not unmixed with disappointment—with which he one day discovered a book on birds in a shop window. He took to reading in the Liverpool library, and soon acquired a considerable knowledge both of birds and plants.

Solitude also developed in him a certain religious optimism, which neither the grim evangelicism of his home, and of his own early manhood, nor the vast inconclusiveness of philosophic speculation, ever succeeded in quenching. When Ward was seventy years old, on the occasion of his portrait being presented to the University of Cambridge, he said of that strange lonely period of his boyhood:

It was here that the optimism began, in those wild wastes absolutely untouched by the hand of man, with no sign of his presence save the ships in the offing speeding out west as the tide ebbed. The scream of the sea-gull, the piping of the ring-plover and the cries of the peewit—to this day the sounds of all others that stir me most—were ever around me. The lovely grass of Parnassus, pimpernel, eyebright and speedwell, the gentian-like centaury and the rare *Pyrola* or winter-green dappled the herbage under my feet; the west wind fanned my cheeks; "the lark was singing in the blinding sky"—all was beautiful, all was good, and I was one with it all. If only I could have got yoked on to some kind traveller and walked in the footsteps of Darwin or Wallace, I might have been strong and happy.

But no such help was forthcoming: he remained the

only one interested in nature in a little society whose absorbing passions were business and sermons. When he was fifteen his father started upon the invention of a special kind of pump, and set his son to make the drawings for it. These drawings were so excellent that the idea occurred to the parents of apprenticing their son to an engineer or an architect, and before he was sixteen he was articled to a firm of architects in Liverpool. There for four years he remained—little interested in his work, but increasingly interested in the political and religious discussions that went on in the office around him. The part he took in these discussions apparently convinced his fellows that he was "cut out for a lawyer or a parson." He started a debating society, began to educate himself as much as possible in his leisure hours, made the acquaintance of a pious young Wesleyan with whom he studied Greek and Logic, took to teaching in the local Sunday school, and by his nineteenth year was beginning to dream of the ministry.

Ward was not of a calibre to do anything by halves. The study of nature was not enough—it had been so much by himself and for himself. Any wide intellectual interests, scientific or artistic, were simply outside his world: clever, ambitious, idealistic, restless, he *must* do something: and something which he felt would benefit his fellow-creatures. In a letter of self-confession which he sent to his minister when seeking admission to the local church, he owned that he had at first felt a hypocrite when he began to teach in the Sunday school. Ardent religious zeal soon swept any such feelings entirely out of his conscious mind. But it is possible— even perhaps probable—that some hidden dissatisfaction with his position continued to depress his spirits and weaken his health for all the years in which he remained an active member of the church. His in-

stinctive way of combating them was to throw himself
still more ardently into the work he had chosen; and
when doubt at last began firmly to root in his mind
it caused him inexpressible pain—the more so because
his passionate intellectual honesty made it impossible
for him to turn away from it for a moment.

For several years, however, his religious enthusiasm
seemed entirely to absorb him. The faith he embraced
—the faith of his home and friends—was a peculiarly
narrow one. We find the youth of nineteen exhorting
the boys and girls in Sunday school to think of the
Judgment, and reflect upon the eternal fires: and
writing to warn his sisters that not the most virtuous
life is of the slightest use for salvation without the direct
intervention of Christ. A faith of this kind—pernicious
in any soil—was particularly harmful for a character
which was naturally dictatorial and critical. The element of hardness in Ward's nature was doubtless encouraged by it, and the habit of judging harshly of
human weaknesses and follies made into a duty. But
he certainly dealt hardly also with himself. Working at
his office all day, he was either studying, preaching, or
helping at clubs and Sunday schools in the evenings.
He was perpetually ill, with colds, and giddiness, and
attacks of headache and sickness, and at one time
feared he was developing consumption. It was in the
middle of 1862 that he first spoke to his father of his
wishes for the ministry. His family were delighted. It
seemed a career truly worthy of the son and brother
who was already in his own home the leading light and
stern authority on most matters. It was decided that
money must somehow be raised to enable him to go
to a Congregational college. Various members of the
family contributed. But Ward had to control his im-
patience—which he did with great difficulty—and work
on by himself at home for a whole year before he was

able to obtain admission to Spring Hill College, near Birmingham (afterwards incorporated in Mansfield College, Oxford). He left the architect's office for good in January 1863. In September of that year, after months of severe study, he went up to Spring Hill and a very new life began.

II

It did not begin however with much *éclat*. Mr Barker, the Principal of the College, was a man of liberal views for his time and position, and when he came to recognise the uncommon ability of his new student, he, and still more Dr Bubier who joined the staff, gave him a good deal of help and encouragement. But to begin with the newcomer may have been rather a puzzle, with his sensitiveness, brusquery, and pride. Many of his fellow-students also were kept aloof by his intense reserve and seriousness; and the fact that he outdistanced them all in class, and was impatient of being kept back to their level, did not tend to improve matters. His poverty was another difficulty, and one which his pride no doubt exaggerated. For the first term he was continually penniless, and would have to write to implore his father for a few shillings to pay for firing or boot-mending. He had at first no carpet in his room, no table, and only one chair. He worked for part of the time at least with the top of a step ladder for a table. The life was a hard one in any case, the students having to clean their own rooms as a rule, and only having such firing as they could afford to pay for. Sunday was often spent walking miles across country from one village to another to take the different services. The country round was open and beautiful, but the love of wild nature seems to have deserted Ward at this stage of his life; he felt lonely and depressed, and his thoughts turned continually towards his home. He wrote to his father and sisters almost daily—and they replied in the usual strain, giving him detailed accounts of the latest sermons, and vague accounts of the state of the business, which was usually bad, but believed to be improving—and telling him of the many friends he had left behind in that queer little narrow society in which he had played a leading part: how the young man who had once gone to the bad, and been helped out by James, and to whom he had written so many helpful and encouraging letters—how he had gone to sea; how the Sunday school classes which had been so attentive under James's ardent teaching were degenerating, how the father's latest invention, a diving-apparatus called the Sea-Searcher, was within an ace of being finished and making a tremendous success; how anxious the sisters were about their souls, and how eager that their wise and wonderful brother should write them all in turn a religious letter, however severe.

"Dear James," wrote his little eleven-year-old sister, Lucy, afterwards the dearest to him of all his family, "supposing I asked God to make me sure I was His and all the time I wasn't.... Please tell me what you call idle words and what singing praises is.... I have such wicked thoughts and horrid feelings, I do pray for them to go away. It says in the Bible that Jesus Christ was tempted as we are yet without sin. Did He have horrid feelings do you think, and it says too that the wind bloweth where it listeth and I do not know what it means.... I have had a nice little book given me; it is called a *Ful Christ for empty sinners*, it is just the book for me."

The brother wrote back the religious letters, full of austere evangelical advice, but sometimes he wrote playful and teasing letters, and sometimes merely grumpy ones—but always he *wrote*. He was very glad when the Christmas vacation took him home again, and when he returned to college, in January 1864, life there began to open out for him vistas into a larger and wiser world.

At this time his father owned a china shop in Bold Street, Liverpool. Business was bad enough, and he was running into debt. His hope was that the situation would be entirely saved by the success of his diving-dress, and he ran further into debt in order to keep on re-modelling it. In the meantime enough was scraped together to make James fairly comfortable, for the whole family were united in the determination that, whatever happened, he must have every possible chance in life. They were a generous family, and through all their financial anxieties they did their best to be hospitable and helpful to their friends and relatives, wherever possible: "so many people and so little money," sighed one of the elder sisters after an un-usually crowded (and servantless) Christmas.

With some necessary comforts, and a room to which he could now invite his friends, Ward settled down to years of steady work. He decided to take the London B.A., in addition to the Arts and Theological course at the College, and he matriculated 1st class in the summer of 1864. During that half year he made several close friendships with men of a culture and width of outlook very different from any he had hither-to known, who like himself were distinguished from the mass of the students by the earnestness of their attitude to life and their life-work. We get from letters a rather touching picture of this little group, Spartan, devout, hard-working, and all so much at peace with respect to their creeds: doubtful at this stage only about the way, never hesitating about the goal. Yet in a very few years, two of them had been driven out of the ministry, one had reacted bitterly against all religious faith, and one was dead. In the meantime they met in one another's rooms, to criticise one another's sermons and discuss their ministerial ambitions, supplying in turn the tea and sugar and bread on which they supped. To Ward it seemed that knowledge, always more knowledge, was the equipment needed. In the intervals of ill-health, he worked incessantly. Quite fearlessly he committed himself to his own truth-seeking intellect, and explored every channel that opened itself: these at first were not very easy of access, for his teachers were somewhat chary of assistance in his explorations—a fact he both then and afterwards resented, perhaps unjustly. He felt he had far to go, for the goal at which he aimed, that position of preacher and teacher, of worker with God, was to him something very great indeed. He sometimes feared the secluded college life would unfit him for work in the larger world: sometimes he even feared he might degenerate from a man of action into a mere book-worm. In February 1864, at the age of twenty-one, he writes to his mother:

My dear Mother,

I'll just tell you where I am—you know what I'm doing. I have had my dinner just half an hour and have been sitting in that easy chair behind me—I am now sitting on a hard one writing at my desk—my room has just been cleaned and everything is in apple-pie order and tolerably comfortable, but I was looking through the window and it is miserably dull, bare, and wintry, not a twig stirring—stay, I just see a magpie shaking its tail at the bottom of the grounds, but now he has vanished, and all is still and lifeless.... I have got through all the hard work of the week and after looking back upon it, look forward to next week—next year and the next five years, and the thought of being here like a monk for a long time made me feel weary and sad. It is a great change from the noise and bustle of Liverpool, from being somebody in Hay's office, from being at home and moving about among friends, to come to this quiet secluded place where I have few friends and no domestic society and stand once more at the bottom of the list.... Again it is a change to have nothing to do on the

Sabbath, I cannot teach in Sunday School, I should be knocked up with walking: I have very little village preaching. ...You may easily see that the influence of college life is not in many respects a good one—shut up with books and students, feeling that one is literally withdrawn from the world—as I feel when I think of you pegging and bustling away in the middle of a busy town, while I am here in the wilderness— and deprived of the means of engaging in works of Christian usefulness, or if not positively deprived of them, they are very much out of reach: under these circumstances students are apt to become very unnatural, very unfair in their opinions and remarks on men and things, very formal and professional in the solemn work they seek to enter upon—Now there is no one more likely to suffer seriously from these things than I: the turn of my mind is such that if I don't take care, I shall be fit for nothing but to play with an inkhorn among book-dust.

Mrs Ward may well have thought that her remarkable son was remarkably hard to please: what was it that he wanted? He wanted to be both at home and in college and also in the world: he wanted to hear oftener from his family: he wanted more money.

"My dear Aunt," he writes in April of the same year, "I am exceedingly displeased that I have not heard at all from one of you since I left home a fortnight ago; and I really should not write now except that I feel sometimes so painfully anxious that I cannot do my work. Since Saturday morning last I have looked expectantly for a letter, and this morning was so much disappointed that from 9 to 11 I did not do half an hour's work. For all I know the business may have gone to the dogs—Pa have broken his legs squeezing into his new-fashioned Eureka, or Mr Barney [alias Ward's sister Polly] turned crazy with novel reading, be barking at the moon and eating coal and cabbage-stalks in the asylum at Tuebrook. From such a state of lamentable ignorance on matters so important and interesting to myself I pray you by some means to deliver me and that by return of post, unless you would compel me to tramp to Liverpool to enlighten myself!"

This unusual silence of a fortnight may have been due to impending calamity. About this time the father's letters which had before been full of advice on the treatment of some text set for a sermon, or discussion of some passage in the Bible, became scarcer and more mundane: business worries loomed larger: father and son discussed the diving-dress in considerable detail: the Deity was mentioned mainly in his relations to this great scheme. "The subject is fraught with danger on all sides," writes James Ward, Senior, "to the Diver, and requires more than common vigilance to see that all is right. I do believe I have been directed by God to understand all things connected with it thoroughly. Praise Him for all the success." But the praise was premature. That summer the poor man was for a second time declared bankrupt, the invention was sold for a few pounds, and may have helped some more practical if less pious inventor to plumb the depths of the sea— as far as its originator was concerned it was not heard of again. The son was at home when this new blow fell, and there is no record of how he took it. The position was saved sufficiently to enable him to continue with his college course, and in October he is back at work again, while his father with a buoyancy almost as remarkable as his instability, has bobbed up in the cotton trade. By the following Christmas all seems much as before, and James is once more corresponding with his sisters about their school life, correcting their exercises, teaching his little brother, and advising and consoling a number of relatives; but henceforth business occupies a chief part in all the family letters, and we see that acute anxiety about his father's affairs is never again long absent from the son's mind, where it conflicts most painfully with a studious and meditative life.

Early in 1865 when skating, of which sport he was very fond, he fell on the ice and hurt his head—how seriously he did not realise for many weeks afterwards, but he suffered in consequence all his life, and particularly during this year, from occasional severe attacks of giddiness. He was poorly most of the spring, and in the summer, to his own infinite disgust and grief, and the consternation of his teachers, he failed in his first examination for the London B.A. He did not brood over this misfortune, and was soon working hard again—sometimes sixteen hours a day—though continually unwell. Early in 1866 he had to return home for a time as the hard life at the college was knocking him up. He was in some ways ready enough to go, for he was discontented with much of the teaching, and though attending a Hebrew class at 7 a.m. felt the days were not filled as they should be. The spirit of the place too was rather flagging, and Ward and several others made great efforts to revive it—instituting debating societies, magazines and so forth. While Ward was studying at home one of the moving spirits in this effort, an intimate friend, died suddenly, and most of the schemes had to be abandoned. Later in the year he took Honours in the London B.A. and when he went back to Spring Hill College for the autumn term, he turned again, for the first time since his boyhood, to the study of science, and began to work for the B.Sc. His Principal had congratulated him early in his college career on his "scientific mode of thought"—he was soon developing this by a keen study of mathematics and physiology, and we find him once more enjoying long rambles in search of birds and plants.

From round about this period the first signs of any change in his religious opinions appear to date, though it was a long time yet before the natural kindliness of natural science got to work on that inhuman creed. Where he still stood in the autumn of 1866 can be clearly seen from a letter describing a visit to an aunt, then dying of cancer. She lived near Birmingham, and it was thought by all her relations that it was the duty of the young would-be minister to visit her, and join them in assuring her that she was not ready to die; an opinion which the poor suffering creature did not share. He too thought it was his duty and in the midst of much hard work went continually to see her.

"I saw Aunt S. on Saturday," he writes on one occasion, "for a little while. Her mind is very dark and she is in no way fit to die, though indeed she is sinking fast and cannot last long. Her one word for God is the Almighty; of the work of Christ she knows nothing; her only business she supposes is to be patient and 'pray to the Almighty to take' her; she does not think she is condemned because she has no fear. Real sorrow for sin she has none, she does not trust Christ, she does not love God, at least not as far as I can see. A despairing look gleamed from her eyes once or twice when I endeavoured to point out the lost state of all without Christ and referred to him as the Rock of Ages."

She died soon after this visit; but James Ward was destined to recover from his Calvinism.

About half-way through his college course Ward reached the stage when he was allowed to accept invitations to preach in different places and be paid for doing so. By this means he eventually earned enough to supply his own most urgent needs, and also to help with the education of his young brother, in whose development he continued for years to take the deepest interest. After considerable struggle and much hard work, and when his creed had widened somewhat, Ward shewed signs of becoming a remarkable preacher —though not perhaps a very popular one. Those who could follow him in his intellectual discourses came away deeply stirred by the clear profound thought, the vigorous delivery, the earnest appeal, and not least by the impressive presence of the young preacher—his

full-toned voice, his tall, thin form and remarkable
head, lit by such piercing and commanding eyes. But
his sermons were not suited to an average congregation,
and the enthusiastic praise of the few did not blind him
to this fact. "I have not warmth, nor imagination, nor
sermonizing tact enough for a preacher," he wrote
once to his father; and again, after reading a sermon
for criticism at College:

I am very sad and unhappy about it. I shall never get on
as a minister, for I shall never make popular sermons. Some
here stigmatized my sermon as an "essay." One good fellow
said he should like to read it three times before he gave an
opinion. Oh how I long to know what my work in life is to be!
I must try to be a College Tutor [he means presumably in a
Nonconformist College]; I should like it very well in some
respects, though it is higher work to be a successful minister.

In 1868, feeling at length that he was getting towards
the end of his long climb up the educational ladder,
with the London B.A. and the first B.Sc. examinations
behind him, he began to think of a wider life—though
still of a life of study: for, as he wrote to a sister who
inquired when would he finish his studies, "I shall
finish my studies when I lose my wits or my vital
spark." He still felt himself insufficiently equipped for
the work of an enlightened and enlightening preacher.
He applied for and obtained the Dr Williams Scholarship, which made it possible for him to go abroad.
He had thought somewhat longingly of Oxford, but
his teachers seem to have feared the sceptical spirit of
the place and to have dissuaded him. In that same
summer of 1868 a college friend of Ward and of his
great friend, Henry Wolstenholme, and like them of a
speculative and philosophic turn of mind, had gone for
a session to Germany, and attended Dorner's lectures
at Berlin. He was carried away by the philosophy of

Hegel, and wrote glowing letters to the two friends about his experiences.

"You will think," writes the young man, "that I have gone Hegel mad—but the truth is I have found him daily nearest to the spring of the great intellectual movement of the present century.... When an infant first begins to see he sees everything double. Are there two things? He must learn by practice to focus his stereoscopic machine, and then he sees everything *solid*. In going into the Hegelian philosophy I feel just as if everything stood out in solid adamantine beauty. What was to me before full of doubt, contradiction and confusion now so far as it is honestly worked out becomes a real living Being.... My few months in Germany have taught me more than all my previous college course.... You, Henry, say that your heart often fails you in the pursuit of truth— I believe that the intellectual expression of faith in the prevailing philosophy and theology is behind the times and one *must* be shaken."

This was just the sort of letter to fill Ward with enthusiasm. *His* heart did not fail him—though he little knew whither he was rushing. He determined to go to Germany, and he left Spring Hill College in the summer of 1869.

The six years that he had spent there had been on the whole happy ones; but they were certainly not so sheltered and secluded as they might have appeared to an outside observer. Neither in mind, nor body, nor in spirit had he ever been at rest. The greatest outward cause of disturbance was of course his home. Ward's relations to his home were somewhat unusual, as the reader may have gathered. It was not only that he was turned to by every member of the family in all business perplexities, rash quarrels and religious doubts, and was regarded by them all as their pride and glory, and his prospective ministry as their dearest hope; it was not only that his father's ceaseless crises and his young sisters' practical and religious difficulties kept him for ever suffering anxiety or writing advice; it was that the family as a whole, himself not least, consisted of difficult, hasty, sensitive characters—and that he loved them all devotedly. The letters that passed between him and his sister Lucy, eight years his junior, and which continued till the time of her death, were written in a spirit of earnest affection and confidence which makes some of them read like love letters: and they had often the playfulness and charm of love letters as well. To this sister, and to two others, slightly senior, to correspond with him, to talk with him, to be near him, seemed the most desirable thing in life. And certainly he for his part eagerly looked forward to their letters and was more or less always lonely when separated from his home, despite the gloom and anxiety that often reigned there. For his father he long retained a true filial affection, attributing his failures mostly to bad luck, and believing him to be a man of genuine goodness and piety—as indeed with nine-tenths of his nature he was. To behold this father involved in almost hopeless debts, and having to mortgage in his own interests the little school which the plucky elder daughters had started, imperfectly educated though they were, and to have himself to continue for years in part dependent on him, all this was indeed a painful matter to the eldest son, struggling on year after year to fit himself for what he believed to be the highest of callings. He was acutely aware also of the hardships of his mother's life—a mother whose own mother's misfortunes had been the cause of her being herself, to her great distress and humiliation, uneducated—so uneducated that she would sit and weep because she hardly knew how to reply to the intimate, eloquent, affectionate letters her clever son so often wrote her.

In addition to the anxieties and preoccupations about his home, Ward was constantly troubled by his

2-2

own delicate health, and by the severe ordeals of continual examinations—ordeals which almost always reduced him to a state of physical collapse, overtaxed as he was by incessant and often feverish study, and spare living. There was also added the restless torment of self-questioning and self-reproach, of vain struggles with his hasty temper and proud will, and consequent remorse and despondency. For he shared with his father and sisters that curious faculty for seeing clearly, and suffering deeply from, faults which seemed nevertheless to be ineradicable. When the sisters confessed themselves to him their prevailing tone was often one of hopeless but perfectly honest self-condemnation. You will be ashamed of us for all these weaknesses, they would say, and we are miserable about them—but for all that, you must know us as we are. The same determination to find and face the truth about himself was rooted even more deeply in the brother's nature—and the same inability to alter. And he too in rare moments confessed himself to the dearest of his sisters or to his close friend, Wolstenholme. More often no doubt he sought comfort from his religion—but already by the end of his Spring Hill course this comfort was becoming harder to find.

His family feared nothing for him as yet, and sent him off to Germany confident that he would soon realise the great wish of their lives—on which they had staked so much. In Spring Hill College itself he left others, both students and teachers, almost equally devoted and confident—men who had found him with all his faults, his reserve and irritable pride and fits of coldness, an inspiring influence as well as an intimate friend. One of these in particular, Henry Wolstenholme, gave himself up entirely and with passionate admiration to a friendship which had matured through their college course together, and which continued, much changed, and in sad enough circumstances, to the end of his long life. To Wolstenholme the very ground on which he stood seemed to be the faith which he shared with his friend. What doubts they had had so far had been shared in common, and resolved in common. When Ward set sail for Germany the object of life for both was to fight together in the army—a newly equipped and enlightened army—of Christ. This is how Wolstenholme wrote to him a few weeks after he had reached Berlin:

If I might ask anything of God for myself—and yet it would not be altogether for myself for I should be worth more to others, I think it should be that I might share with you the difficult but glorious warfare; that hand in hand we might go forth in divine strength, "for the help of the Lord against the mighty," giving mutual encouragement and inspiration. A thrill of longing, nay almost of prophetic hope, passed through me as I read [i.e. in Ward's letter] what my consciousness of differences and of our relative positions would hardly allow me to think without the assurance of words, that such a union of heart and hand, of work and warfare, would also realise wishes and dreams of yours.

But in reality the turning-point in his friend's life had come, and he was to pass in the next few years not only far from that union of heart and hand, but out of reach of old beliefs and old ambitions.

III

Ward settled in the Dom Candidaten-Stift in Berlin, a college for young German ministers to which foreigners were sometimes admitted. He conducted English services in various chapels, attended functions at the Court, which patronised the Dom Stift, went to the lectures of Dorner and Trendelenburg, and read philosophy. It was not long before his father began to be uneasy. "Don't let philosophy lead you into 'By-path meadows'—depend upon it you will have to come back and take up your 'roll.'. . . You appear to be in some difficulty about the inspiration of the Scriptures. I see no difficulty in it myself." His son was not quite so ready as of old to discuss his problems, even with so confident a guide: he admitted that he was in suspense on several points which might make the pastorate impossible to him, but he reiterated that his heart's desire was still as ever "to do something to serve the Church of Christ." The sisters had to put up with getting fewer "religious letters"—though when these came they were as eloquent, and perhaps even more earnest than before. Sometimes the note of personal pain and misgiving breaks out, as in these words to his sister Lucy:

I have read your last letter many times, and always with very mixed feelings—sadness at the forgetfulness and distrust of God which it reveals and which have occasioned the despairing tone of so much of it. . . . Instead of going to God through Christ you are living alone. . . . You talk of not being able to believe in Christ as you ought as if it were necessary for you to produce a certain degree of faith in yourself before Christ would accept you. . . but he has said "Whosoever cometh to me him I will no wise cast out. . . ." You do not see the simplicity of the message.

These words are sincere enough, but the simplicity of the message was at the same time provoking sheets upon sheets of argumentative, wavering, desperate letters between Ward and Wolstenholme. The intellectual life into which Ward was plunged was an intense stimulus—conversations with Dorner, lectures or talks with other students, all these thrilled him. "In a state something between sleeping and waking," he writes on December 22nd, 1869, "I wrote the foregoing sheet so long ago as Saturday last. Since then I have been so far enamoured of philosophy as to lack courage to break from it." Yet he continued to feel that philosophy was betraying him. His belief in the verbal inspiration of the Scriptures he easily renounced —he had indeed renounced it before he left England; the philosophical difficulties of conceiving immortal life were his next obstacle, and the problems of the relation between mind and matter began to press upon him.

The immortality of the individual is a vexed question—and as the difficulty springs from a psychological ground so do also my doubts as to the distinction of matter and mind. I cannot find both, and as matter seems to make at times the best claim to be all, I have no foundation for an examination of Christianity, which, however, taken by itself apart from presupposition for its establishment to the reason, I accept very cordially. In fact I am like a man who has got a right formula and finds it serve him well, but he cannot work out the proof. I could go smoothly enough empirically and contentedly if it be *proved* that the empirical way is right, but I want something *proved*, a foundation somewhere. Tossed to and fro I seem as if I had lost the power to believe, and this is the real danger.

And again he writes a few months later:

Thanks, many thanks, for your timely words about the sort of proof possible to a soul in doubt about religious matters. ... Christianity satisfies with practical proofs—but the *reine Vernunft* she satisfies not. And oh I have starved my soul in seeking food for the reason—it is a very waste, bleak and cold. But I have chosen my path, and there is no return: a sceptical spirit once evoked cannot be hushed, it must be accompanied on its wanderings till it find rest. Yet happily I think the worst is over. I almost think I see how I shall come out, and feel now more at a loss for a method. As to the relation of mind and matter, I said in my last that uncertainty here deprives me of a basis for the examination of Christianity. But here my unsound method exposes itself. I spoke under the feeling that I had to elaborate a philosophy before proceeding to deal with a revelation because philosophy deals with the presuppositions of a revelation, e.g., the existence of God, the possibility of a criterion of truth etc., etc. And logically this is the true order but chronologically it is the false. When we hush the buzzing within and listen to the two voices, the cry of Reason for a philosophy and the call of Christ for admission to the heart—mighty instincts bid us attend to the latter first. Verily I have been attempting creation—O fool that I am— my problem has been, "Given nothing, to construct everything"—to start in chaos by making my own instruments and from thence and with these to find out God.

But he seemed only to get further and further into that waste of which he speaks and of which Wolstenholme had once said: "As Christ is life, so to part from him would be death. What blank and desolate misery to have for the sole occupation of one's religious faculties —Silent worship at the altar of the Unknown and the Unknowable!"

"I feel it is absolutely necessary for me," Ward wrote again in February 1870, "to study for some time in quiet, and free from all doctrinal restraints, and the ministry is incompatible with this. My sympathy and my hopes are with the Evangelical section of the Church, but I can serve it best in retirement I feel sure.... The only thing I have now to say that can be said in a pulpit is 'Let thy light shine.' If men would only show that Christianity is a life instead of using the phrase as a mere shibboleth, Vogt and Moleschott, and Taine and Mill would disappear."

But giving up the ministry meant giving up any clear aim in life for Ward, and the uncertainty of his future preyed upon him.

My present longing is for rest—I am out in an ocean of darkness where neither sun nor stars have for many days appeared: the whole horizon round in turn seems at every point to be brightening for the dawn, but all is cheating fancy. In the world there is plenty for me to do, if only I had mental rest, nor am I afraid of finding my level and my work, but I'm uncertain how to begin. Dr Simon tells me I am a pan-

theist. Dorner has said to me, "You are on the best way to
Rome"; a Unitarian student here has invited me to preach
for his people in England...the fellows here laugh at me
sometimes and call me *ein grosser Ketzer* and yet think my
scepticism the most harmless in the world so long as I retain
religious faith and feeling. Mrs Davies...is a religious mystic
and in our Sunday evening talks we are often agreed, while
Davies assails our dreams about life in Christ and future glory
from the standpoint of common sense—in fact I am everything
in the wide world but Evangelical.

Continuing still through all these struggles "enamoured of philosophy," he determined at the close
of the session at Berlin to attend Lotze's lectures at
Göttingen. He had made several true friends in
Berlin, whom he was loth to leave: he had even been
invited to become pastor of the American Chapel there.
But as he had said, there was no stopping in mid-stream.
Poor Wolstenholme for his part, in melancholy in-
activity, was watching his faith slip from him. He had
already decided that the ministry was not for him, and
having nothing to put in its place his whole life seemed
—as indeed in some ways it proved to be—henceforth
without a clear purpose. *His* misery was of the same
nature as his friend's, but more unalleviated.

"I am sitting," he writes one Sunday, "in my own little
home amid Sabbath stillness with sweet flowers by me and
summer beauty all round—yet even the sense of Sunday
brings with it something of melancholy reflection. It gives
a lost and lonely feeling of void to think of the Christian world
at worship, the Christian world at work, and to feel a shadow
thrown over one's fellowship and sympathy with those we
have regarded as the salt of the Earth, to whose faith and
zeal we have looked for the regeneration of the world. Yes,
you may well say 'my faith in Christianity is still great' and
I say it with you. I will cling to it till it is torn from me, and
in the bewildering vacancy of that bereavement I hardly
think I should care to live. It is hard to clear away the wreck

of what hitherto has made up life, given to it its significance and hope, and to form a new and chilling view of the world and of oneself, to feel that to be here, and to be a man is so different a thing from what we had ever thought it."

Much of the vast correspondence between Ward and his friend was taken up with Wolstenholme's prospects —or lack of prospects. In spite of all we find Ward strongly urging him to remain in the ministry. His reasons for this were sound enough. The contradictoriness and unwillingness of his own position had been increased by what he had seen of life in Germany. He had been very much shocked by the materialism, the vice, and the irreligion that he saw everywhere in Berlin, the militarism and monarchic pomp had shocked him too, and he already acknowledged a fear that Germany was set upon a ruinous course. At the same time he was deeply impressed by the sheer superiority of real learning and knowledge that he found there. More and more clearly he felt that if Christianity was to survive it must be through a tremendous broadening of the Churches, and that far more able minds must take up its defence. In one letter he describes at length the condition of things in Berlin—where he found neither missions nor charities, nor Sunday schools, nor any real Christian life, only efficient bureaucracy.

"In the midst of all this," he writes, "it would be a supreme consolation to know that after all things were mending, though slowly still mending. The prospect of a break-down of our modern civilisation is distressing enough to contemplate. ...I long to know which way things are going. The question has pressed upon me ever since I came here. Of course once Apologetics were to be the great restorers of the power of the church, but I am not so sanguine now of leaven of this ingredient alone."

He felt more and more certain that the one hope for religion was by noble living and fearless thinking to establish it on a foundation that mere sceptics could never shake.

"Who are to be the initiators of this better state of things," he asks, "if those who see the effeteness of the old retire because their opinions no longer square with modes of thought they have outgrown? A call to the ministry is in the resolve of the whole soul devoutly and unreservedly to consecrate and concentrate its whole being and influence to advancing the highest good of man and the glory of God....Such a calling is not to theological dogmatizing....I say to you what I would say to myself—go on, find out all the truth you can, and live out and press on others all you find: if you who can at least handle those difficulties turn tail at the sight of them, who is to guide the untrained and illiterate when these very difficulties are urged upon them as signals that Christianity is no more and the era of the Religion of the Future is to begin?"

Ward was not, then, without a mission, however undecided he might be as to its form, when he prepared to leave Berlin and explore further into philosophy. But he still found no rest—the vision was ever changing —and changing ever, it seemed, for the darker.

"Now," he writes, "about James Ward and Pantheism. I believe if everybody had their right name he would have been called a pantheist for the greater part of the past six months. The intellectual foundation has long been laid... always dabbling in philosophy, reading in its history one after another various ontologies, Schleiermacher's *Glaubenslehre* (a wonderful book), uncertainty as to a future life, these have absorbed both energy and thought while the soul's truest instinct and the light that comes from action have been first neglected, then lost. And yet looking into the matter as an outsider it seems to me that this path lay inevitably before him and yet he has trodden it so as to increase his guilt.... My faith has not been wholly eclipsed, but how near it I can't say. I have experienced an approach to utter spiritual death...not directly referable to my course of thought but only indirectly through the changed attitude all has

assumed in consequence of this. Can I ever again compact
my shattered self into a definite ego whose mind shall reflect
the mind of Christ? Probably an ill-defined view of the world
that grew up like a weed in my soul did more harm than anything else.''

And again:

if you can realise an individual with no proper faith in his
personal immortality feeling that too this life was so far largely
a failure, with no doubt as to the Divine Personality but as
much of Spinoza as possible along with this, admitting the
ethical worth of Christianity but uncertain as to anything
else in it, and living where it has but the merest name to live
while in truth it is dead indeed, then set me in his place and
think again and you will perhaps divine better than I can tell
you the black chronic misery of the last three months.

And so he went to Göttingen, and came under the
magnetic influence of Lotze, an influence destined to be
permanent not so much in the way of definite doctrines,
but rather for some leading ideas and perhaps in the
general attitude to philosophical problems.

Lotze combined the interests—scientific, philosophical, and religious—which were struggling in Ward's
mind and which dominated his career. He empha-
sised the exact methods of science and defended
their applications to phenomena of all kinds: he stood
for mechanism as against the methods of the Hegelian
idealists. At the same time he maintained that mechanism did not explain reality: reality could not be understood without taking into account aesthetical and
moral values. Hence the fundamental characteristic
of his thought appealed to Ward who was equally alive
to the demands of exact science and to the claims of
moral and religious values. It is possible also that
Lotze's emphasis on the idea of personality diverted
Ward's mind from pantheism—though it is hard to believe that pantheism could have taken permanent hold

of a man whose temperament was so thoroughly individualistic. Lotze may also have directed his study to
Leibniz and monadism. By Lotze, as well as by Herbart
and the Herbartians, Ward was considerably influenced
in working out his psychology[1].

A few weeks after reaching Göttingen Ward is
writing once more, in a slightly more cheerful tone,
on the subjects which were ceaselessly occupying the
minds of himself and his friend, and which had indeed recently provoked a serious quarrel—if brief—
on the score of his apparent pantheism. "God alone
essentially exists, matter and mind are only through
him—all that is is a modification of God. And here
I am now, and here I am likely to stop, and my business some day must be to elaborate the whole. This is
a sort of pantheism, but it is a long way off being
materialism." But obviously upon this course any
sense of the personality of God was likely to grow dim,
and this he clearly felt to be the most serious danger.
"My position is wrong somewhere," he wrote, "for
it threatens to exclude personal communication with
God from the world altogether."

Before the close of the summer session in Göttingen
the Franco-Prussian war broke out. The students departed, lectures ceased, and Ward decided to make his
way home. By this time he had come to be very fond
of many Germans in both universities, and to feel a
considerable affection and esteem for the country as a
whole—which he never quite lost. The rumours and
signs of war which met him on his way home made a
lasting and painful impression upon him.

By the middle of August he was in England again,
and visiting his old teachers and counsellors at Spring

[1] For this passage on Lotze's teaching, as also for subsequent
passages describing my father's works and philosophical ideas,
I am deeply indebted to his old friend, Professor Sorley.

Hill College in the hope of receiving some definite help and advice as to his future. The prospect was anything but cheering. On every side men who were honest thinkers were leaving the churches—heart-broken in many cases, but leaving none the less. A close friend of Ward's had been forced to abandon his pastorate at Shrewsbury: several others of his college companions were in similar difficulties. The thinkers who remained in the church were using discretion almost to the point of paralysis. Ward put his case clearly before his advisers; he was not without schemes.

I feel I have two impulses, one that springs from my individuality mentally and that is to pursue a certain line of study, and here my first love Natural Science would receive a large share of my regard and the question here would be how to resolve the present general laws of Physics into a higher—in short what might be called cosmology philosophically considered. But another question that has more recently put in its claim is to make good the position and claims of Christianity against all opposition of the day, and to work out the lines of an apology for Christianity...that shall rest on first principles. And then again I feel at times a sort of enthusiasm for the Elijah life—so to style it....I have in the first case what I feel is my calling according to nature, my bent, in the second the call of the ages as it shapes itself to me, and in the third case, I don't know, perhaps I seal my death warrant in saying it—it may be the invitation of Christ to be an instrument in a possible spiritual awakening—it may be mere enthusiasm. ...Shall I after all turn to science and revel in its delights and try to unfold something more of the glories of nature, and unlike other inquirers proclaim Nature as a Revelation of God, and by living a Christian life though retired shew that Science and Faith can go together?...What I might do in Science I don't know, not more than an average brain and strong predilection can do of course. It is quite certain that the predilection exists and I trace it back to my childish inquiries, and see it in my father. As to the second case it wants a man of very marked abilities and considerable scholarship—a man with not only philosophic acumen but a rarer gift, philosophic breadth, so that in going deep he may not forget to range far;—yet still a life spent in this direction might do something to prepare the way or gather materials, but where and how am I to set about such a work? As to the third case, my prayer has often been that it may not be said of me, "Once I would but you would not, now it is hid from your eyes."

Those familiar with Ward's mature work will possibly recognise in it something of a synthesis between the first and second of the aims here vaguely outlined, and they may feel also how the natural predilection for science gave to the philosopher that rare gift—the power to go both *deep* and *far*. In the meantime however it was the third of his dreams which seemed to be the one destined for realisation.

The reply of his directors to this and similar appeals, written and spoken, was not very encouraging. They were not sure if they desired him to remain at Spring Hill to continue his only too thorough studies, as he wished. One patriarch suggested that he should study in Germany, supporting himself by journalism at the rate of £5 a month. In general they seem to have felt they would like best to keep this powerful personality in the church, if only he could be tamed: but they feared that untamed he might bring discredit upon their institution. They really didn't know what to do.

Ward felt very bitterly that not a hand was held out to help him: he no doubt exaggerated a little, as was his wont when angry, the indifference of the College tutors, who after all were themselves, poor men, in no very easy position. This is his account of an interview in a letter to his sister Lucy:

Their conduct may be put so: *College* Do you believe as we believe? *J. W. Jr.* No. I believe the New Testament, but I don't believe the creeds. *College* Sir, please to walk out at

that back door: we commend you to the devil, although we
are very sorry for you. Your readiest way to find him will be
by hanging yourself and to this course we recommend you.
J. W. Jr. We shall meet again at Philippi. Heaven reward
your charity and help me.—There, I have no doubt they
mean well, but the above is the impression they made on me.
How often I have wished I had never known Spring Hill
College, and how earnestly do I wish it now. And yet folks
look upon me as decidedly above the average, which only
makes my annoyance the greater, for if any life is left in me
after such a course of mental suffocation and repression what
might I not have hoped for where my mind had been stimulated and fostered?

His attitude—as Wolstenholme pointed out to him—
was not quite reasonable. An evangelical Foundation
could hardly be expected to continue to assist anyone
with views so unsettled as Ward's were at this date.
His real distress was probably owing to the fact that at
heart he was still very loth to give up the idea of the
ministry. He had aimed at it and toiled for it for eight
years, and he could not yet believe that no church
broad enough could be found or made, which he could
fitly serve.

The pastorate at Cambridge, which had been practically offered to Ward before he went to Germany, was
still vacant: the congregation had as a matter of fact
waited with its eye upon him. In October 1870 he was
invited to preach there for a month, and he accepted.

His general views on the connection of philosophy
and Christianity and the idea of a Christian Church
without rigid doctrines found full expression in a long
letter he wrote to Wolstenholme, immediately after his
return from Germany, from which I take the following
extracts:

Aug. 25th, 1870.

...I got home here on Friday night (i.e., from Germany).
My mother, about whom you kindly inquire, is much better

than she was a year ago, though a good deal depressed with the state of my father's business, which is very bad indeed just now. She cried when I told her it was possible I should return to Germany: she said, "You are 27 now and I looked years and years hoping to see you something and now I never shall." My father is also troubled about it, and tries to persuade me "to settle," thinking that then I shall soon be right. He wants to know what my difficulties are and is confident that he can resolve them, or at any rate that they would be no difficulties to him.

He then continues to discuss at length, and in the light of his own struggles, Wolstenholme's altered prospects and spiritual uncertainties.

Do you not believe that the world has known many noble lives, that at least a large proportion of mankind are capable of being influenced for good? Let what will come of original sin, moral depravity is a fact, and so is moral regeneration, let doctrines of grace be what they may. It is possible then it seems to me to determine in what the worth of men consists and to increase that worth in ourselves and in others;...it seems to me there is ground for starting in the way I suggest, and also for a ministry for the moral regeneration of men.... A system of truth is not the first thing to seek; no, not even a theory of knowledge...it is I think, though I cannot enlarge here, possible to fix this point that a life which realises the broad lines of Christ's and a society pervaded by the spirit of Christianity are generally the ideals of men individually and collectively....The doctrines held by Christians will I believe undergo a process of developing and purifying and supplementing through all time, a complete system of Christian truth and philosophy is as little to be expected as an exhaustive science and philosophy of nature—nay less to be expected...and till it can be shewn possible to set God and man in a higher moral light than that in which Christianity sets them, or to have ethical principles higher than such as flow from the Christian representation of God and Man and their relation to each other, so long will it be safe to say Christianity is the absolute religion. A religion which says,

as Christianity does, God is love, Love is the bond of per-
fectness, the Christian is a law unto himself etc., etc. admits
of development in forms and doctrines, but I can't see that it
fails in anything. Its very absoluteness leads me to expect to
find it in any one time and people one-sided and imperfect.
And according to my present way of thinking I should apply
this remark to the Apostles and their time among the rest....
    ...To me it seems Christianity tells a man his worth, his
position and his goal, but it does not further do more than
supply the main principle of action. There is still room for
what one might call a science of life: Christianity no more
supplies this than it does a code of morals....The great
essential principles of Christian truth are obscured by human
expositions and applications of them, and by their complex
working and inter-working in history. It is the same in
nature. Who sees one plan in every class of mammalia? who
sees but the consequences of three simple laws in all the
varieties of motion? If a few of the 'shalls' and 'shall nots'
of the New Testament were changed for once into 'musts' and
'cannots' and this made good by shewing the necessary connection between these and the nature of God and Man, a new
light would be let into many minds and they would see a new
worth in Christianity....I cannot but think that a Newton in
Theology would be a blessing to the world....
    Working among natural phenomena a very respectable
section of mankind believe they have established certainly a
number of laws of nature. Here we learn that men's faculties
are so far trustworthy that they deduce results afterwards
verified by a reference to the data. And will you say that the
sphere of moral things is an absolute chaos? I grant here progress has been smaller, but this is explainable without tossing
up the whole in despair. Now on the one hand it is as useless
to refer the deductions of Science to the senses, as on the other
it is impossible to deny that there are facts of the inner world
quite as certain as, nay far more certain than, the facts of the
outer world. Now it is with these highest generalities and
their relations among each other that Philosophy has to deal.
How then can you say "it is as much a matter of probability
as any other region of truth"? To begin by seeking the worth
of 'objective standards' is a mistake in method. The most

immediate knowledge we have is that of our own mental
states—of ourselves: on the analogy of ourselves we build our
knowledge of things without....So knowledge grows, one
part acting and interacting with another....Is it not possible
so to connect knowledge with knowledge without a break as
at last to see in the Macrocosm such a resemblance to the
Microcosm that it shall be recognised as the expression of a
Mind, whose image we bear?....A realistic idealism may yet
prove the solution of philosophy. Anyhow the talk of *objective* standards involves an enormous assumption. Whence
the right to that word '*objective*'? Is there not a theory of the
world assumed in its very propounding at the outset? We
have no business with that yet. There are laws of evidence on
which men agree and not a few valid ideas, let us work
scientifically in sorting the material before us and building
up the Sciences, then critically in the discussing of their
principles, ground ideas and results. Who says that such a
notion as purpose has not helped to explain much in the
world? Grant that it be subjective. Still it helps us on. Does
not the like hold of worth, a far more difficult idea, and many
others?...Let all be provisional, yet if a whole, a perfect
cosmos results at last who shall say then that these ideas are
mere tools?...It is because our savants work with one eye,
without perspective and chiaroscuro that they present us with
those flat Egyptian pictures of the world with which no soul
can rest content. But get both eyes at it, let the notions of
worth and end play their part, and you may have a stereoscopic photograph of the whole, united and complete. How
then about the objective standard? Nobody wants it here,
nobody believes it possible there. Thought and its object
must ever be distinguished but when both are found to be
thoughts they may perfectly agree.

...I have my own notions and feelings about the ministry.
I quite expect I shall try your charity and that of others some
of these days and shew myself very inconsistent, yet all I have
said has been the expression of my feeling as to a matter in
which so far as act goes I have been unfaithful. My impulse,
except when alas I have fallen below myself, has ever been to
do something for the highest good of men, something to help
on the world's true progress. Speculative doubts have often

weakened this, but cannot stand against facts. "There is a worth in man, he is bad and can be made better: ground for action cannot be far to seek and is it wise to wait till this be brought into connection with a philosophy? It is already my conviction that a doctrinal reformation is needed. To be sure I am in terrible uncertainty just now, but it cannot be that I shall never find the light of day again.... Granted my views, where determined, are against those of the people among whom I minister, but it is my business and my responsibility toteach them, not to preach what they dictate. Why then may I not hope to find my work even yet where I thought to?" So I have soliloquised often enough, and so spoken to you, and if I do not act consistently with this it won't be because I cease to feel thus, but because I yield to a temptation which has long been strong and to which perhaps I have listened more of late, the temptation I mean to seek the walks of Science and Natur-philosophie.

A month later he went on his trial to Cambridge and preached a series of sermons on the text "God is Love" which so shocked one or two of the congregation, and so deeply moved a number, that they remembered them all the rest of their lives. One feels it was indeed a risky venture. He certainly did try the charity of several persons: his inconsistencies were many: his secret hankerings after the life of a student would not be quelled: as for *teaching*, rather than preaching what his flock dictated—the idea was excellent, but he had surely forgotten that a democratic control is one of the foundation stones of Nonconformity. "Now mind," wrote a certain postmaster or gas-fitter, one of his prospective flock when he was finally called to Cambridge, "you are invited on the distinct understanding that you believe that the Death of Christ was for the purpose of expiating the sins of men."

Before actually accepting the call Ward suffered a good deal of inward storm, culminating—it might interest some of the 'modern psychologists' to know—in a fearful nightmare, in which, in conflict with some mysterious opponent, he broke a chair, damaged the wall of his room, roused and frightened the sleeping inmates of Spring Hill College by beating on his door with the broken chair leg, and finally "struggling with the wretch on the floor," twisted his own clothes and his carpet into one inextricable mass, in which state they were discovered in the morning, while Ward himself, ill and trembling, was found with a smashed knuckle and a bruised foot. Encounters of this sort (though never again so violent) happened at intervals all through his life—to the alarm and subsequent amusement of himself and his children: and it must be admitted that the enemy often took the form of the devil.

Overriding all obstacles, and inward misgivings, whether wise or foolish, Ward definitely accepted a warm invitation from the Cambridge congregation, and began his work there in January 1871. The leading spirit in his chapel was Mr William Bond, "a fine specimen of an earnest, honest, manly Christian tradesman....I could work with him splendidly." The Bond family on their side took the greatest interest in their dangerous new minister and shewed him every kindness. Unfortunately Mr Bond, who had been the chief means of getting him to Cambridge, and to whose intellectual and highminded religious conceptions the young pastor's sermons were bread and wine, was not the congregation. This was, as Ward wrote,

a very peculiar one—many of the people are just those you meet with in any country-town, narrow, ignorant and old-fashioned...others have come into contact with the thinking of the time, know what is stirring in the minds of men and have brushed against University people...then we have all the Scotch in Cambridge with us, and there are a good many of them, travelling tailors for the most part....Some poor people, a few disaffected Baptists and a sprinkling of students [undergraduates] completes the medley....How am I to cement such a mixture?

Mr Bond had hoped that a broadminded and intellectual ministry would bring the chapel more into touch with the life of the University: he had reckoned without the more militant section of Nonconformists. Difficulties soon began—mostly at first in Ward himself. He was hypersensitive to the unfriendly element in his flock, he was indignant to find himself regarded by some, as he put it, "as public property," and he was only too much aware of the growing conflicts in his own mind. "Our friend, Mr Ward, has got wrong again," wrote Mr Bond to Wolstenholme in the middle of the year, "if he *will* throw us up, why he must—he's an awful lot of trouble, and yet he's worth it." Mr Bond "was determined not to let him go if he could possibly help it"; while Mrs Bond, who had become a devoted and intimate friend of his, did all she could by wise and spirited appeals to reconcile him to himself and to his work.

Thus the first crisis in August 1871 was tided over, and he set himself with renewed determination to his task. One of his sisters came to keep house for him— a veritable opening of the gates of Paradise for her, out of her cramped existence—and the autumn began favourably enough. But soon the unsatisfactoriness of the whole position shewed itself in a practical way. Appeals were being made to the Nonconformist body all over the country to help in building a new chapel for their important centre in Cambridge. The question soon arose: what teaching are we asked to support?— if this new Cambridge minister is a heretic, as rumour says he is—why should we build a new chapel for him to spread false doctrine in? Letters began to come in— "Do you believe in...etc., etc., etc. If not I shall not subscribe to your Chapel." Ward had by this time gained a considerable reputation and attempts were made by certain opponents to expose him in the *Independent Press*. Kind inquiries about the state of his opinions poured in upon him: some of them, it is possible to affirm, he answered with extraordinary patience and forbearance, but the fever of his proud spirit under all this can well be imagined. "It troubles me a good deal to have to make the following communication to you," wrote one of his flock, "viz., that I feel impelled to absent myself for the most part from your Ministry because I believe that your pulpit discourses are calculated to disparage the word of God." "I narrowly watched all your sermons and prayers," wrote another, "and there was nothing in them (except an occasional allusion to Christ's sonship) which might not have been said by a Unitarian." Disapproval sometimes expressed itself, both in Cambridge and when he was preaching elsewhere, by members of the congregation "rustling out." Mr Bond became very much worried, and wrote frequent letters, affectionate, admonishing, scolding, encouraging, irritated letters, to try and convince Ward that the greater part of his congregation clung to him and that the work he was doing was the best possible. He took him to task for being somewhat inhuman, and for being impatient of the narrow and commonplace elements in his congregation whom it was his special calling to teach. But Ward doubted it more and more, and his eye and his heart strayed ever oftener to the studious College courts and the vast possibilities of the University Library.

I have wished till I am tired of wishing that it were not too late for me.... You know what a trial it is to me to be here, seeing every day new proofs of the golden opportunities I have lost.... If I had come up here four years ago I might have got through safely. It is a great disappointment to me that I have

no time for study...my congregation is very ordinary, intellectually—I get no advantage of the University beyond the
air of the place. Pastry cooks are said to fatten in steam,
perhaps I may get culture and discipline from jostling gowns-
men on the pavement. I do not think I shall stay here long.
I will not leave the people in a worse plight than I found them
in—but my work is not preaching, and if I keep long at it I
shall lose for ever the chance of humbler but more congenial
work. I am too selfish, too cold, too dreamy, too lazy for a
life requiring so much self-denial, tender sympathy, prompti-
tude and perseverance despite discouragement.

He resolved to take any opportunity that offered for
studying at the University, but as he threw himself with
zeal into his ministerial work the opportunities never
came. "My work is hard," he wrote to his father, "but
I am more helped than I thought, and feel very much
my responsibility. I shall not get on fast: it will be well
if I do not exhaust the patience of the people." But,
as he confessed often enough to Wolstenholme, "the
greatest evil, and the real source of my weakness is my
heresy, which in certain directions is fast hardening
into shape...the question is whether I ought on this
account to abandon a denomination whose watchword
is Progress." And again:

I have certainly no special anxiety to identify myself with
the Unitarians and this not from any want of sympathy with
their intellectual position generally considered but because I
shrink from their coldness and worldliness of life, and feel
further that there is so much truth in the notion of one organic
unity and growth in the Christian Church as to justify me in
looking for progress within the Church and not without it—
not that I exclude Unitarians but yet they seem rather an
offshoot than part of the parent stem. Have you seen Matthew
Arnold's Article in the *Cornhill*?...What he says of the false-
ness of the antithesis "natural and revealed religion" accords
exactly with my thinking. All true religion is natural...all
truly natural religion is revealed. The two are one and their

proper antithesis is the artificial, the manufactured, the religion of creeds and formulas.

You see whereabouts I am: too heretical in theory for the Evangelicals, too evangelical practically for the Unitarians. There is but one place where I should be at home, i.e. in the *Broad* Church section of the Church of England, and from this, having a conscience as yet unschooled in casuistry, the XXXIX articles forbid me. Of course I don't want to push my opinions down folks' throats *nol. vol.* The question is then, shall I get a hearing? Will there really be a broad Church amongst us? O Weh! O Weh! es ist eine böse Aussicht!

He was far from happy, though he continued to find much of his work "very enjoyable."

"Many of the people here," he wrote to his father, "are very kind and very much attached to me, it will cause some of them great pain if I leave. It makes my heart sick to think of the trouble I may give to them and to you, but as I can make neither party understand my position I must leave it to time alone to defend the course I take.... The Bonds, without exception the kindest people I ever met, are in such a commotion. They are very broad in their views, and cannot see that I do wrong to remain."

To his sister Lucy he wrote still more unreservedly:

I am a minister among strangers, and not perhaps strangers merely but suspecters too in many cases. I do not care either for death or life, what I prize is truth. Sometimes I feel that I could almost shout to God and ask for but one sign that I am right—but I know it is foolish, even sinful. "Do and thou shalt Know"—But oh it is weary work. I feel it already—to talk and talk and neither to live as I preach myself nor to make others do so. One naturally despises a man who spends his life in talk, let it be never so fine. I have ever had a love for deeds, and yet I do nothing and talk continually, set people to sing stirring hymns, read the most solemn passages of Scripture, utter fervent prayers, preach to the full conformity to the petition "thy will be done on earth as it is in heaven," and yet nothing done. Incomparably the most wretched men on Earth now are Christian Ministers.

And then some of his congregation began to pray at him.

Mrs Bond's account of things here is all *couleur de rose* and not to be trusted. I know what the people think when they pray at me on Monday evenings. "Lord grant that thy servant may not labour in vain, may have seals to his ministry, grant Lord that he may be earnest, and humble, not too proud to do thy work. Lord give him a word in season for the poor and the desponding and the ungodly etc., etc., etc."

It could not continue.

"I believe it is my own fault," he wrote to his mother at Christmas time, "but the loneliness and disappointment I feel is almost more than I can bear. I only hope I shall never look back upon another year like the last. As soon as ever I can see my way to the means to maintain me for a year at the University I shall give up my post here and resume study. I just feel that I am doing little more now than making a tool of the ministry to earn money enough to get out of it. Elsewhere I could be happy and useful but standing to preach to others before one has got truth for oneself is worse than any torture."

In early March 1872 he tendered his resignation. He had never been ordained. The Church with only six dissentients refused to accept it and begged him to reconsider it and they would wait if necessary for some months.

I could hold out no certain hope of my position changing ...and so at the end of a fortnight I sent a second letter expressing my adherence to my first decision. In anticipation of this I joined the University on the very last day possible to enable me to keep this term. Bond has undertaken to lend me [he had as a matter of fact wanted to *give* it] what money I want till I can determine whether it is possible to secure a scholarship at one of the Colleges.

It was done—but it was a shattering business, and left its mark for ever afterwards. The rumour that the resignation was impending had distressed a wide circle of family and friends. "What is to become of the churches," wrote one friend, "if everybody who has a God-given insight into the truth, and what is more a rare and precious knowledge of his own ignorance, is going to resign. I shall be most terribly grieved if there is any truth in this report." At least half the congregation were warmly, even enthusiastically upon Ward's side, and vowed they would rather stay for ever in their old quarters than lose their pastor for the sake of the new chapel. Letters expressing real grief at his decision, and of gratitude for that "clearer vision and widening of the spiritual horizon" which he had brought to some, added to his present distress. Certain members of the chapel banded together and made him a generous gift.

"Such an expression of good will," he wrote to Wolstenholme, "seems to lay hold of me just when it is most painful and most dangerous to be alone. But I am deeply thankful for it. To feel that so many of the people here think me worthy of their esteem will help me to maintain moral equilibrium and save me perhaps alike from the sourness and the extravagance of many incipient heretics. . . . One does not know what a privilege and what a blessing it is to work for others till one is suddenly laid aside from it."

Another letter to Wolstenholme (of March 9th, 1872) shews still more clearly what a shock he had suffered in thus throwing up the work and aims of his life at the late age of twenty-nine.

For the present I am pulling myself together again and so thinking of nothing in particular, although working as hard as I can at Philosophy and Theology. I did not know before how utterly I had been crushed. I cannot tell you how I feel, how one great ruthless heel of fate seems to have stunned and flattened me and my prospects. The pain of the shock of it is to come, will come by and by—and yet the other day I thought my heart would burst—it was on the Thanksgiving day, and all the people were taking holiday. I went a walk over the Gogs, the sky was bright and the larks were singing, and somehow, as fresh as if it were the reality, the old feeling of James Ward the would-be Naturalist of ten years ago rose up and confronted the self-excommunicated sceptic, who had turned himself and his sister out of doors to-day....

...Dear me! Ward, Wooding, Wolstenholme, we have all wandered, are we all to waste? There is nothing I dread so much as getting out of the stream of life to strand and rot in some stagnant shallow....Here in the busiest, grandest time —a Spring-time and not an Autumn in the world's life, full of the ferment of a new spirit—to have to stand aside and do nothing! Oh if there is a God at all he won't suffer it, surely he will find us work and lead us to the truth that shall make us strong for it....For myself I am not afraid of intellectual stagnation, but moral stagnation is a real danger. To see that is something and yet it is no way easy to do much work in Downing Street, without making mischief[1]. A little thing would sunder up the place, and my presence here is anything but a cement....I must wait till everybody has come to regard me as a mere undergraduate and then perhaps I may venture to teach and preach occasionally—at least that is what I should like. I feel as much as ever I felt that I have *something* at any rate to say to people—it is not perhaps all they want, nor all they need, but something it is which my life and study prompt me to utter. Anyhow now that I have stopped it will be better to be silent six months too long than to begin again only to get afresh into the fogs and bogs of scepticism. All my doubts philosophical and historical notwithstanding, I am sure of this as a practical truth—reason, conscience, experience back me up as I say it, I say it with my whole soul —I have no doubt of God's infinite fatherly patience and love: when I despair of myself I find new hope in what He is.... Self is one's bane—self it is which deflects the will, the needle of our spiritual compass. How are we to know? Were the

---

[1] The reference is not, as might easily be supposed at first sight, to No. 10 Downing Street, London, but to the Nonconformist Chapel in Downing Street, Cambridge.

heavens for ever dark we would not perhaps at once, but there are stars and light above even the dreariest sea of doubt. Spiritual shipwreck to an honest man or to any man unconsciously is doubly impossible. In all this, in the practical, what I want is not light but grace, to be taken up into a higher life and delivered from the treacherous self. I tell you Wolstenholme, I have no dread of God, no fear of the Devil, no fear of man, but my head swims as I write it—*I fear myself.* Oh God deliver me or I perish! There it ends. To this I come back: "Beloved, if our heart condemn us, God is greater than our heart and knoweth all things."

IV

In the autumn of 1872 Ward attended the University as a non-collegiate student. He learned that a Scholarship in Moral Science was to be offered by Trinity College. This he won, in the spring of 1873, and was soon established in the great college with which his connection remained unbroken till his death. He had thus at last attained that life of study which he had so often felt at heart was his true vocation and for which his intense thirst for knowledge as a child, his untiring pursuit of truth, and his wide and varied reading had fitted him well. His practical struggles were over. He had discovered his new country, and his work was henceforth to explore and develop its possibilities. To the outside world it was the second half of his life which was interesting and profitable; and it may seem that I have dwelt rather too much upon those early religious experiences. And yet these were to a very great extent the formative experiences of his life and character, though they remained utterly unknown to the larger number of those who became his friends and familiars in later life. He buried the past, he burned his boats: but he remained for all that a native of other shores. He served the world much better as a philosopher than he could ever have served it in the ministry—for after all, for one thing, "the Elijah life" (by which he meant a life of Christian example) was not in him: he had too impatient and violent a temperament, as at heart he knew; and in any case the Church was not broad enough to take what he could have given. And yet I think it is true that whatever he gained in other respects, he did permanently suffer in some ways from the abandonment of a faith which nevertheless *he* could not honestly have retained. His was always a difficult nature with its perpetual internal warfare between the spirit and the devil, that is, in his case, between high principles and earnest love of goodness, and a hasty, domineering and irritable temper. He had found in prayer and in the belief in a divine father ever ready to guide and forgive, his surest help in subduing this conflict. As it was he was left with no weapons against it, except his instinctive faith in goodness and his love of truth: and the latter was a double-edged sword, for it wounded him with the knowledge of faults he could never wholly overcome. He sometimes confessed to the feeling that there were two men in him; and being thus more or less always at war with himself it was no wonder that he was apt to be at war with other people.

In the first few years following his resignation of the ministry he seems to have hardened in several ways. Human nature was always something of a closed book to him, and one of his gravest faults was his lack of ready insight into the feelings of others. He was easily led to take a melodramatic view of people's characters: to see them in the light of sheep and goats—oftener goats—and to be very hard on any defects; while at the same time capable of deep and humble admiration for what he saw to be noble and good. When he was in the position of a spiritual father, the difficult riddles of character were perhaps oftener spelled out before him, and he was given both the clue to understanding and the right to help. Then, family, friends, members of his flock, all had looked to him for counsel—and rarely looked in vain. He never refused help to anyone who asked it, and all through his life would take endless pains to advise and assist; but his help must first be sought: and the intellectual world of Cambridge did not seek it. Consequently he felt aloof, and was sometimes liable to be cold and distrustful and to misunderstand or misjudge his fellows. He became more than ever prone to take offence, especially at any indirectness or well-meant but obtrusive tactfulness. "All the people in Cambridge seemed to me to tell lies when I first went there," he used to say—"I like the downrightness of the northerners who say what they think." He felt in himself a lack of social gift and graciousness and would sometimes be deliberately and defiantly gruff—yet in truth no one could make a more delightful host when in the right vein, and there must be many persons in many parts of the world who have happy memories of his hospitable home. To some extent he consciously isolated himself—and yet felt and resented that isolation.

A year or two after he became a Fellow of Trinity a disaster occurred which tended further to harden and isolate him. His father had a complete and discreditable business collapse. Ward was in the full tide of his successful new career; a public scandal was only narrowly averted, averted mainly because he agreed to shoulder for the rest of his father's life (which proved to be a very long one) a yearly payment of certain sums due to creditors: he also eventually undertook to contribute largely to the support of his parents, on the condition that his father signed a solemn declaration in the presence of his two sons never to engage in any independent business undertaking

again, but to remain, in short, permanently 'a mouse'
—a church mouse, and in this there was further ground
for bitterness. For his trust in the genuineness and
worth of his father's religious character had never till
then been really shaken: he had ceased to discuss religious problems with him, but he respected the firm-
ness of that faith. In old days he had often written to
beg his father to cling to this as the greatest safeguard
in the troubles of business life. "I think of you to whom
I owe so much and pray that though your path lies
through the bustling heartless world you may still
keep the straight and narrow way." Now it seemed
once more perhaps that religion was being discredited.
He never forgave his father—unchristian perhaps, but
under all the circumstances only too comprehensible.
His close and affectionate relations with his family,
which had inevitably been already loosened by his new
wide and intellectual life, began after this last blow to
break up. With his sister Lucy he continued in close
friendship till her death in 1892 and with his mother and
one or two other members of the family he remained
on affectionate terms—but the simple and intimate relationships of home began to give place to the more
intellectual and deliberate friendships of his academic
world. The knowledge of his father's fault remained
always as gall in the secret depths of his proud and
highly honourable nature, and tended perhaps to
make him more suspicious and intolerant, especially
of anything at all underhanded.

There can be no doubt that all these various events
of the first forty years of his life acted very powerfully
upon his already strangely complicated and original
character, and helped to produce that extraordinary
personality—austere and of iron will, yet also often
uncontrolled; attractive, and yet aloof; often moody
and unreasonable, while loving reason and justice

above all things; tender-hearted, yet sometimes so harsh and dominating; whimsically humorous, practically pessimistic, fundamentally full of hope, which exercised so strong an attraction and influence over many persons of various ages and nationalities, even though some of them were made to pay for their roses with a thorn. Those who desired and won his friendship had to reconcile themselves to being on intimate terms with two men, one of whom would frequently hurt and anger them, while the other could be the most entertaining, genial, kind and wise of companions.

But from one common effect of the abandonment of long-cherished religious beliefs, Ward never suffered. He did not react to the opposite extreme: he "maintained his moral equilibrium," and remained free from "the sourness and extravagance of many incipient heretics." Unlike some of his comrades in revolt, who came in time to curse religion, Ward never spoke of any honest religious view or sect without respect and sympathy. A certain melancholy regret for his lost life remained with him, and also, and more permanently, a vein of true religious feeling. I can only speak with the greatest diffidence of any matter connected with his work, but it has always seemed to me that just as his wide knowledge of natural science gave width as well as depth to his philosophical survey, so this religious feeling may have given his philosophy a greater balance, may have, as it were, corrected the bias of an otherwise too abstract and theoretic mode of thought. He always recognised, and often said, that philosophy alone could never greatly ease "the burden of the mystery." His own courageous attitude to life and death was not due to philosophy, but to that instinctive faith in a God which his philosophical writings were largely an attempt to justify.

The last word in the story of his brief ministry was

not written till the year before his death. The new chapel which had been the immediate cause of his resignation had been completed a few years afterwards, and in May 1924 it held its Jubilee Celebration. To this Professor Ward was duly invited, and he replied to the invitation in these terms:

> 6, Selwyn Gardens,
> Cambridge.
> 10 . V . 24.

Dear Sir,

I have to thank you for your friendly invitation to join in the Jubilee Celebration of Emmanuel Church. But the memories of my connexion with that church—which happily the lapse of more than half a century has softened—are too mixed to make me want to revive them. My ministry in Downing Place lasted less than a year and it was the darkest and the saddest of a long and eventful life.

I shall never forget the personal devotion of those who were ready to stay on in that unpretentious 'chapel,' if I would stay with them; nor the earnest appeals to me of men like Baldwin Brown and Campbell Finlayson to do so. If I had done so, and I am by no means sure that I ought not—you would not be celebrating the jubilee of the fine building in Trumpington Street a week hence. It is a monument to two men, Henry Allen and William Bond, but it is the tombstone of a buried life to me.

> Yours faithfully,
>
> J. WARD

V

Ward did nothing by halves as we have seen. He now devoted himself to his undergraduate life—a life he found difficult at his age—with desperate energy. "Hard engrossing work, getting stuff behind you, tunnelling your way, this is the healthiest thing I know, at least for myself." After obtaining the Trinity Scholarship in the spring of 1873 he at once began to work for the second part of the London B.Sc., studying philosophy at the same time and attending Sidgwick's lectures. He was ill as usual during the scholarship examination and was miserable at the idea that he had failed and was to disappoint the many high hopes that he had roused in well-wishers, and be "branded a humbug." When he went up for the examination for the London B.Sc. in the autumn he was in a nervous flurry, arrived late for the stiffest paper, worked for an hour on a question he couldn't manage, "with the idea of certain defeat dancing like a demon through my head"—and did in fact fail, to his great disgust and humiliation. However in 1874 he took a first class in his tripos and soon set to work on his Fellowship dissertation. The examination required in addition to the dissertation was a more important part of the test in those days than it is now. He took this in the autumn of 1875, driving himself through it with the aid of quinine and strong tea. His dissertation was the result of many months' work. This was the first occasion on which Trinity had offered a fellowship for distinction in the "moral sciences." The competition was unusually keen. There were four candidates, all of whom had occupied the highest place in the Moral Sciences Tripos and three of whom were afterwards among the forty-four original fellows of the British Academy. Ward's dissertation was on "The Relation of Physiology to Psychology." A part of it afterwards appeared in the first volume of *Mind* (1876) as "An Attempt to interpret Fechner's Law"; but the dissertation as a whole, although printed, was never published. The psychophysical investigations which Ward set out to interpret were at that time little known in England; in the unpublished portions of the dissertation the discussion was markedly original, and shews that he had by that time reached the view of the nature of mental fact which he afterwards maintained without essential change. The dissertation was of course unintelligible to most of the electors, but they had expert guidance; they were impressed by its originality; and in the end Ward was elected.

On the 9th of October he wrote to tell his parents of his success.

You will both of you say little, but your satisfaction will be none the less true and deep. All my wavering and wandering, my restlessness and worry must have been rather a trouble to you. I cannot promise even now to be always contented and docile, for every position gained only awakens new desires. I am pledged now to pursue the life of a thinker, the life I began when quite a child. Certainly I have had some fights and been out of all sight of the goal I seem to have reached at last. I remember how it was my childish ambition to be a philosopher and now the way is clear for me to do what is possible towards making my dream come true.

"*Denken ist schwer*," as he often used to say in later life, holding his head in his hands and swaying to and fro in his study chair after a day spent wrestling with some stubborn riddle. One of the first effects of that life of a thinker to which he pledged himself was that he ceased to be able to write long, intimate, argumentative letters. There were still a few to Wolstenholme in the years between 1873 and 1875 and one or two after, but there the record of his speculations and struggles practically ceases, while the fruit of it all begins to find expression in print. As they are the last of those fluent letters written almost without an erasure, pouring out in page after page speculations and opinions, sympathies and jokes and judgments on all manner of topics, it is perhaps worth while to give a few more extracts, even though these will only reveal once more the perpetual restlessness of his mind and spirit—a restlessness which, as it had continued till he was over

Photo by V. H. Mottram

JAMES WARD IN 1911

thirty, was likely to continue longer. Whether the life of a thinker ever did completely satisfy his nature and his ambitions is a question. At times it probably did, and at times, especially at the beginning of his Trinity career, it certainly did not.

July 13th, 1873,
from TRINITY COLLEGE

To H. J. W.

... There is a good deal of reform wanted in our universities —but for the "time-honoured acts" and the like I could get on very comfortably. Matters are not mended by the determination to which I have come not to preach any more for the present. I could easily have filled up this vacation, but I find people will persist as long as I preach in saying: "Oh! you are pretty much where you were, and you'll be taking a charge again in a year or two." I have resolved therefore to break this false continuity when and while the break looks honest.... In fact for the time, much to my own discomfort, I have ceased to attend any place of worship at all, and this just because I see my prospective action is hampered while I remain outwardly what I was....

Trinity in the 'Long' is a very quiet place....But for the sound of an occasional footstep across it I could fancy I had the whole Great Court to myself....The stillness of everything is charming when the day is bright, as now, but wretched when it is wet and cold and windy as it has been. But now with a gentle breeze through the open window, a clear quiet sky and the tinkling of the water in the fountain just sounding in one's ears, it is as easy to be contemplative as it is to sit still and do nothing when moving about means melting and running out of one's skin. I am afraid I have done sadly too much sitting and dreaming since I have been up.

The doubting phase is pretty well passed for me now. I reject the whole system of Christian dogma from beginning to end and rationalize the history. Yet I see more clearly than ever that Christianity can do more for the world than it ever has done. The Evolutional philosophy seems the only one that fits and explains the facts. My next business is to know something of the so-called "religion of humanity" and of the

Christian forms of Pantheism.... The next turn thought will take, I think, will be toward a fuller examination, a more earnest attempt to understand the relation between the so-called individual soul and its fellows and the universe generally. I seem to see more and more clearly that no man is an absolute individual, and try sometimes to conceive a consciousness of a higher potence in which without the sense of continuity and identity disappearing the limits which mark me off as an individual may be transcended. The mode in which since the far far distant ages of flint-chippers the human race has multiplied individuals is against the permanence, i.e., the reality of the individual. Let us see what we can make out of 'the solidarity' of the race, as the phrase now is: as for this segregation *ad infinitum* after the fashion of the vinegar plant, it does not seem very divine. Some day perhaps Paul's figures, as I often fancy, about body and members, and Christ's about the vine and branches may have a deeper meaning. It was by endeavouring to exhibit Christ as the typical man in this sense, taking as text "The name of Jesus—the name which is above every name," that I got myself and Hunter into such hot water at York[1].

May 24th, 1873]

You will be interested to hear, if you do not know already, that John Stuart Mill has left behind him, besides a complete autobiography, a work giving his views on religion. We used to talk of his silence on this subject, and I have more than once thought of writing to him about it. Now it appears many persons actually did this, and that his answer was he could serve his generation best by silence. His thoughts on religion are to come to us from the grave. Perhaps this is a little fanciful, and yet as a matter of fact they will have more weight, be more generally and dispassionately read than if they had appeared before—especially now that the picture of

[1] Ward had been invited to preach for Dr John Hunter, a well-known Nonconformist Minister, at York, and the sermon he delivered was too broad-minded for a large section of the congregation. It caused a good deal of disturbance in his friend's Chapel, and was followed for some weeks after by controversial letters in the York papers.

the man in his domestic and moral aspect is becoming known and turns out to be so admirable. I must confess I do not think Mill had an intellect of the very finest mould, although one far above the average cast. Still he had the good English habit of thinking wisely and soundly, was not guilty of speculative freaks of thought. His best and last thought on the subject which has wrought such varied threads of joy and sorrow into my life and into yours should be an interesting legacy to us both.

[December 25th, 1872]

As to my speculations, either theological or philosophical, which you do me the honour to invite me to communicate, I think I can best tell you where I am by comparing myself to an oyster. Time was when I roved at large, a vagrant in the ocean of knowledge. Now my tentacles are atrophied and I lie at the bottom like a stone, conscious of gravitation, and able only to deal with such facts as connect themselves with my habitat. Perhaps my most ambitious dream now is to be able to arrange and concatenate these into something like a system....As might be expected too, now that I am at leisure with myself, I am become more distinctly conscious of the need of knowing this self better, before I can better know other things. From the little world to the big the order must be. In psychology and even in ethics I am more disposed than ever to be empirical, even what some people would call materialistic in the one, utilitarian in the other. I still hope to come at length to the theological questions which were my first love. Your closing sentence raises them nearly all. "Whether reason will sanction or not, the demands of the spiritual nature will not be repressed." Is this a necessary antagonism? If a man—having of course the brains and culture needful—dares to entertain any and every rational inquiry in this region of things, must he be without a faith, or hold one that is as they say 'above reason,' i.e., non-rational? Is it any solution to the difficulty to say, (1) that reason is related to this (hypothetical) spiritual nature as intellect is to sense, and therefore our spiritual experience must always be in advance of our rationale of the same, while

the probability is that as the world of sense is more than we
can intellectually comprehend though we are continually
experiencing it, so might it be with our spiritual life—faith
being thus paralleled with common sense in a common
opposition to philosophy—and (2) that this being so, theory
must wait on fact, the speculation of reason on the facts of
spiritual life: that in other words the conclusions of reason
can only be hypothetical, since however truly we have
reasoned, it cannot be surely known that we have other than
partial premises, and certain necessary truths, as they may be
some day called, are missing? I once worked out the line of
thought I can but imperfectly suggest here in a sermon from
the text "And there fell from my eyes as it had been scales."
...But a more serious difficulty remains....We speak of
spiritual facts, facts of a subjective experience of course I
mean. Now suppose we treat these facts as Mill and Spencer
treat the facts of man's moral life or the facts of his social life.
If the result should be that we decide that these facts are subjective not only relatively (to the individual) but absolutely
(for the whole race), how will the case stand then?...I am
not furnished for the fray and must leave it to others...yet
from what I do hear I seem to gather that the Old Faith is the
losing side. In entertaining the thought of its final defeat,
the question returns "What will be the worth of our subjective facts after the explanations that Evolutionists may
then put upon them? Would religion—or rather must religion, gradually die out?"—I cannot see why theism—a sort
of pantheism you may call it if you are spiteful—is not still
possible. I assume that man is practical rather than speculative. Self-preservation and not philosophy is the first law
of life....Christian morality, the belief in a Divine Love and
in an existence after death, all I believe 'work well.'...So then
I conclude that Christianity will spread by virtue of the
principle of Evolution alone....And all this time I am supposing that there has been no such thing as what I roughly
termed an 'objective religious fact'—God manifesting himself by overt act, as man always manifests himself to man. Is
this then to go on for ever? Are God and man never to meet?
What if they have been gradually meeting all the time? Becoming leading at length to Being, Development, Growth,

Evolution. The tendency has been for a deepening sense of God to advance *pari-passu* with a greater shyness at attempting to describe him.... There has been along the line of religious progress an increasing tendency to feel God within accompanied by less and less expectation of seeing him objectively without. From the consciousness of the brute man has advanced to self-consciousness, from this to God-consciousness, fitful, inadequate, and projected by imagination outwards into Nature etc. Then comes a God-consciousness within, but still distinct and without organic connection with the self-consciousness. Perhaps in the Christian conception of a Holy Spirit and all that belongs to that conception we see the beginning of such organic union. Why then may not the consummation be a God-Self-consciousness?... On this view the age of types is not yet gone by: the present form of Christianity having been but typical of the truer "Christ that is to be"; and so regarded our faith is the less tried and we are the less disheartened to see it apparently dying out.

May 6th, 1873. People here call me hard names because I don't visit them more frequently and you—philosopher though you are—have allowed yourself the same indulgence. My intercourse with you has simply suffered as my intercourse with everybody else has—home and friends alike—from the terrible exactions of the age on one trying to wriggle his way up on to a new platform with such odds as there are against me.... The dissatisfaction you express with the present course of your life is, I am persuaded, but an indication of the one-sidedness... it is a pain consequent on the unhealthy regimen circumstances have half forced upon you. I am coming to see more clearly every day that man is only half free, or rather that his freedom is not what I once thought it. It is not the power to choose anything, but only the power to choose between alternatives offered, and what these shall be circumstances determine quite as much as will. However this partial relative freedom avails for much more than it otherwise would do because of the power intellect gives to us to survey the field of life... and we can set our faces in the right direction.... This virtuous habit of systematically employing intellect as chart, compass, telescope, sounding-lead

etc., for the true self, the will, is commonly called *prudence* if
directed to the lower ends of life, *wisdom* if directed to life's
chief end. But the names are so hackneyed that it often does
one good to drop them and look at the things....

You are not sanguine and hopeful enough. Worse still you
have the unhappy knack of seeing the evil there is in the
world rather than the good....Well, I doubt if there ever
lived a good man who would have been different if he had
been cheated of hopefulness and forced to lead a life in which
reflection usurped the time and blood which belonged of
right to action. Do try and believe in the good there is in the
world and unite yourself with the many many good men in
England who are working with all their might to help the
world on its way....I am sure you belong of right to them
—yet circumstances may, *if you let them*, cut you off from your
own company. We are living in a momentous age....It is
marvellous what a ferment of thought there is in England,
not only now chiefly on religious matters, but on social and
political questions too. Some of us must soon enter upon the
burden and heat of the day, and shall have to take a strong
stand in the struggles that must come before class interests
can be broken up and a true national life begin.

Though the life of a thinker proved to be too ex-
acting to allow of much political activity, Ward's keen
interest in political movements, which had begun in
his boyhood, continued till his death, and his views
remained always liberal and even in some points revolutionary. In these letters to Wolstenholme he expresses a deeply democratic outlook, involving a belief
in the fullest political liberty and educational opportunity for all classes and both sexes. He was eager to
help with the Extension Lecture Movement, then just
started: he met and talked with Josephine Butler; and
he lectured to working men's clubs.

"Even I have made another beginning at last," he writes
in January 1875. "I am commencing work on new ground—
ground of great interest to me—the higher education of

women. I am to lecture to women on Political Economy in Cambridge from now to midsummer, and next October I am going out into the provinces to lecture both to women and to the working classes."

He was for a long time still—while he had some hopes in the movement—interested in the politics of the Nonconformist body and concerned about the plight of Spring Hill College, but he felt that "the two little facts, (1) that man is inert brute matter and (2) that when he moves it is round his own axis," were seriously in the way of progress. His interest in the national character and future development of Germany had been aroused as soon as he had landed there for the first time, and he had some shrewd guesses, or rather fears, as to her course.

"There is an art," he writes [September 25th, 1879], "of making happy which is understood better there [i.e. in Germany] than here, and in every German there is a dash of sentiment, domestic, patriotic and pious, which works marvellous transformations in the hard facts of life. This vein of sentiment it is I think which has preserved Germany from all the ill that must else have come from the free thinking. It is a good thing that just when England is being threatened with the same epidemic there should be signs also of a like antidote.... People now are ritualistic, admirers of Tennyson and the Brownings, have a passion for flowers and music, and what is even more important, cheap locomotion has made us all lovers of nature as she is, of the beautiful in landscape, cloud, and sea. Such influences... are fitting us to bear, with comparative impunity, a shock which, if they could have experienced it, would have shivered the whole fabric of Puritan goodness, substantial though it was.

Are you of the opinion of some of our English papers that Germany is drifting towards Imperialism? What an odd thing it would look in history if in this respect Germany and France should change places and some fifty years hence the

French republic by providing a Sedan for a German Caesar
should inaugurate the political majority of the German
people, till that time under tutors and governors, i.e.,
Bismarcks and Wilhelms!"

And every now and then, through these manifold
interests and activities, the old restless dissatisfaction
of spirit revives, and is revealed again to Wolstenholme,
the friend of past and present, the only one to whom it
could all be confided.

[*November 9th*, 1873.] When I look back upon the times
when you and I prayed and talked together at Spring Hill
or upon my brief ministering here in Cambridge I see a wide
difference between what I was and what I am....Though
I hardly know how to go to work to regain my old self, I am
at any rate conscious of its superiority. Part no doubt of my
former healthfulness was due to the greater exercise of human
sympathy and to direct contact with the souls of men. Now
I have no one who is such a friend to me as you were at
Spring Hill. H—— is as kind and friendly as a man could be,
but so hopelessly cynical and befogged himself as to be as
much a hindrance as a help to me. I always feel the better
for a talk with Mr and Mrs Bond but never see them except
in the way of casual intercourse now....I am conscious that
whereas once I felt that God was with me in life and that the
good of it was a fuller communion with him: now I feel alone,
believing in God indeed, but for myself I cannot find him,
don't know how to address him, how to think of him. From
having tasted what seemed a supernatural life and felt impulses and promptings that I took for those of a Holy Spirit,
I now lead a life natural and commonplace enough, without
any motives that cannot be soon explained—as the prompting
in some form or other of self. My reason bids me seek that
life again, for reason owns the superiority of it—but how, I
keep asking, am I to regain it? The old faith is gone, where
am I to find 'the new,' or when will it find me?...I believe
I am a sort of moral desperado, ready for any wild scheme,
social, political or ecclesiastical, that would absorb me wholly.
But meanwhile nothing offers and the question presses: How

is a disciple of modern thought to be religious? I don't know and there is nothing left but trying, "feeling after him if haply I may find him."

[*January* 25*th*, 1873.] You have been very helpful to me in many ways. Much that you have said commends itself to me. I know, and told you, that I had fallen below my old life— and for the reason that I had lost my old creed, and still further because I had passed under such unfavourable circumstances from an active to a bookish life. I do not say that the old life and a far better is not possible without the old creed, but the two were so connected for me that what affected the one affected the other. Prayer was the secret of everything good there ever was in me. Now I must find other reasons for striving to regain the old paths and keeping to them. What if this be not any belief in what they lead to but in what they are? "Virtue is its own Reward," said Spinoza, but I did not know this once in the experimental way in which I know it now. I believe in the Christian life, but must rest it on new foundations. I would preserve *it*, the foundations for me are gone. Well, there is the story of the tortoise that carries the elephant that carries the world. If we stop at the tortoise, why not at the elephant, why not at the world? But somewhere we must stop; which things are an allegory. The Christian life, as you say, is its own foundation, its own reason, its own credentials. This is sufficient *practically*, no doubt. "Ye shall know them by their fruits." Yes that is enough for action. But alas, alas, man not only acts but thinks, and science can make nothing out of practical proofs. The old questions remain: why? whence? whither? and so the goodly hue of resolution is sicklied o'er with the pale cast of thought. I am a divided being and so unstable.

Gradually as the interests and occupations of his new world spread, he tended to look back less into the past, and to find in various forms substitutes for what he had lost. In the companionship of other brilliant men, in the study of nature, in the ardours of 'thinking things out' he found the best basis he could for his new tabernacle. To Henry Sidgwick he owed most of all.

His thwarted Evangelicism, based on that deeper craving of his nature to teach and serve humanity, found new life and hope in Sidgwick and the work and ideals that he held out. Lucy Ward had been drawn in the wake of her brother's scepticism, and he was often desirous to shew to her as to himself some worthy compensation for the loss of faith. In December 1878 he writes to her:

Once we sink to the level of living among people without either giving or receiving moral and spiritual quickening we begin to die....During the last few years I have been so far stunned by the break up of my early life and my early beliefs that I have been content to drift with the people about me. Now and again it has happened that some chance talk with men like James Stuart or Henry Sidgwick has roused me up ...these things make life seem worthier and wake up higher aims, but then they will not last for ever....So long as one professed Christianity one took steps to keep alive a better life—by suitable reading, by meditation, and prayer, and by striving to do people good. Why should these means be abandoned because we are forced to admit that we don't know as much about God and the future as we thought we did? Are we not still sure that the old life was better than this? And can we not still sit at the feet of the world's noblest and purest spirits and learn of them?

His interest and joy in nature, which had been so early roused, revived almost as soon as he left the pulpit for College. Soon after, the ornithological notes and plant and egg and fossil collecting began again.

"Did you ever read Wordsworth's Excursion?" he wrote to Wolstenholme in 1878. "I have just finished the First Book. It has quite stirred me up. What the world is going to come to without religious aspirations and the old feelings of awe and mystery that Nature inspired in the best minds, is more than I can tell or care to guess. These springs of higher life must revive again or the beggarly elements will starve us back into savages."

As for the pleasures of thinking things out, once his Tripos examination was behind him and the field of original research before, he did not fail to seize these to the full.

"I have been tremendously absorbed," he writes to Lucy, "in the things I am trying to think out. I have not yet got the length of forgetting my own name, but not far short of that....My bedmaker said to me this morning: 'Shall we get you anything before we go, Sir?' I asked her what she meant, and she said: 'You look so ill and worn, Sir.' 'Oh!' said I, 'I am as right as can be, I am only thinking something out.' I very much enjoy burying myself in thought and waking up after a week or two to things about me."

"Life is short," he writes to Wolstenholme, "and at 33 there is certainly no time to spare....I am resolved if possible to work out my own thoughts and indeed now to sacrifice everything else to that....I have been invited to become a candidate for the Philosophy Chair at Owens College, but don't intend to try, just because the work would not leave me leisure enough."

And then again to Wolstenholme a year or two later:

No doubt you are right, we have made a start, both of us. There can be no starting again in such a sense as applies to the start of ten years ago. Yet probably for me at any rate the reluctance to say: it can never be, was the cause of my enduring at this time of life the irksomeness of an undergraduate career in Cambridge. So far I have no great reason to regret the result....I am not trying to persuade myself, still less you, that things could not have been better. I simply feel that here as elsewhere there is good in evil, though not so much as to make me cease to wish the evil had not been. Perhaps though when the end of all comes it may prove true that evil has been the parent of a larger good...only so far I am not conscious that such evil as I have known and done has proved this for me.

VI

It was in this spirit, with its typical mixture of pessimism, resolution and hope, that Ward turned to his new life, and being sustained only, as he said, by "faith in light to come," his instinct at this period was to open his doors to every breath of knowledge from whatever source. He seems to have turned first and most ardently to Natural Science, and in the autumn of 1876 he set off for Leipzig to work at physiology in the laboratories of Ludwig. He took his sister Lucy with him; his old friend Wolstenholme was settled in Leipzig at the time, and he had many reasons to enjoy the trip. But his bad habit of depression and anxiety about the future pursued him. His father's business affairs were rankling in his mind; he felt his own prospects anything but secure, as at this time there seemed no opening for fresh Moral Science teachers in Cambridge. He even began to wonder if he would bury himself in Germany, though the letters he received should have been enough to convince him that he was needed in Cambridge, and when he did return in May he found several pupils waiting for him, and Sidgwick determined to find him a permanent post. His experiments at Leipzig were remarkably successful, but he was irked by faulty instruments and delays in procuring others. And all the time he was homesick to get back to philosophy, while yet, as a passage in one of the following letters shews, philosopher enough to take even philosophy philosophically. He was a little stunned perhaps by a fresh sense of the vastness and inconclusiveness of knowledge; and he was also, as usual, a little lonely, for Lucy was settled in a family some distance away.

"My dear Keynes[1]," he writes in February 1877, "I should not have been quite so long answering this letter if my bed-maker had not come in: I have been trying to explain the eclipse of the moon to her. Otherwise after apostrophizing your worthiness I meant to remark on the inconveniences of space. If old Kant instead of living and dying in the same spot and recreating himself with books of travel had yielded to some of the many attempts that were made to get him out of Königsberg, he might have had his misgivings as to the ideal nature of space, especially if he had left all his best friends behind him. At any rate so it is with me: what would I not give to-night to drop in at the Bonds, see Mrs Bond and Minnie Bond look happy, Mr Bond and Miss Bond look sad, Harry[2] look as if steering an eight was the same thing at bottom as piloting the ship of the State; see Rowe[3] as if he dined on musical-box springs and you with that everlasting roguish twinkle in your eye which one only sees in ordinary mortals when they cry: Checkmate. Here we are altogether perhaps in some '*intelligibler Raum*,' like St Thomas's angels on the point of a needle—but the forms of intuition forbid that we should perceive it. But with one of your wonted dry thrusts you reply: Why then do you not betake yourself to the next best thing and write? I am, but if you want to know why I don't write oftener look to the beginning of the last letter you had and let me go on.

I have positively been here five months now and have done nothing. I well remember telling you when I wrote before, of the time I was losing because there was no apparatus in the place in working order: I little thought then that the mere getting apparatus to work would take me till the end of January. It was a wretched business and many a time I felt disposed to throw it up, but Ludwig at the very outset told me he doubted if my patience would hold out....

There is not the least chance of my forsaking Psychology for Physiology: I simply wish to know all I can of what

[1] Now Dr J. N. Keynes.
[2] Now Dr Henry Bond, Master of Trinity Hall, Cambridge.
[3] Rowe was a brilliant mathematician and very musical: for a time Fellow of Trinity. He died young.

Sidgwick calls 'the margin of psychology'—the physical aspects of the psychical. The experiments I have been making now have as their aim the determination of what I might call the rhythm of central action.... Experiments of the kind I am making have been made before but not with the same end in view nor with such exact apparatus."

And again to the same friend in May:

Prof. Ludwig seems now to consider my work so far as it has gone sound and the work of my predecessor in the same line, which leads unhappily to different results, to be disposed of. So my business now is to round things off and write (i.e. Ludwig write for me) a paper in Du Bois Reymond's *Archiv*. Still in that rounding off what slips may come! As to anything that I have done besides this minimum still to fix I am forced to confess, after deliberately thinking over it, that this has been the most intellectually stagnant year of my life. I have read little and—to any worthy purpose—have thought less: I am not one peg nearer to anything except the final flicker. To have to say this is the more disappointing because I expected the very opposite and with reason, for to my previous twelve months in Germany I knew I owed so much: —that certainly was the year in which I grew most. I do not blame my "self" for this, tho' I feel myself to blame. But for circumstances—largely however of my own making—I might a second time have had cause to rejoice in 'my temporary expatriation' as Sidgwick calls it. The most fatal step has been the exclusive surrender to physiology: it has left me no time or energy for anything quickening and yet has not sufficed to keep me braced of itself. Still I do not greatly dread a total wither-up just yet and hope to find in Cambridge and fresh work the energising I so sorely need....

But oh dear me, when was I ever so lazy! Here is positively the 10th of May, a drenching rain, Bond a model of industry grimly writing letters in the various languages of Europe and biting his thumb like a statesman in a private parlour. But nothing moves me. I neither read nor talk nor write but either sleep or stare thro' the window at the barges and timber rafts floating down the Elbe, four miles an hour for nothing! When Nature does so much, why do anything, says the Elbe boatman, and neither hoists a sail nor plies an oar but sits as light-hearted as his rye-bread and sausage diet will let him, and slowly puffs a $\frac{1}{2}d$. weed. Now this man set me off musing dreamily this morning and I think the burden of it all hung round the question: Is the question Why? How? a mark of perfection or not? Or is it but part of a lower phase in our development and shall we some day be simply active and creative but no longer speculative? It seems reasonable to expect that if the philosophic impulse cannot be satisfied—and how can it be?—it is to be superseded. When I saw the barges floating and thought of the whole mass of the earth as concerned in the motion and then of all the other streams and barges and of all the myriad other movements and strains with which it was equally concerned and then again of all these incalculable motions as being motion along lines of least resistance, I asked why does a particle so move, and fancying that such motion is at bottom really tantamount to the Aristotelian *primum mobile* I began whying and where-foreing this too and so came to move 'the previous question' —Will not the triumph of philosophy be giving itself the Japanese *coup de grâce*?

At the end of the summer session Ward returned to Cambridge, and was soon engaged in almost every form of mental activity that University life could offer. He began lecturing and for several years gave courses of lectures to women students on Psychology, as well as other courses on Modern Philosophy and on Education: in the vacations he lectured fairly frequently to Extension Classes, or working men's clubs. He wrote reviews, papers on Locke and Descartes, also an article, in German, on his Leipzig experiments; he conducted some elaborate investigations on crayfish in Michael Foster's[1] laboratory: he examined several years for Manchester, and for various groups of the Cambridge Locals, also for the Tripos. He was

[1] Afterwards Sir Michael, the great physiologist.

a member, and usually an active one, of innumerable
societies—the *Chit-Chat*, the *Apostles*, and in due course
of the *Eranus*, the *Ambarum* and the *Synthetic Society*: he
was amongst the first members of the *Moral Science
Club* and the *Natural Science Club*. His association with
science and scientific men was unbroken. He records
in his diary many afternoons spent in "Stuart's Shop,"[1]
—and amongst his friends were Foster, MacAlister[2], and
Frank Balfour[3]. In the evenings he seems to have given
a good deal of time to literature, reading English and
Latin by himself, or Dante with Oscar Browning and
J. G. Frazer; other evenings were spent listening to
music or discussing mathematics. Long expeditions,
botanising or birds' nesting, occupied free afternoons
or week-ends, and the beginning of the vacation
usually sent him instantly off either to fish, or more
frequently to study rare birds in the Hebrides or
Sutherland, where he stayed in lonely shepherds' huts
and had himself lowered over cliffs on a rope to hunt
for eggs. He enjoyed his Scotch expeditions intensely,
and never lost his love for those bleak and wild coasts.

"My dear Lucy," he writes from Kearvaig, near Cape
Wrath, in May 1879, "The position of Cape Wrath is no
doubt well known to you—just as the position of Exeter was—
but Kearvaig I fancy you do not know and will not find in
a hurry, though I have no doubt some of your very learned
friends can tell you all about it, if you ask them.

Well then, I am here in search of health and eagles' eggs—

[1] James Stuart, Professor of Mechanism and founder of the
Extension Lectures Movement, had, as part of his laboratory,
workshops both for metal work and for woodwork. In these some
graduate members of the University had the opportunity of
making their own instruments for various experiments.

[2] Now Sir Donald MacAlister, Principal of the University of
Glasgow.

[3] Frank Balfour, a younger brother of Lord Balfour, promised
to be a brilliant biologist, but was killed while quite young
when climbing in Switzerland.

the former I have some chance of finding, the latter I fear
is doubtful. I have been out along the tops of the cliffs, which
in many places are but stone walls 500 feet high going sheer
down into the sea. I bowled stones over the top and yelled
the bush cry but got no answer save from the Kittiwakes at
the bottom. Anyhow an eagle did at length condescend to
shew himself of his own accord and a grand fellow he was—
a couple of ravens who were trying to mob him looked no
bigger than starlings beside him. But, Fräulein, I can't do
justice to eagles: I am too hungry. My word, I am hungry!
I left Durness after an eight o'clock breakfast and walked
carrying my knapsack nine miles through the hills to this place
and found that the entire population with the exception of a
lad of sixteen had gone off in a cart to pay a visit to a place
twice the size of this, viz. the Cape Wrath Lighthouse. The
lad thought they would be back by four o'clock, so I begged a
drink of milk and set off, as aforesaid, in search of eagles.
Would that I had gone in search of my dinner instead; for
it is now after seven and I have been back an hour and still
the tide of population does not set in this way and I am well
nigh collapsing....A couple of lambs have walked in lately
to make my acquaintance: would that they were roast. I
would excuse the mint sauce. Hark, the dogs are barking. To
the window sharp. Petticoat, petticoat coming over the hill,
a red shawl, blue bonnet strings and a maiden with her dress
in her arms. The boy hastens after them, but here they are....

I shall probably put up for a day or two with very humble
fare so that I only see something of bird life and get a further
peep into Nature. But it has just—*May 23rd*. I must have
commenced eating at this point and can't remember now
what I was going to say....We went out this morning, the
shepherd and I, and succeeded in finding the eagle's nest by
the help of our telescopes about 100 feet down from the top
of a terrific cliff. [Here come some potatoes and Mrs M.
speaks of a 'wee bit ham.'] Just as we were discussing how
to get down, the shepherd, whose glass is better than mine,
saw something move at the far side of the nest and there sure
enough was a baby eagle, a little ball of white down with
black beak and eyes—eyes that would probably never have

seen the light had I reached Kearvaig a week earlier. As it is the young eaglet has every prospect of a good time of it and my neck is spared one rick for a twelvemonth. It was a grand sight to see the old eagles soaring high over our heads in the air, mobbed all the while by a couple of ravens, whose young I fancy must have helped to furnish the eagles' larder....

I will tell you what Kearvaig is like. It is a small cove or bay shut in by the hills on every side except that facing the sea.... One can only get a view by going out of doors. The best is up the little valley on the left, which has been, the old dame tells me, as it well deserves to be, transferred to canvas. From this point one looks down a hollow lined with mossy stones and heather on to a patch of bright yellow sand washed by rolling waves of the clearest sea-green which break every minute or two into seething foam and rise in clouds of spray round the base of a quaint-looking stack of rocks, which look as if some giant had been playing with monster toy bricks, and left his structure towering a hundred feet out of the water, its black sides marked with lines of clear white, the breasts of innumerable guillemots and razorbills nestling in the crevices between the blocks."

This year, 1879, Ward added to his other work an article on *Herbart* for the *Encyclopædia Britannica*, and a paper for the Royal Society dealing with his experiments on crayfish, a paper which won the approval of Huxley and remains to some degree an authoritative document. Ward's keenness and aptitude for Natural Science led his friend Michael Foster to lament his decision to be a philosopher: he was, said Foster, "a physiologist spoiled." It was in 1879 too that he examined for the Tripos on an occasion when a certain Newnham student who had attended his lectures, and who was destined to become his wife, was a candidate. Whether from nervousness, or from his natural gloomy habit of expecting the worst, Ward added up Miss Martin's marks at a thousand too few! Fortunately there were more impartial examiners to check his figures, and restore Miss Martin to the First Class which was her due. In 1880 the Chair of Philosophy at Aberdeen became vacant. Sidgwick and the Balfours were eager to obtain the appointment of Ward, but were not successful. In April 1881 "by the good offices of Sidgwick" he was elected to a College lectureship in Moral Science, and his position in Cambridge was thus made finally secure. The relief he felt was very real, for he had no doubt dreaded the idea of being once more cast out into the unintellectual and unacademic world.

He was at this time becoming more and more deeply absorbed in psychological questions; and several of his friends and admirers were urging him to produce a book. He tried to turn his mind to this, but as always was driven by desire for accuracy and completeness into ever new researches. From 1878 he had given courses of lectures on Psychology in Trinity by arrangement with the tutors. His psychological views also took shape in a series of papers read to the Moral Sciences Club, which were printed before being discussed. The first of these is dated October 15th, 1880, and is called "A general Analysis of Mind," and it was followed by others on "Objects and their interaction," "The Law of Relativity," and "Space and Time." These papers disclose his new stand-point and illustrate his method. He had also urged that a laboratory for Experimental Psychology should be established in Cambridge—and this when there was no laboratory of the kind elsewhere. But the proposal had to be dropped at the time and it was a good many years before the Cambridge laboratory was started.

Beginning with Wundt's laboratory at Leipzig in 1879, many psychological laboratories were established in Germany and U.S.A., and the experimental work which was done in them was closely followed by Ward, but his own original contributions were not to any great extent dependent upon their results. At first, at any rate, he was more concerned with the stand-point of psychology as a science. The novelty of his procedure, as shewn in his lectures and in the papers mentioned above, may be said to have consisted in a combination of two features—a strictly scientific method and the distinction which he drew between psychology and the natural sciences (including physiology). The former led him to replace the descriptions of the "faculty psychologists" by a more exact method; the latter led to his criticism of the assumptions of the sensationalist and associationist psychologists. Psychology, he held, is distinguished from the natural sciences by one and the same characteristic. They have all to do with facts; and these facts are all, directly or indirectly, presented to a conscious subject; but this subjective reference does not concern the natural sciences and they tacitly agree to take no notice of it. Psychology, on the other hand, is concerned with just this aspect which the natural sciences ignore—the presentation of objects to a subject. Starting from this point of view he was able to give a comprehensive survey of the whole range of mental life and to shew that, keeping to this point of view, a strictly scientific method was possible.

In 1882, after a naturalising expedition in Norfolk, Ward was suddenly taken ill and was found to have typhoid fever. His sister Lucy was at Newnham College during this year, but another devoted sister took him home and nursed him through. At one time he was so ill that he was hardly expected to live. He used to relate in after-life, with some gusto, how he was one day left seemingly asleep, and opened his eyes to see on the table beside the bed a letter his sister was writing in which she expressed her doubt of his recovery. "I was so angry," he said, "at the idea of their disposing of me in that fashion, that I resolved to get well after all just to spite them"; and he began to recover from that time. He was back at work after a few months, but his delicate digestion had probably suffered, and a buzzing in his ears, which he had had for some years, seems to have increased. It never quite left him, and led probably to the deafness which in later life troubled him a good deal, though it gave his humour much scope; for he would attribute impossible remarks to the members of his family and develop out of them an inimitable conversation of nonsense and cross-purposes. In the autumn of 1882 he became a member of the College Council and from that time took an active part in College and University politics, fighting always on the side of liberty and reform.

During the whole of 1883 his health was very uncertain, and his spirits, in spite of a most successful trip to Spain with J. G. Frazer, very low. A bachelor life in College had never suited his home-loving nature: he was forty, and he was anxious to marry, while afraid that his uncertain health made it wrong for him to entertain the idea. He attempted, about this time, to insure his life, and to his consternation he did not succeed—nor did he ever—in passing the medical examination. Meantime he was struggling to get his ideas on psychology written down for the proposed article in the *Encyclopædia Britannica* and wanting to get ever deeper into his subject before committing himself. Already some years before he had written to Lucy:

Sidgwick and Foster urge me strongly to write a book and Foster thinks I ought to do it within a year! They very rightly say that I am at present living too much on the credit I have and that it is time to perform. I distinctly hate rushing into print in a hurry and in my own mind fixed five or six years as the time, but I must bend to circumstances and bestir myself accordingly at once.

In 1883 he writes to Lucy from a Sutherland cottage:

I wonder if I really shall retire to such a place in thirteen years time[1]....Take care of yourself, Fräulein, and you can come and pay me long visits and see my flowers and my pets. But after all nothing would make such a life tolerable but worthy and successful occupation. If I had vigour enough left to think hard and write books I should like it. I am coming to feel more and more that the most solid pleasure lies in work: that gives me a sense of worth and dignity that nothing else does. I am very keen on getting some work done now, and if my health keeps up I quite think I shall get a book ready in the next two or three years. From 1875 to 1883 will always remain a dark and barren period in my recollection: but—always supposing my health is not seriously undermined—I may perhaps outlast it. A great deal will depend on other people: Cambridge must prove less of a wet blanket than it has, and I suppose I must grow less sensitive to the wet blanket treatment, or more genial so as to dispel it.

Other letters of about this date shew him feeling lonely and depressed:

You need not always ask my forgiveness, Fräulein, for saying what you "feel and think about me." If more people took even this interest in me I shd. be happier than I am. Moreover what you say is perfectly true. I do get worse instead of better and often wonder if I shall ever wake up again and live to some purpose....The Xmas in which the—— business happened marked a sad turning pt. in my life. The utter collapse of home has been too much for me....I seem to have nobody behind me or belonging to me....

He then goes on to make one of his shrewd statements about the religious and intellectual life of the time:

As to Theology, when those who believe in God at all say God is not a person, what they often mean I think is not that

[1] When he would have been fifteen years a lecturer and so entitled to hold his fellowship for life.

he is less than a person but more, and inconceivable and unknowable because the highest life we can grasp is personal life.... Hence in all the higher religions intercourse with God has been represented as a spiritual communion, as internal light or manifestation.... Religion must thus ever transcend Science, which *can* never prove it false nor yet shew it to be true. The infidelity of the present generation which tries to dethrone religion by science is the perfectly logical and natural outcome of the mistaken endeavours of the past generation to establish religion by appeals to science.... Just now the intellectual world has not faith to grow.

[*January* 1883.] I am not very well and not in good spirits. Niven[1] has gone now altogether, and I suppose you have heard Dale[2] is dead. Cambridge is lonelier than ever: I cannot even expect your somnambulistic knock and the wonted apparitions that used to be such a sauce to my mutton chops and custard to my puddings. Verily I am like a bottle in the smoke (*vide* O.T.).

But the following winter the clouds lifted: his health improved again; he became engaged to Miss Martin (who was by this time a Lecturer at Newnham College), and he got well started on his article for the *Britannica*. He was married in July 1884 and that autumn settled in the Huntingdon Road, while waiting for the house which kind Miss Clough, the first Principal of Newnham, in her motherly interest in the newly married couple, was arranging to build for them by an easy method of loan and repayment. The new house was a great source of interest, activity, and conflict. Ward had not forgotten his years of apprenticeship in architecture, and soon disconcerted his own architect by his knowledge and acute criticisms. Several violent battles occurred, out of all of which he emerged triumphant. His reward was the rather original and picturesque

[1] Afterwards Sir W. D. Niven, Director of Naval Instruction at Greenwich.
[2] Thomas Dale, Fellow of Trinity, and Third Wrangler, 1862.

house in Selwyn Gardens which he dearly loved, where he lived for nearly forty years, and in which he died.

In 1885 the Psychology Article appeared, and in a very short time established its author's position as the leading English psychologist. It was a comprehensive survey of the whole field from the original point of view which Ward had been developing for years past. Its effect was immediate, and it is not too much to say that it revolutionised the teaching of psychology in Great Britain. Its leading doctrines soon permeated the literature of the subject, and often their origin was forgotten. Bain, whose teaching it was destined largely to supersede (though the importance of his work was fully recognised by Ward), welcomed it with generous praise. Though critical of many of its doctrines and "staggered" by what he called the "aggrandisement of the Subject," he summed up his opinion of it in the following terms (*Mind*, 1886, p. 477):

There is force in everything that he advances; and, for my own part, I have been always instructed, and often convinced, by the arguments in favour of his positions, whether new or old. The form of the treatise, as it now stands in the *Encyclopædia*, has obvious disadvantages. When the matters excluded by the narrow limits are filled in, when the illustration of the whole is duly expanded, and when, finally, the exposition of subtleties is transferred from *brevier* to *pica*, Mr Ward will have produced a work entitled to a place among the masterpieces of the philosophy of the human mind.

The "masterpiece" was long delayed. For some years he had been contemplating a book; and, by agreeing to write the article, he says, "I rashly sacrificed my book...and so, as it has turned out, destroyed one of the dreams of my life." Thus he wrote many years afterwards, recording at the same time the successive stages in the growth of his work. "The article was begun late in 1884 and completed in 1885; then, in 1902, a supplementary article was prepared for the tenth edition of the *Encyclopædia*; and finally, in 1908, these with omissions and additions were hastily amalgamated into the new article of the present edition" (published 1911). But at long last, in 1918, the dream came true and his volume of *Psychological Principles* appeared.

After the publication of the famous 'Article' honours began to come easily to Ward, but writing never did. He would often spend a morning over a sentence, weighing the truth of every word, delete it in the afternoon from a belief that it was insufficiently accurate, and come down to dinner in the evening groaning in spirit—and aloud—and protesting that every page he wrote was wrung from him in torment "I can think of nothing I have learnt to do," he once wrote to Lucy, "in which my pride and my patience have not been sorely tried." Patience was a quality in which, in daily life, he was singularly deficient: to wait for a person, a train, a meal, irritated him furiously. But in building up his psychological or metaphysical theories he could endure any labour better than an imperfectly considered or partial view: and to gain impartiality and the width of view necessary for the philosophy which was to him the consummation of all science, meant a knowledge of all other branches of science. Ward was as ready to enjoy a discussion with a physicist or mathematician on his subject as one on his own, or as a chat with a Highland shepherd on birds—and the enjoyment and profit of such conversations were usually mutual. But the sheer mass of mental labour required by such standards and by such wide interests left little room for other relaxations and pleasures, though not perhaps for other pains.

"Did you ever consider whether a 'thinking machine' was a possibility?" he wrote once, shortly before his marriage:

"I doubt it....It is all very well at first blush to talk of
intellect developed at the expense of heart, but man is far
too intimate a unity for that....Can a man be a profound
thinker and yet lack depth of feeling? Can his thought reach
out into the immensities and the eternities and survey the
inmost seeds of nature and leave him without imagination or
emotion, untouched by aught that concerns this human family
of ours in its struggles and aspirations?...What stirs feeling
so much as thought? Did you ever get any new insight into
things without emotion being stirred at once? I am sure I
never did....So pray don't talk any more of preventing me
from making 'a thinking machine of myself.'...My soul hasn't
been starved by thinking, or, I would rather say, by trying to
think; but thought and feeling have failed me together,
crushed by shame or disappointment which I lacked the
energy or the means to repel....But you will say I run to
sermons, so I will stop."

This was one mood. Several years later in a letter to
the same person, he expressed a hope that he would be
held in loving remembrance after his death and could
break off with: "Ah, why should a foolish man wish
to live in others' memory who has never lived in his
own soul"; and in his last year he more than once declared that "barren philosophy" had rendered him
inhuman and cut him off from life, and wished that he
might live to a hundred to try and mend matters! And
this was another mood.

In 1889 Ward received an Honorary Degree at
Edinburgh, the first of the long series of Degrees and
Memberships of distinguished Societies, English and
foreign, which were conferred upon him (he became
one of the original members of the British Academy and
also a member of the *Institut de France*). In 1894 he
was offered and accepted the Gifford Lectureship at
Aberdeen. The subject of the Lectureship is Natural
Theology, and the most complete freedom of treatment
is left to the lecturer: provided only that his method be

scientific and independent of any appeal to revelation. For some years previously Ward had been lecturing on metaphysics as well as on psychology for the Tripos. This appointment gave him the opportunity and stimulus which he needed to bring his scientific and psychological work into a synthesis with his philosophical speculation.

The task he set himself required a mastery of the methods and results of physical science and biology, as well as of psychology, as the preliminary to his philosophical inquiry; and it is not surprising that the delivery of his twenty lectures was spread over a longer time than usual. They were published in 1899 with the title *Naturalism and Agnosticism*. "They only attempt," he says in the preface, "to discuss in a popular way certain assumptions of 'modern science' which have led to a widespread, but more or less tacit, rejection of idealistic views of the world." This is perhaps too modest a statement of what he aimed at and what he carried through. The greater portion of the work, however, is occupied with these assumptions; it shews that they are due to a confusion between the scientific and philosophical stand-points. The former is necessarily abstract, aiming at expression in mathematical formulae; and the value of science is not affected because it does not or should not, like philosophy, attempt to express the ultimate nature of reality. But Ward is not content with exposing assumptions. The book is really a philosophy of nature; as he afterwards said, it might have been called "The Realm of Nature"; and it ends by setting forth a view of the nature of the real world. Thus he passes from a theory of the nature of scientific knowledge to the construction of a philosophy. Here the results which he had reached in his analysis of individual experience in the "Psychology" come to his assistance. The ultimate at which we arrive in

analysing experience or reality is neither sensations nor
atoms, nor a dualism of the two (or of mind and matter),
but the duality of subject-object. The world is spiritual;
and he calls his theory Spiritualistic Monism: but
by 'monism' he means not that all things are modes of
one substance, but that they have all the same ultimate
nature—that, in varying degrees, they are spiritual.

The thoroughness and lucidity of Ward's argument
in this book—considering his great reputation at the
time, it is odd to remember that it was his first 'book'—
established it at once as a classic. Of course there were
criticisms in plenty. These came in the main from two
sources: from men of science who inclined to naturalism
or agnosticism, and from metaphysicians who were at
one with Ward in giving a spiritual interpretation of
reality but who followed the tradition of Spinoza and
Hegel in stressing the unity of the spiritual reality instead of (like Ward) the tradition of Leibniz and Lotze.

Ward took criticism very seriously, as one who held
that truth would emerge from discussion, and he replied
with great care and candour to all important objections
—the essential passages in these replies being appended
to later editions of his book. When it was first published
Herbert Spencer's system was still the most outstanding
representative of the views which Ward opposed; and
Spencer came in for elaborate and relentless criticism.
To this he replied at some length in the *Fortnightly
Review*, alleging 'animus' on Ward's part; he also
silently corrected a number of the offending passages
in his *First Principles*. These corrections remain, but
his replies were finally and fatally disposed of by Ward.

In 1897 Ward was elected to the new Chair at Cambridge of Mental Philosophy and Logic. In order to
accept it he had to resign his Trinity Tutorship and for-
go a good deal of income both present and future (in
the form of pension), but the honour, and still more the

promise of increased leisure for his own work, decided
him to accept. The Professorship brought him also new
personal relationships of a kind he greatly valued: it
brought him into closer touch with learners and teachers
and other thinkers all the world over, and gave fresh
scope for his inborn instinct to enlighten and to guide.

This instinct of his had been perhaps the greatest of
the many links which bound him to his sister Lucy. In
1892 Lucy, who was almost equally dear to Ward and
to his wife, and who had spent most of her holidays at
their home, had died suddenly after a short illness, at
Bradford where she taught. Everything that was hers,
even down to her botany notes, her brother arranged
and kept, and thus the huge mass of correspondence
in which he had taught and scolded and encouraged
and argued with her came into his cupboards, where
it remained till he died. With Lucy's death one of the
few really intimate ties that bound Ward to the human
world was broken. There had been a hidden kinship
between her passionate, unsatisfied, rebellious nature,
and her brother's.

"I miss Lucy—as we all do—just now very much," he
wrote one Christmas to his mother. "Some of the pleasantest
holidays I ever had were those I took with her, in Wales,
Scotland, Germany, Switzerland. She really had a poet's
soul though without the poet's expression. She was always
striving after what was highest and best, always hungering
for love and rarely got it. That was why we put those words
of Heine's[1] on her grave....I can think of no better picture

[1] A translation of Heine's lyric:

> Der Tod, das ist die kühle Nacht,
>   Das Leben ist der schwüle Tag.
>   Es dunkelt schon, mich schläfert,
> Der Tag hat mich müd' gemacht.
>
> Ueber mein Bett erhebt sich ein Baum,
>   Drin singt die junge Nachtigall;
>   Sie singt von lauter Liebe,
> Ich hör' es sogar im Traum.

of Lucy's 'long sleep' than that of rest after a dusty, sultry day, the song of the nightingale, melancholy and yet sweet, seeming to shape her dreams into dreams of love. Whenever she was here in the early summer she made a point of sleeping with all her windows open that she might hear the nightingale sing."

The unsparing self-criticism which made writing so hard a task for Ward, made lecturing also a strain. He was intensely sensitive to any feeling that he had disappointed his class. It does not appear that he often did so, and his relation to his pupils was an almost unfailingly happy one, and one of the best things in his life. In a memorial notice for *The American Journal of Psychology*, one of his old pupils, Mr F. C. Bartlett, gives a vivid description of the first lecture of Ward's which he attended:

He came slowly into the small room—there were only about eight or nine students—his long, spare form struggling into his gown, his very keen and penetrating eyes taking us all in. It was the first lecture of the year, and there was a certain ritual to go through before he could begin to talk. He must find out who we were, and what we proposed to do, and he must discourage us a little so as to put us into a proper frame of mind. "Well, I don't know why you come to me; I don't know what you expect to get out of me; but whatever it is I expect you will be disappointed." Then he sat down. Out came half a sheet of note-paper which he by no means needed, and for an hour he talked and we were literally held in spell. There was no hesitation, the right word seemed always to come, the illustrations were frequent, brilliant and human, the asides and reminiscences were full of fun. There was little formality. Nobody could do much in the way of taking notes....That was not all. We met him at other times in his own home. Then, when he was in the vein, he would talk, as few can talk, about anything and everything....

Of course there were some pupils with whom he did not hit it off. Dr Montagu Butler, with characteristic generosity, once wrote to a friend about Ward, then just elected Tutor:

I have seldom been so anxious for a friend's success in public work as I am for his. He is not an *intimate* friend of mine, and probably never will be—his intellect is so far above mine and so differently constituted—but I really love the man, and feel that he has a kind of greatness in him which may—or may not—catch and lift the young fellows[1].

Yet it was in vain for the same wise well-wisher to admonish Ward, as he did, that he should 'suffer fools gladly': for pretentious folly always roused him to outbursts of satirical contempt. To simple-minded ignorance, on the other hand, honestly seeking knowledge he could give lavishly of his time and thought. He would have his students frequently for long talks in his study: he would try by the hour to explain abstruse philosophical ideas to persevering Indians and Chinese who had hardly learnt the elements of English: he would carefully criticise and correct first attempts at philosophising on the part of total strangers: he would write long letters to try to enlighten and encourage honest spirits who were clinging as he had once clung to Christian doctrine and finding their reason at war with their faith. He grumbled—sometimes fiercely—but he did it.

One of the most interesting and enjoyable events in Ward's later life was his trip to America to lecture, in the summer of 1904. Here he found himself again almost like a pastor with his flock. His audiences were frequently unintellectual but always they were keen and perfectly confident that he could give them new light. He addressed a large gathering at the St Louis Exhibition, lectured in various other places, both east and west, and spent a whole term giving a course of

---

[1] See *Henry Montagu Butler, Master of Trinity*, p. 54.

lectures at Berkeley where the glorious climate and hospitable people brought him much enjoyment, though during most of his trip he was far from well. He saw and did a great deal, and on his way back visited the Yellowstone Park, a thrilling experience to so ardent a lover of nature.

"I have had a grand time this afternoon," he writes to his wife from Lake Tahoe in June, "starting out about 3 and expecting to be back by 5.30....But I got lost in the forest and did not get back till nearly 7....The pines here are splendid, I never saw such trees before....I got down into some swampy ground and found heaps of lovely things, but the mosquitoes were rather too friendly. I am happy to say they do me no harm....I found many plants that we have, and many that would grow with us, such things as..." (here follows a long list of Latin names).

Writing from the Yellowstone Park in September of the vast tracts of plain and mountain he has passed through, and of the great irrigation works undertaken around Washington, he says,

But what is already done in the way of irrigation is nothing to what will be done: as the train passed along "where the mighty Missouri rolls down to the sea" I could not help trying to picture the thriving population there will surely be there—all young and hopeful, with no old world pessimism—long after I am gone and forgotten. The world after all is far from played out yet: surely there *is* a good time coming.

And from the Yellowstone Lake, a few days later,

Spite of many interruptions I have just finished the address which I am to deliver a week hence at St Louis. Hurrah! I am sitting on the shingly beach of this beautiful lake...with an old log for a table....It is so quiet that I can hear the rustle of the grasshoppers' wings as they fly about on sails of black and gold. Two huge pelicans are floating about hard by....In a willow bush just overhead a family of pretty yellow wrens paid me a visit, twittering as they hung from the boughs in the most friendly manner....*Grand Canyon*—

Sept. 14. It is possible to get out in three or four places on huge precipitous cliffs and look down the Canyon...on the tops of pinnacles I counted half a dozen ospreys' nests and several of these fine birds were sailing about in grand circles with outstretched wings hundreds of feet below. I saw one alight on its nest and eat a fish....I spent four hours this afternoon on the Canyon and saw and enjoyed it thoroughly. ...I started later than the crowd and went on in front, so I had it almost entirely to myself. I got out on to a crag at one place which they call Grand View. I had been sitting there some time when a party came along: there was not room for two on my perch so I rose to leave. "Keep your place," the first man said, "I don't aspire to that."...Yes, the Canyon is fine, but what ages it must have taken the river to carve it out—the river itself bound all the way to the Gulf of Mexico. Nature is very great and very patient, and what an ephemeral thing is this man that comes buzzing about and occasionally pretending to philosophise!

A good deal of patience however had been required of Ward himself in his attempts to philosophise to a mixed American audience.

"My audience," he wrote from Berkeley, "is mostly women....The numbers keep up so far—60 or more....Two days ago a strapping damsel came up at the end of a lecture to complain that she feared she did not understand. 'Well, but have you not some general idea of the drift of it all?' I said. 'Yes, indeed I have, too many ideas,' she replied. Today she floored me with the remark: 'Can't you explain to me the difference between subject and object: I don't see any!' I don't know which to wonder at most, the eagerness of these people or their superficiality....An Oakland engineer wrote to me to know if his wife could attend my lectures. Here is an extract from his letter: 'You will understand why I ask when I tell you that she is a psychic being especially sensitive psychometrically, the peculiar effects of the practice of psychometry on the solar plexus, the brain and ganglia, and the many facts she has gathered from various fields of inquiry has made her anxious for knowledge on the subject from some eminently successful psychologist.'"

Ward never lost the friends he made in America, and their letters and occasional visits were a recurrent pleasure to him.

In 1904 he was once more appointed a Gifford Lecturer, this time at St Andrews. The lectures were delivered in 1907–10, and published in 1911 as *The Realm of Ends*. This book carried the argument of *Naturalism and Agnosticism* further, indeed to its natural conclusion. *Naturalism and Agnosticism* had issued in an idealistic or spiritualistic view of the universe. But, so far, the universe might still be described as 'pluralistic'—an aggregate, or a society, of monads which manifest varying degrees of life or mind. But this view was only a starting-point for further speculation. "From a world of spirits to a Supreme Spirit is a possible step," he had said in *Naturalism and Agnosticism*; *The Realm of Ends* shews how this step can be taken. It starts with the hypothesis of a pluralistic universe and tests its consistency and adequacy as a final explanation; then, after the way to theism has been opened, it exhibits the changed aspect under which nature and human life are seen—the cosmology of theism.

The human interest of this book made it appeal to an even wider circle than that reached by his previous works, and coloured its reception even by the expert.

"It is superfluous," wrote Professor A. E. Taylor at the outset of a long review (*Mind*, 1912, p. 427), "to summarise the argument of a book which all who care seriously for philosophy in Great Britain may be expected to study closely, sentence by sentence, for themselves, and elaborate criticism is hardly possible to a reviewer who agrees so thoroughly with all the main positions contended for that his natural impulse is simply to thank God that we have such a philosopher as Dr Ward among us."

The preparation of these Gifford lectures and of the book had been a hard fight. Ward was suffering from a distressing ailment all the time, and had postponed the necessary operation in order to carry through his undertaking. As soon as the lectures were over, after two years of severe nervous strain, he went to London for an operation in the autumn of 1910. He had an idea that he might not survive it, and took something of a last farewell of his friends on the afternoon before he left. He was dangerously ill, but did slowly pull round, and for the remaining fifteen years of his life was both stronger and more serene. In 1912 he delivered the Sidgwick Memorial Lecture at Newnham College entitled *Heredity and Memory*.

The faculty for just and dispassionate judgment, which undoubtedly sometimes failed Ward in his personal relationships, was never wanting in his attitude to larger issues. The war—which affected him the more owing to his intimate knowledge and love of Germany —did not unbalance him as it did so many of the older generation, even when they were spared, as he was, any close personal loss. Through it all his outlook was sane, hopeful, and without bitterness. Though his own enthusiasm for his country's cause and for those who defended it was unassailable, he opposed himself to any attack on freedom of thought, and fought strenuously in his own College to prevent what he felt to be the unjust treatment of Pacifism.

The last ten years of his life were probably the happiest and most peaceful that he had known. Though they lay between the ages of seventy-two and eighty-two he retained an extraordinary youthfulness, both in mind and body. His erect carriage and light firm step never flagged: and the width of his interests narrowed but very little. Through the middle years of his life his greatest pleasure had been in his garden which he had planned and planted with his own hands, and in which he knew every hidden bud and blade. It was only in the last few years that he gave up working in it: and only then too that he began to be less quick and sure in detecting a rare bird from its song or its flight. His love of nature and knowledge of her ways was a source of constant enjoyment to his three children. A mile's walk with him was worth ten miles with any ordinary human being of only average powers of observation. His hearing was against him; but his eyes were hawk-like, and his sense of smell very acute. Every strange plant, every rustle in the hedge, every rapid flutter of a shy bird, every rare shell on the shore, every unusual geological formation, he would notice and discourse about in the most fascinating manner. If the walk were incorrigibly dull, then he would find some interesting information to give about the clouds, or start some Sherlock-Holmes-like investigations, based on foot-prints and fallen hairpins. That blend of knowledge and alertness, with his quite peculiar ironical and whimsical humour which is wholly impossible to re-produce but which was continually flashing out un-expectedly in his own home, in some comic remark or prank or impromptu rhyme, made him a delightful com-panion to his family, whenever he was happy enough to be companionable. Two things only removed him entirely out of reach—bad moods, and chess. His passion for playing chess did not develop till middle life but his utter detestation of being beaten dates from his first attempts. In a diary for 1881 there are two very telling entries on the occasion of his spending Christmas with a brother-in-law. "*Dec. 24th.* Played at chess and lost all the games this time. *Dec. 25th.* Miserable Xmas. The ——s don't understand mak-ing relatives comfortable." This childish weakness he never overcame, and his absorption in a game of chess was so entire that it needed a catastrophe to divert his attention from it.

JAMES & MARY WARD
In their Cambridge Garden during the War

Another interest he developed in his children and shared with them, was a love for strange pets. At one time as many as seventeen odd creatures inhabited his house and garden: owls, herons, seagulls, jackdaws, snakes, hedgehogs, tortoises, with always a cat or two and a dog, were quite usual lodgers. He was unfailingly kind if any of these creatures—or any others—were in distress, and would at once come down from his study to their aid, armed with surgical or medical appliances. For he added a considerable knowledge of medicine to his other gifts, and one which was always increasing, since whenever any of his family were ill he used to fetch armfuls of medical books from the University Library and study the case: and when he was ill himself he sometimes disconcerted his doctors by the extent and accuracy of his knowledge. The last and dearest of his pets was his collie dog, Jan. This dog went with him to his lectures, leaving him at the door and returning at the exact hour to fetch him home again: accompanied him on all his walks, and spent the evenings under his study table, ready with silent canine sympathy, shewn by a great brown head laid on his knee, if some sigh or groan had betrayed that *Denken* was more than usually *schwer*. On one occasion Jan actually succeeded in attending one of his master's lectures. It was an important occasion, and the dog seems to have realised it[1]. Ward was giving the Sidgwick lecture at Newnham College: Jan followed him into the College unobserved, silently padded upstairs to the gallery of the hall, put his snout through the railing, and gazed earnestly and wistfully at his master talking to the human crowd below. Ward missed this dog greatly during the years that he survived him, and

[1] As he had done once before, when he took himself to Great St Mary's, arriving only a little late for the marriage of Ward's elder daughter.

often said he felt his ghostly presence following him upstairs, or waiting under the table.

The old ministerial instinct to advise and help which made Ward so invariably willing to answer his children's questions and doctor their pets brought him also on many occasions into close and affectionate relations (not unmixed with a certain dread on their side!) with his servants and other members of the working class; he often took great pains to help them in any difficulty; and being very democratic at bottom, he won many a simple heart by discoursing of politics and natural history over the flower beds or the paint pots.

The recognition which his work won so widely towards the end of his life had also a softening and cheering influence upon him. His sensitive pride had always led him to underrate his success. In February 1914 his portrait was presented to the University by a group of friends and admirers, and in his speech of thanks he quite openly confessed to having felt a shadow over him for many years until that day, from a sense that his work in particular and philosophy in general had not been much valued in Cambridge.

"I do not say that without this expression of your approval and goodwill," he said, "I should have felt self-condemned. I believe in philosophy, though Cambridge as a whole doesn't or didn't. I know that philosophy can bake no bread, but I know too that man does not live by bread alone, and I believe that philosophy ministers to higher needs than science ever can. So I have worked loyally and whole-heartedly in the service of this ancient queen of the sciences, though I have had to share the contempt till lately accorded to her in this place."

After a short autobiographical passage he concluded his speech by saying, "If I am anything at all, I owe it to two men, Hermann Lotze and Henry Sidgwick."

Again ten years later, on his eightieth birthday, many letters and congratulations reached him from different parts of the world. All these tributes gave him a very real happiness, for they convinced him that he had not lived in vain. They shewed that for many people he had succeeded in doing what he had grimly set himself to do those fifty years earlier when his own Temple of Faith crumbled and he started in the waste to build another that should stand on a firmer foundation—firmer at least for those minds which, like his own, needed a rational and intellectual basis for their beliefs. The extent to which he had succeeded in this was perhaps most fully revealed, however, in the letters written about him after his death.

"I regard it as one of my greatest privileges to have been his pupil," wrote one: and some others: "Dr Ward's teaching was an event in my life." "I have always counted my association with him as his pupil during my fourth year as one of the great influences for good in my life...and such humble contributions as I have been able to make to philosophy were due to the inspiration and encouragement which I received from him." "His teaching and his personality have been a lasting inspiration to me." "For thirty-five years it has been a proud thing to have been a pupil of Dr Ward's, and to all that that meant there has been added the incredible kindness of his welcome whenever one went back —the flame of interest and friendliness that never seemed to fail however much time passed. He taught some of us not only what the search for truth meant but what the encouragement of young and unimportant people might mean too." "What I have thought and written in Psychology and Philosophy," writes Professor Stout, "has always been closely connected with his teaching and largely dependent on it. My debt to him in this way is too great for me to measure. Yet it is my settled belief that there is much more in him of lasting value than I or anyone else has yet assimilated and used."

In 1918 appeared what was in a sense Ward's *magnum opus* and contained the fruits of forty years of study and preparation, his *Psychological Principles*. Four years later he delivered the Hertz Lecture to the British Academy. The subject of the lecture was Immanuel Kant, and in order to prepare it he set himself with his usual thoroughness to read Kant's works over again as well as much recent Kantian literature. As a result what was meant to be a lecture grew into a book; the delivery of the lecture had to be postponed for a year; the book, *A Study of Kant*, appeared first and then the lecture which was founded on it.

It was to be his last book, for though he had much else that he still wished to write the remaining two years did not suffice for the production of more than a few articles. The last thing he wrote, a few months before his death, was an article for the *Hibbert Journal* on "The Christian Doctrine of Faith and Eternal Life." A very serious illness of his wife's which she was hardly expected to survive caused him prolonged anxiety in the last year of his life, but she rallied, and his last months were made happy by her recovery, and by various enterprises of his children in which he felt an interest and pride. In the winter of 1924, not long before his eighty-second birthday, he was knocked down by a careless motorist when walking home from College at night, and was picked up suffering from slight concussion. He was very much shaken, and though he seemed to regain something like his normal strength after a few weeks, he was unable to lecture during most of the next term and suffered from increased attacks of giddiness. By the end of February however he seemed to be quite recovered, and little more than a week before he died had a group of his students to lunch with him and talked to them with all his old keenness and vitality. A few days after heart trouble shewed itself. He soon learnt for himself what the symptoms meant, and realising his danger remarked, "So I am to have an easy death." Yet he would gladly have lived on. It was not long since he had suddenly burst out to an old friend in the middle of a walk, "The days of our years are threescore years and ten: and if by reason of strength they be fourscore years, yet is their strength labour and sorrow...but *I* have not found it so!"

The day before he died (when his condition seemed to be steadily improving) his mind was running on Shakespeare, and he made merry with his elder daughter over some passages in *A Midsummer Night's Dream* in which he had acted as a boy—then suddenly broke off with a favourite quotation, "Lord now lettest thou thy servant depart in peace." He died suddenly on March 4th, 1925. The news, an old friend said, "came like the shock of the death of a young man." His body was cremated; and a memorial service of a broad simplicity and beauty, which perhaps his own work had done something to make possible, was held in Trinity College Chapel on March 8th. A very remarkable figure had passed out of the Cambridge world. Few men have had so strangely complex a character; and few perhaps a more striking exterior. His thoughts and not his conflicts were expressed in old age upon his face, the harmony and beauty of which increased with years. "He had too much philosophy," a distinguished admirer of his said to me, a few months after he died, "that we might all have a little." Yes— probably he had had too much. But not ten different lives would have wholly reconciled his nature, or exhausted his eager intellect and ambitions. As it was he had found in philosophy not a life of easy meditation but a hard and strenuous pursuit, and with that perhaps his fighting nature was content.

UNANSWERED

Ah yes I know where the rayed sundews grow
  And small pink gentian stars the salted grass:
The sad sea-voices of the birds I know,
  And I could pace the shore and never pass
The tern's nest in the stones: for long ago
  You taught my childish sense to hear and see.
And now along familiar sands I go
  With no one on the wild wide shore but me.

Dark spreads the tide across the drowning strand,
  And day streams fading through a narrow door
Curtained with storm. Piping above the roar
  The rosy-footed plovers skim to land.
One strange grey bird, all ghost-like, dares the swell;
  What kind of bird it is I cannot tell——
You would have told me. I shall never know.

O. C.

ESSAYS

I

CAN FAITH REMOVE MOUNTAINS?

THE time was when such a question would have seemed as impious as now to many it must seem imbecile. The victors by faith were then a great cloud of witnesses, whom none could gainsay, whom all could emulate: then the reign of Law was unknown as modern science understands it: "the whole choir of heaven and furniture of the earth" were but the language of a Father of Spirits addressed to created spirits free and intelligent like himself.

It was a true foresight that led the immortal thinker on tar-water, whose words I just now quoted, to discern in our modern savants or 'minute philosophers,' as he terms them, the uncompromising opponents of that conception of nature on which the theistic faith has been wont to rest. He essayed to do them battle but it must be allowed that he was foiled: indeed we may regard the Idealism of Berkeley as proving only the futility of engaging in speculation for practical ends instead of solely in the interests of truth.

Nowadays the 'minute philosophers' are supreme. The uniformity of the laws of nature, the continuity of all the changes of nature, shut us in like mountains, which mock at prayer and convert faith into folly or even sin.

 here is God, and there is God.   Tho' old Religion shake her head
lieve it not, O Man;   And say in bitter grief,
 such vain sort to this and that   The day behold at first foretold
he ancient heathen ran.   Of atheist unbelief;

> Take better part, with manly heart
> Thine adult spirit can;
> Receive it not, believe it not,
> Believe it not, O Man.

So complete is this revolution that some of the earnest
men of our day, like a departed member of this society,
even preach the duty of rooting out religion, name and
thing. Speaking of the authors of one of the latest
attempts to reconcile science and religion he says:

"Only for another half-century let us keep our hells and
heavens and gods." It is a piteous plea; and it has soiled the
heart of these prophets, great ones and blessed, giving light
to their generation, and dear in particular to our mind and
heart. These sickly dreams of hysterical women and half-
starved men, what have they to do with the sturdy strength
of a wide-eyed hero who fears no foe with pen or club? This
sleepless vengeance of fire upon them that have not seen and
have not believed, what has it to do with the gentle patience
of the investigator that shines through every page of this
book [*The Unseen Universe*], that will ask only consideration
and not belief for anything that has not with infinite pains
been solidly established? That which you keep in your hearts,
my brothers, is the slender remnant of a system which has
left its red mark on history, and still lives to threaten mankind. The grotesque forms of its intellectual belief have survived the discredit of its moral teaching. Of this what the
kings could bear with the nations have cut down; and what
the nations left, the right heart of man by man revolts against
day by day. You have stretched out your hands to save the
dregs of the sifted sediment of a residuum. Take heed lest
you have given soil and shelter to the seed of that awful
plague which has destroyed two civilisations, and but barely
failed to slay such promise of good as is now struggling to live
among men[1].

But is it after all quite certain that a fearless and truth-
loyal man must renounce religion or else, like Faraday,
refuse to make his creed amenable to those canons of
reason by which he is guided in all matters beside?

[1] W. K. Clifford, *Lectures and Essays* (1879), pp. 252, 253.

Now this is the question to which I would fain have an answer and for the sake of which I propose to inquire whether faith can remove mountains not in the high *a priori* fashion which is now out of favour, but according to the most approved style of our modern prophets, who believe in space of *n* dimensions and gaze in awe at globigerina ooze.

But first for a definition of terms. By 'faith' I mean not the intellectual acceptance of a creed but that personal trust and confidence in an Unseen Being to which the religious in all ages have attributed their power to 'overcome the world.' No one with a grain of psychological insight can doubt that the actions of men like St Paul, St Francis, John Wesley or Henry Martyn were as really shaped by such a personal trust as were the actions say of the soldiers of Wellington or Napoleon by their confidence in their leader. Nay it is not too much to say that the faith of the Christian saint as truly determined his action as the urge of nature determines the action of the most wisely scientific of our day. That we doubt whether they had the same rational justification of their faith is quite another matter. The only thing we have to lay hold of now is that their actions could hardly have been more conformed to their belief if that belief had been exchanged for the face-to-face knowledge which they were assured would one day consummate it. And by 'mountains' I mean chiefly all that in the light of modern science and philosophy constitutes the impossibility of this consummation. But I do not include physical impossibilities such as making the past present, turning water into wine or making hatchets float on the top of it. Neither on the other hand would I include mere moral impossibilities, if there be such—e.g., the attainment of a more heroic standard of virtue or greater internal freedom and peace of mind than mere mundane motives ordinarily ensure. By 'faith removing mountains' then I mean realizing its object and so justifying itself by the actual experience and knowledge of what has been hoped for while yet unseen. When for the sake of argument St Paul contemplated the possibility of his faith being groundless he declared himself in that event of all men most miserable: if such be indeed, as some aver, the melancholy outcome of the theist's hope, then, however heroic and holy may have been his life, I for my part should say that his faith had been a failure and no mountains were removed.

So much by way of explicating terms; it now remains to ask by what method we shall conduct our inquiry. As we eschew the transcendental and cannot directly know what lies in that undiscovered country from whose bourn no traveller returns, nor even if there be such a country at all, we must needs content ourselves first by a brief critical examination of the prevailing dicta concerning the nature of the mountains that frustrate and falsify faith. And then, should we see reason to reject these, we may take a hint from Butler and consider how far the present constitution and course of nature, as modern science positively conceives it, shew us anything analogous to this power of faith to transplant mountains.

First then as to the grounds on which faith is nowadays declared absurd and irrational. The unbroken chain of physical cause and effect we are told excludes any real communion with any extra-mundane being now and the complete interdependence of mind on body forbids the hope of such communion hereafter. Now I am not going to deny either of these premises although I am not prepared to accept the conclusions. But it is one thing to believe a general proposition inductively established and quite another thing to know all the particulars it will cover. It is precisely because

of that difference in fact that there is still so much for
a science to do when it has risen to the rank of a deductive science. What appeared at first sight quite
beyond the range of its principles or even as a provoking
and ugly exception turns out at last a most charming
corollary at once a consequence and a verification of
the fundamental law. I do not quarrel with modern
thought for insisting on physical continuity or on the
inconceivability of disembodied spirits. But I must
protest against that finality which regards our most
general conceptions as if they were handcuffs on a once
vagrant body of facts now at length secure and well
known to the savants, or as like the crystal sphere of
the ancients enclosing a finite and definite region of
particulars leaving nothing but the fools' paradise beyond. There is, I imagine, but one kind of knowledge
which would enable us to say what is or is not possible
in the future, and that is such absolutely perfect knowledge of the present as would amount to intuition, and
this in turn implies as condition of its possibility a like
previous knowledge of the past. But the very method
of all our knowing necessitates ignorance: to know we
must abstract, i.e., ignore as comparatively irrelevant
details with which we cannot cope; and so we spin over
'the solid ground of nature' the thin webs of our
systems and think we have comprehended the universe.
The swinging of a church lamp, the falling of an apple,
were such irrelevant details till Galileo and Newton
saw in them the very foundations of physics. The heat
developed by friction was a detail that escaped even
Newton, and yet on the experiments to which this
phenomenon led Count Rumford rests in large measure
the modern doctrine of the conservation of energy. The
variation of domestic pigeons was an irrelevant detail
till it set Darwin to investigate the origin of species.
Surely then if our boasted uniformity of nature is worth

anything it should lead us to expect that in the future as in the past innumerable new facts that lie outside the meshes of our present science will furnish the starting-points for fresh lines by which we shall comprehend nature more completely without doing any violence to those fundamental conceptions by which alone we can comprehend it at all. Allowing then to the full the continuity of nature I cannot see that modern science is entitled to the proud boast I once heard made by the German Tyndall[1] on her behalf: *endlich haben wir das Universum entgöttert.* It is possible nothing exists at all answering to the God in whom the religious put their trust and in whose likeness they look to rise from the dead. But such negative is at most possible. There is nothing in our present knowledge to make it certain.

But I may go further. Keep strictly to the scientific standpoint and you will find no evidence of consciousness of any sort. The reasoning which led Descartes to regard brutes as automata was scientifically unimpeachable and is more cogent to-day than ever; but then we are bound in consistency to apply it to man too. And though the fact is little known, Descartes did so apply it albeit with certain untenable reservations in favour of reason. To talk of *conscious* automata, as Huxley does, is sheer nonsense. No man knows himself as an automaton and no man knows any consciousness but his own. On the strength of this he *interprets* certain material forms and movements as manifestations of a consciousness, but such interpretation is no part of the facts presented nor necessary to their scientific formulation. That consciousness is a possible concomitant of the antics of certain automata is all that science can say. A sufficient knowledge of the laws of matter and motion and of the course of evolution would explain the phenomenon now making a noise: but stick well to your

---

[1] Du Bois-Reymond.—Ed.

measurements and further than that you will hardly
get. But what Prof. Huxley was polite enough to do
for his hearers at Belfast the theist's faith leads him to
do for the world as a whole: the one inferred consciousness back of human organisms, the other infers God as
the Life and Source of all. Science can disprove neither
the one position nor the other.

Again, though all that we know of consciousness forbids the belief that such consciousness could exist out
of connexion with a material world of some sort, yet
there is nothing in our present knowledge to shew that
there may not be other forms of embodiment besides
that with which we are familiar; nay, there is nothing
in our present knowledge to shew that consciousness
has not manifold other relations with the existing organism and environment than we can as yet explain.
If we knew nothing of embryology and if it happened
that the process of dying consisted in a gradual reversal
of the process of growth and differentiation, so that a
corpse should be nothing but a tiny and apparently
homogeneous speck of protoplasm so small that a
pillbox might almost furnish grave-room enough for
all the dead of London—we should, I fancy, be quite
as sure as we can be now that the renewal of such
a life was an idle dream. And yet in such a speck we
have

> Although the print be little, the whole matter
> And copy of the father,—eye, nose, lip,
>
> .   .   .   .   .
>
> The very mould and frame of hand, nail, finger[1].

And what is more we have the trick of his frown and
very often the bent of his mind and character too.

If then it is reasonable to demur to the scientific
dogmatism which proclaims the absurdity of religious

[1] Cp. *The Realm of Ends*, p. 398.—Ed.

faith, we may proceed in the next place to consider what analogies there are to justify that faith, so far as analogy can justify anything, and under what circumstances such analogies will apply.

The worst we can say of religious faith is that it leads to a line of conduct that present facts do not warrant, that it is not rational in the sense of being clearly deducible from anything that we certainly know. Now I think if we glance at the past history of the organic world as Darwin and Spencer expressed it, we shall find that almost every forward step could be formulated in this way: it was an act of faith not warranted by aught within the ken of the savant at that point. There was little for example in all that the wisest fish could know to justify the belief that there was more scope for existence on the earth than in the water and that persistent attempts to live on land would issue in the transformation of his swim bladder into lungs. And when as yet there was not a bird to cleave the air there was surely little in all that the most daring of saurian speculators could surmise concerning that untrodden element to warrant any risk to his bones to satisfy his longing to soar, although when he did try his fore-legs were changed to wings at length and his dim prevision of a bird became incarnate in himself. No doubt with perfect knowledge all this would be otherwise, but the point is that with such knowledge as ours the maxim holds: nothing venture nothing have. We trust and try first and understand after, till at length we are almost at one with Anselm's *Credo ut intelligam.* The whole history of man and indeed of all animate nature seems to me to teem with instances in which mountains that reason or, if you will, that science could see have been surmounted or levelled by blind faith, encouraged it may be or awakened by vague promptings to which reason, having—as has been well said—eyes but no

ears, had no clue and gave no heed. I know nothing
more wonderful than this unscientific trustfulness that
from the very beginning seems to have been ingrained
in things, likening them to Abraham the type and
father of the faithful who "when he was called . . .
obeyed and went out, not knowing whither he went."[1]

There is then in this respect nothing unique in religious faith at all; and the only question that remains
is to inquire whether or not it has the marks that in
the past have distinguished false faith from true. The
only test we can apply from our present point of view
is that of success, survival of the fittest. Any piece of
daring on the part of nature that issued in the annihi-
lation or degeneration of the adventurer may be said
to have been inspired by mistaken faith. Before the
first lowly beast that began to use his limbs in feeding
could attain to the possession of distinct foot-jaws he
must have been able to succeed in the struggle for
existence during all the stages of the transformation.
And all that we can ask concerning religious faith prior
to its consummation is whether even now obedience to
its dictates entails defeat and degeneration here. The
founder of Christianity was prepared I think on the
whole to stand by this test: "Ye shall know them by
their fruits: do men gather grapes of thorns, or figs of
thistles?" But whether or not, it is the test that men
will apply. Nothing that science can say will ever
quench men's faith in God if they find that on the
whole they make the best of this world by it, while on
the other hand atheism will assuredly prevail if here,
take him all in all, the atheist proves the better man.
There are plenty who would spurn this as a very
grovelling sentiment. But I take it it is not sentiment
at all but fact—the simple truth that however much in
theory men consider premisses; in practice, which ever

[1] Cp. *The Realm of Ends*, pp. 415 f.—Ed.

precedes theory, they consider only results. But the practice which justifies itself by results is also in the end at one with the theory it has helped to complete.

It must be allowed that we have had religion of one sort or another in the world for a long time now whereas atheism has not yet had a fair trial. By all means let those who regard it as the wiser doctrine live it out and see what they can make of it; and there is no reason why we should not own that among the few who have done so there have been noble and high-minded men. But on the other hand we ought not to overlook the fact that most men are atheists not so much from choice as from necessity, i.e., as it seems to me, under the mistaken notion that God has been proved an impossibility. Nor is this strange, when we remember how rudely the old supports have been shaken on which the belief in God was made to rest. The tide that seems to have overwhelmed the legends of the church and the dogmas of the school will I verily believe turn out to have left the essence of religion purer and plainer than before. I suspect a careful study of history would shew that atheism has never been an independent growth but always a symptom of suspended faith disappearing when faith resumed its function. Our Du Bois-Reymonds and our Tyndalls tell us that atheism has hardly lost its hold on Europe for three hundred years. But long as this time appears it is short in the history of our race, and it is equally true that during that same three hundred years a religious reformation has been in progress which is even yet but half complete.

If then the causes of the existing unreligiousness are temporary and if there is really nothing in modern knowledge incompatible with religious development, we may ask if it is not conceivable that in the course of it mountains may be removed and new possibilities

of existence revealed which scientific induction would
never discover and to which no secular projects would
ever lead us to attain. Let us imagine two races of
intelligences living originally side by side—the one
acting only on evidence seen and temporal, the other
led by a faith in the unseen and eternal—is it not
possible that by and by the two may be as wide apart
as we now find *Homo sapiens* and the Social Ascidian,
whose ancestors we are told were Tunicata together in
the long long past in 'the clear green sea,' and the
latter of which we know is among the Tunicata still?[1]
And as the creatures that strained towards the light
now have eyes to see while those that cleave to the
primal slime remain full of darkness, may it not be that
those among men who trust their religious impulses
will attain in the end an insight as superior to all the
inferences based on sight as sight itself is to the gropings
of the blind? Much that must puzzle a creature that
can feel but not see must be plain to one that basked
in the sunshine till the light had kindled for it eyes: the
one would find a wide world and plenty while the
other would pine and grovel in a ditch. There was a
time, the evolutionists tell us, when consciousness had
not appeared on the scene, and the development of
self-consciousness out of this was a process long and
slow. But is self-consciousness the highest form of
psychical life conceivable? Is there no meaning in the
conception of a God-consciousness too? Those in whom
self-consciousness is most developed are the readiest to
admit that the light is dim when they seek to penetrate
to this self: if this darkness should clear away might
there not be something revealed of which our philosophies as yet scarcely dream? And may not the
straining after God to which faith in Him leads,
quicken this new consciousness into life and shew at

[1] Cp. *The Realm of Ends*, p. 414.—Ed.

length that it was from Him the impulse sprang? For if we regard the world as a whole as the Unknown struggling into life, may not religious faith be a higher phase of this struggle; and if so is it not as likely to be consummated as those lower and blinder impulses have been?

* * * * *

[1]If, then, the criteria of faith and knowledge are distinct, if the one is justified by its worth in the living experience of the believing individual, and the other is verified in the universal experience to which thought pertains, the two in their pure forms might co-operate, but should never conflict. Adopting the common representation of faith as blind and confiding, science as deaf and suspicious, might we not picture science—that can see the storm, the fire, and the earthquake—as ministering to faith as that follows the still small voice? From the merely perceptual consciousness of the brute, man has risen—and risen, too, through faith in his kind—to consciousness of self, and has attained conscience and reason. From these in turn his faith in God has sprung. Is God-consciousness then unrealizable, incapable of development: or may not faith here, again, usher in a higher level of life and an insight passing the scientific understanding? So the theist reasons; but as we all know science at present does not minister to faith or allow that it has any message, but denies it all right and room, not only with an *Ignoramus*, we do not know, but with an *Ignorabitis*, you will never know, which means that faith is delusive and worthless.

This situation is readily explained historically if we had time to deal with it. Religion has been, and still

---

[1] The following paragraphs are taken from the conclusion of a lecture given in 1904.—Ed.

is, unwarrantably dogmatic. The so-called knowledge that Kant spoke of abolishing—the rational psychology and theology of dogmatic metaphysics—owed its existence, it should be remembered, to theology, and not to science. On the other hand, science has, what we may call for the present, a counter faith of its own. It is in this *impasse* or deadlock that philosophy can effectively intervene. Such intervention we find, I think, in the reflections that made Hume sceptical, and Kant critical, in regard to scientific knowledge. The result, stated briefly but with sufficient accuracy for our purpose, is that the whole fabric of science—so far as it relates to reality—can be shewn to rest upon a theoretical postulate, our primitive credulity methodized. And we may add that its entire organon of real categories—substance, cause, and end—are anthropomorphic, projections of ourselves. But once projected, their source is forgotten, and their significance dwindles. So we get first a dualism of nature and mind, and finally a supposed evolution of mind from nature. The opposition between the faith of religion and the faith of science is then complete. But philosophy, too, has its postulate—that of the unity and rationality of all experience, theoretical and practical alike. Science itself becomes intelligible only if the knower and the known are not utterly disparate, if nature, too, is ultimately and essentially spirit. Evolution becomes intelligible only if the groaning and travailing of the whole creation is not doomed for ever to be subjected to vanity. Its earnest expectation of 'redemption' is seen to be a faith at one with reason itself.

THE PROGRESS OF PHILOSOPHY

THE words of Schiller which the Glasgow Philosophical Society has taken as a motto—

Welche wohl bleibt von allen Philosophien? Ich weiss nicht.
Aber die Philosophie, hoff' ich, soll ewig bleiben—

might, at first blush, be regarded as a confession at once
of the hopelessness of the attainment and of the worth
of the pursuit of philosophical knowledge. Hamilton,
as we all know, held substantially this opinion, and
supported it in his usual style with a wealth of illustration drawn from all quarters. In his first lecture on
Metaphysics he says: "The last worst calamity that
could befal man, as he is at present constituted, would
be that full and final possession of speculative truth,
which he now vainly anticipates as the consummation
of his intellectual happiness. . .and the man who first
declared that he was not a σοφός, or possessor, but a
φιλόσοφος, or seeker of truth, at once enounced the true
end of human speculation and embodied it in a significant name." Now, I do not propose at present to
controvert this position either wholly or in part, but
merely to suggest that in whatever respects it is true of
philosophy it is true of the several sciences. We might
just as well ask, Which of all the physics, or which of
all the chemistries remains? as ask, Which of all the
philosophies remains? No exposition of a science, no
matter what, that is a century old, would be considered
adequate to-day; and the science, absolutely regarded,
is as much as ever an ideal. We talk of the sciences as
if they were completed wholes, whereas all that exists
in fact is but a collection of approximations—partial,

inchoate, imperfect. Archimedes, Galileo, Newton, are immortal names in the history of physics, but Newton's *Principia* is no more *the* science of physics than Euclid's *Elements* is *the* science of geometry. The progress of all the sciences shews the same essential features: isolated truths come first, and principles last of all; working hypotheses, like rudimentary organs or temporary scaffolding, lead to the establishment of laws by which they are refuted and superseded, or they themselves are confirmed as permanent constituents of knowledge by a more or less gradual process of verification; resemblances undetected at first relate the many with the one; closer scrutiny discloses composition and complexity in what had long been regarded as without parts and without structure; and even that thickest of all veils—familiarity—is pushed aside, so that boundless fields of inquiry stand revealed where never a question had been asked before. With many differences in detail, this and the like is what we find, in the main, in every department of knowledge; and it seems fairly obvious that it must be so, since Mind is one essential factor in knowledge, and the only one that is the same in all. What I would venture to maintain, then, is that philosophy, as regards its history and development, does not differ *in genere* from the body of the sciences. In intent it is as legitimate as they are, and, allowing for differences of subject-matter, it has advanced about as much. Just a word on each of these points.

Without wasting time in any discussion about the precise definition of philosophy, it ought to be allowed to us that the problems of philosophy, whether soluble or not, at least start from and arise out of knowledge that we already have; and more than that cannot be claimed for the problems of any science whatever. Perhaps the true character of philosophy is nowhere more conspicuous than at its very dawn, when we see it, as Ferrier has remarked, in immediate contrast with the mythology it supplanted. The one, directed solely by poetic fancy, provided a deity for every hill and stream, for every wind that blew, and every star that shone; the other, possessed by the idea that there is an ἀρχή or first principle underlying the endless variety that appears, though it failed utterly to find what it sought, nevertheless "inaugurated a new epoch, and gave birth to science among men." The problems of philosophy and science were at that time merged in one general attempt to generalize and simplify the endless particulars and bewildering diversities of sensible experience. In these later days, when many sciences in succession have been differentiated from that nebulous beginning, though the central problem still remains, it is now separated by a vast system of orderly knowledge and far-reaching law from the concrete manifold of sense. And since it is assumed that all we know is to be found in this imposing circle of sciences, philosophy is once again brought into comparison with the mythical; but this time only to be identified with it, when proud *savants*, forgetful of their sires, ring the changes of their despite, as they consign first the mythical, then the metaphysical, to a common oblivion. Both, they affect to believe, are the creatures of imagination, with this only difference: mythology is the inflorescence of fancy, metaphysics but the cobwebs of the brain—that sort of mouldy, cryptogamic inflorescence that a fungus will produce. For all such conceited *persiflage* there is not, I believe—at least if we look at the history of knowledge broadly there is not—one iota of justification. We cannot, of course, deny that philosophers did often lose themselves in a world of dreams, abstracting when, as Bacon says, they had better have analysed, and concerned about the phantoms of the cave or the schools when they should have essayed to interpret nature by the dry light of reason. But all this, rightly regarded, was but a mistake of method—a mistake that vitiated all investigations alike—being, in fact, almost, if not altogether, inevitable. For just as childhood precedes manhood, so preconception, dogmatism, deference for authority and tradition come before the cautious, critical, all-exacting spirit that yields to evidence and nothing but evidence, owns no bias and no fears, and bids even reason to justify herself and disclose her limits.

Listening to contemporary detractors of philosophy, one might suppose that the sciences had accomplished their own emancipation, while philosophy alone remains still befooled by empty but imposing conceits. The truth is rather that all the emancipation the sciences can claim was wrought for them by philosophy; wrought not by those who were the representatives of the modern *savant*, but by men who in these days would be stigmatized as 'genuine metaphysicians.' When the history of modern thought lies far enough in the past to be comprehended as a whole and in its true proportions, it will be seen, perhaps, more truly than we can see it now, that what might be called the dogmatic stage ceased and the critical began at the same time both for science and for philosophy; it will be seen, too, that the men who inaugurated the change were really philosophers, i.e., men of reflection, though they were often scientists or men of research as well. Galileo (in 1610), at the age of forty-six, said that he had spent more years on philosophy than months on mathematics. Descartes' account of himself (in 1637), when he was only a few years younger, shews that philosophy had a similar preponderance with him. By these two men, it is allowed, the foundations of modern exact science were laid. Nor can it be said that they

were great physicists spite of their early philosophy, as
one might perhaps say they were great thinkers spite
of their early scholastic training, which both alike soon
outgrew and cast aside. Dühring, in his *Critical History
of Mechanical Principles*, shews at some length that
genuine speculation was throughout the prompting
and informing inspiration in the ascertainment of these
principles. In Galileo and Descartes, certainly, we find
no traces of the over-vaunted Baconian method: it was
from ideas, not from facts, that their insight came.
Instruments and industry were all very well, as La-
grange has said, for the discovery of Jupiter's satellites,
the phases of Venus, the solar spots, and such like; but
to analyse and unravel the primary laws of nature
called for genius of a philosophic mould. It shews
nothing but ignorance, though unhappily ignorance
that is very widely spread, to suppose that, whereas
modern science is a new birth, separated by a catastrophe from the astrology, alchemy and magic of the
dark ages, modern philosophy, having learnt nothing
and forgotten nothing, is but the survival of Scholas-
ticism. Flippant references to angels dancing on the
point of a pin, or to chimaeras buzzing in a vacuum and
fed on second intentions, are still considered not an
unfair parody of the 'genuine metaphysician's' inquiries. It would be easy to retaliate. Anyone who
would be at the trouble to search the Royal Society's
Transactions for fifty years back and more would find
as much arrant nonsense as, and more bad reasoning
than, he would easily discover in as many pages of the
old Schoolmen. Modern philosophy is quite as truly
a new birth as modern science; and the founders of
modern science in breaking with the old philosophy did
not abandon philosophy altogether. On the contrary,
they founded the new science on a new philosophy, and
but for this new philosophy the new science would have

been a very feeble thing and its future would have been most precarious and uncertain.

It has to be remembered that, although—wherever the human race has been sufficiently advanced—the philosophic impulse has invariably been *one* factor in human life, it has never been a factor independent of all others. As I have said, the *quaesita* of philosophy have always been determined by what were regarded as *data* at the time. Thus the business of philosophy being primarily formative, any defects in the empirical matter supplied must have told disadvantageously on the system constructed. Moreover, philosophy has to take account of much besides the current *knowledge* of the time—ethical and religious ideas fall equally within its ken. And there is still another point to note.

Looked at broadly, the history of philosophy may be regarded, to borrow an idea from the late Prof. Harms, as philosophy experimenting. The experiments were very different in kind from those of physics and chemistry. Still they are entitled to be called experiments, in so far as they were so many mental manipulations of the theoretical and practical stuff of life with a view to the discovery of its hidden springs and inner unity. In these experiments we observe a twofold procedure, sometimes one, sometimes the other, being the more prominent. At one time, that is to say, philosophy was mainly intent on organizing. At another, the failure of such attempts led to a new scrutiny of the material to be organized; in a word, constructiveness yielded to scepticism or criticism. The longest and the dullest period in the whole history is that preceding our own —a Sahara of 1000 years, which Hegel advises us to traverse with seven-league boots. In this period, say, from the sixth century to the sixteenth, a powerful Church, the sole depository of knowledge, was bent on constructing out of the traditions of the Greek schools and the dogmas of the Christian faith one harmonious and rational system. The very endeavour is itself a most impressive proof that the philosophic spirit once there cannot be eradicated, and cannot be smothered. Under any circumstances, there must have been much that was transitory and provisional in the philosophy of such a time; but, as it was, there seems literally nothing of all the vast fabric that has remained. Yet there was progress—the only progress possible with such material. For one thing, the formal apparatus of thought was enormously improved in 'precision and analytic subtlety.' It is noteworthy that J. S. Mill quotes the testimony of Condorcet to this contribution of the Schoolmen to the progress of good philosophy as a fitting motto for the opening of his *Logic*; and it is perhaps not generally remembered that Mill himself, disgusted with the superficiality of Aldrich, applied himself instead to a careful study of scholastic logic. But to the Schoolmen we are indebted for progress in another respect. It was they who began the struggle for the emancipation of reason; at first, more or less peaceably under cover of the doctrine that there are two kinds of truth—book-keeping by double entry, as it has been profanely called—a doctrine that could hardly stagger theologians wont to talk of a sevenfold interpretation of Holy Writ. The attack on authority thus covertly begun led on, of course, to the open rupture which ushers in the modern period.

But neither the logical apparatus of the Schoolmen nor the emancipation of reason can be regarded as properly parts of philosophy. However vitally they concern it, they are still but circumstances outside it; so that, as regards the actual succession of philosophies, there is nothing between the ancient period and the modern. But what we now call science, as distinct from philosophy, was, if anything, in a worse plight. The historians of science do not forget this. Thus Bacon refused to take account of more than six out of the twenty-five centuries he reckoned from the dawn of history as either *scientiarum feraces earumve proventui utiles*. Again, Whewell's name for the middle ages is the stationary period. When philosophy is talked of, this sterile waste is most unfairly included with the rest. In fact, what hindered the advance of knowledge in one direction hindered it in all; and so soon as freedom of thought and inquiry was achieved, speculation and positive science moved on apace.

This brings me at length to the second of the two points mentioned just now, viz., that, allowing for differences of subject-matter, the advance of philosophy is quite comparable with that of science. Of course, anything like direct comparison is impossible, just because of this difference of subject-matter. Who can say what philosophical truth is to be set off as equal in importance with the law of gravity, or how many scientific theories can outweigh Kant's formulation or solution of the question, How are synthetic propositions *a priori* intelligible? In these days of universal examinations, no doubt still stranger comparisons are made: when, e.g., *A*, who writes a sonnet, is adjudged equally deserving of a fellowship with *B*, who has ascertained all the primes between 19,000,000 and 20,000,000, or with *C*, who has discovered that in the tadpole's economy there is a special class of cells for the absorption of the tail as soon as that juvenile appendage is done with. But in all these cases what we really compare is the ability of the worker: and we assume that the best work in one department is equal to the best in another; and, generally, that excellence of about equal rarity is of about equal value. When in this fashion we compare philosophers with other men, we have nothing to fear; and, fortunately, in almost

every case a circumstance comes to our aid, which perplexed examiners always hail with especial delight: the
best philosophers were what we in Cambridge call
'double firsts.' Leaving aside Plato and Aristotle, and
confining our notice to modern times, when philosophy
is regarded as a distinct pursuit (so to say, as a profession), we have, along one line, Bacon, Locke,
Berkeley, Hume; along another, Descartes, Leibniz
and Kant—all unmistakeable 'double firsts.' Everyone of these men would remain highly distinguished on
the score of literature, science or politics, if all their
philosophical work were counted as nothing. But what
we have now to estimate is not the men, but their work;
and the question is, whether the men of philosophy
have advanced, as the men of science have; or whether
they are only marking time on the old ground, and are
now left far behind.

What the truth is in this respect might perhaps be
effectively realized if we were to imagine one of those
old sages from Miletus—or even a thinker so recent
and of such abiding influence as Descartes—to come
to life again, and hear all that has been done in science
and in philosophy since his day. He would be told
that all the varied forces of nature are but various
modes of transformation of an energy that is changed
in form continually, but never destroyed; that all the
so-called elements furnish evidence that they also are
but modes of one primal stuff—inert, impenetrable and
indestructible; that, in an equation involving the three
fundamental units of time, space and mass, a complete
account could be given of all that really happens in
any material system, large or small, as it changes from
one given configuration to another; that life, *for the
spectator*, is ultimately resolvable, without residuum,
into such a series of physical changes or reflex actions;
and that mind, for the spectator, is in like manner

ultimately resolvable into life. The Ionian philosopher would probably be a good deal less impressed than we should expect. The sublime generalizations, the splendid analyses of modern physics, would seem only to bring us back again to where he was in the sixth century B.C. Then it was the simplicity of ignorance; now it is the simplicity of knowledge. The countless phenomena carefully ascertained by thousands of observers and experimenters, which might have defied all attempts at system, are no obstacle after all: there *is* a principle underneath phenomena, and all change is according to law. The naturalness of this result, so to say, would prevent astonishment in one who knew nothing of all the inductive methods, experimental devices, elaborate instruments and tedious calculations by which so very obvious and necessary a truth had been empirically won. *Artis est celare artem.* The master-key is, to look at, the simplest key of all, and is most a wonder to him who has made it. Similarly here.

As for Descartes, he, no doubt, would fully appreciate the triumphs of modern science, and the narrative would fill him with pride. Did I not say, he would urge, Grant me extended substance and motion, and I will start afresh, and reconstruct the world? He had not hesitated to extend his mechanical theory to brutes, and even to man—so far as sense and imagination are concerned. On every side, he would see only the substantial confirmation and consummation of his own views. Thus, neither for the father of ancient philosophy nor for the father of modern would there be anything altogether unfamiliar in a summary of the present state of science: they would not, as is sometimes supposed, be comparable (let us say) to a couple of trilobites of different silurian eras reappearing in a cretacean sea. They would see that knowledge had advanced, but the standpoint of exposition would be the same.

But, in turning to philosophy, the situation would be quite otherwise. The ancient who would readily take in 'the recent advances of physical science' would probably have seen in these all the philosophy for which he felt a need: at any rate they would follow on, and fill out the formal outline of knowledge he had himself conceived. But in the philosophy of these days he would find previous questions raised, of which he had never dreamed. To form any idea of these he would have to learn to regard knowledge itself as a problem, and to surrender the very δὸς ποῦ στῶ of all phenomenal achievement for analysis and conscious reconstruction. He would need to see that it is not enough to understand the world as it is given, to organize and unify experience, but that this systematic unity must be itself understood. Like some fabled artificer who, as he polishes his rough silver slab, finds the dull and opaque turn bright and translucent, till at length he discovers himself reflected in it and sees beyond and through his work his own form revealed, the Ionian thinker might surmise that the perfecting of the objective hemisphere of knowledge had revealed the subjective, making it possible to test the accuracy of the external by its perfect reflection of the internal, or to examine the internal thus projected and made large. This would be to him a most impressive advance.

To Descartes *redivivus* the changed face of philosophy would seem less strange and more intelligible; but the change would perhaps strike him more, and would certainly please him less, than the changes in science. *He*, of course, would fully understand the problem of knowledge, and might see at once that his own solution had been in part false, in part superficial. His sole criterion—*logical* clearness and distinctness—he would see ravel out the whole tissue of knowledge into the meaningless identity *A* is *A*, and end in the *reductio ad absurdum* of the Wolffian philosophy, poised like an inverted pyramid on the principle of contradiction—only stable, because it is empty and bound to topple over in search of a base the moment it receives the smallest real content. The distinction of pure intuition and pure understanding (of which he had had an inkling, but which, as alien to the leading idea of his own system, had remained only an unfruitful excrescence, atrophied and ugly), he would see developed by Kant into the cardinal doctrine of the two stems of human knowledge—whereby an escape was possible both from the empty formality of his own rationalistic successors and the blind scepticism of their empirical opponents. He would realize that there is more in geometry than clear thinking, and see that a philosophy wrought out *more geometrico* is for ever an impossibility: since geometry must rest on intuition (i.e., spatial perception), and philosophy start solely from the analysis of notions. It is true, I should say by the way, that Descartes only attempted the treatment of philosophy according to the geometrical method as an experiment on the suggestion of his friend, Mersenne, and was careful to point out that, "in so far as that method is synthetic, it is not so applicable to metaphysical truths as to the elements of geometry which have a relation to the senses." Still this only amounts to the inkling I spoke of just now: Descartes did *try*, and was afterwards not unsatisfied with the result, leaving it as a suggestion to be developed by Spinoza, who represents the inevitable outcome of one aspect, at least, of Cartesianism. Besides the recognition of two factors in knowledge, which, in his imperfect analysis, he had almost overlooked, Descartes would perforce acknowledge advance as regards another point likewise hidden from him by his geometric manner—I refer to the necessity of the conceptions of Cause and End (or Purpose) to give

unity to experience. Geometry knows nothing of experience, and nothing, therefore, of cause or process in
any guise. What Spinoza did completely, Descartes
had almost done, i.e., identified cause with reason, and
rejected final causes altogether. Again, even if we put
the most favourable interpretation possible on his doctrine of innate ideas, it is still only an assumption that
cuts the knot: it does not make necessary and universal
knowledge *intelligible*, and a necessity that is not intelligible is only a contingency after all. In a word, his
doctrine of innate ideas is only a sort of a preformation-
system, to use Kant's phrase. As Reid put it: "The
power of judging in self-evident propositions may be
compared to the power of swallowing our food. It is
purely natural." We do it, just as "dogs delight to
bark and bite, for God hath made [us] so." This is
better, certainly, than the *generatio aequivoca* of Mr
Herbert Spencer's book-plate, for it does recognize
that knowledge cannot be explained out of the perpetual stimulations of sense, any more than a chunk
of wood can be 'licked into shape' as a top, and made
to spin, by continually whipping it. Yes, it recognizes
the problem certainly, but it does not solve it. Descartes
would have the less difficulty in acknowledging Kant as
the Copernicus of philosophy, because everyone would
admit that a psychological solution was the one naturally to be attempted first; and because, further, there
was not in his day—what, in fact, he had largely contributed to produce—a body of natural science which
could prompt to a careful reflection on knowledge as a
product, and make a transcendental logic possible. In
Descartes' time, the only science there *was* was mathematics; and this, as we have seen, would lead away
from any attempt to frame a theory of experience in the
Kantian sense.

This second mention of the philosopher's tendency,
one might say, his function to set out by reflecting on

the existing body of knowledge, suggests another line of remark concerning the advance of philosophy as compared with the advance of science. If we might illustrate the advance of knowledge as a whole by the figure of a clock, then science might be called the minute-hand, and philosophy the hour-hand, of this clock. They are both really connected and moving in the same direction; and, though their rates of movement differ, this is compensated by a difference in the significance of their motion: one stage onwards for philosophy means a whole cycle of scientific progress. Now, that philosophy is never much behind we may see in another way, and that is by taking note of the little excursions into the groves of Academe in which men of science occasionally indulge. There is altogether quite a literature of this sort—a good deal of it in British Association addresses and the like: in that and other ways men of such eminence as Huxley, Tyndall, Cayley, and I must not forget Prof. Tait[1], with Helmholtz, Du Bois-Reymond, Claude Bernard,

[1] One instance of the spirit of this famous triton among the metaphysicians, this seer of the Unseen Universe, may perhaps be allowed as a note. In his excellent treatise, *The Properties of Matter*, there is a chapter on Time and Space that opens thus: "We begin with an extract from Kant, who, as mathematician and physicist, has a claim on the attention of the physical student of a different order from that possessed by the *mere* metaphysicians." Here follows about half a paragraph from Sec. 7 of the 'Transcendental Æsthetic' in which Kant is endeavouring to clinch his epistemological argument as regards mathematics. The 'therefore' (*demnach*) of the opening sentence is however omitted, and without further word or comment Prof. Tait proceeds: "On matters like these it is vain to attempt to dogmatize. Every reader must endeavour to use his reason, as he best can, for *the separation of the truth from the metaphysics* in the above characteristic passage." On reading this, one wonders (1) whether Prof. Tait has any sense of humour; (2) what the residuum of truth is when the metaphysics is winnowed or washed away from this 'characteristic passage'; and (3) why the physical student is called upon to exercise his reason upon it without a hint of the premises to which it is little more than a conclusion!

and many others abroad, have discussed various marginal questions on the confines between their special subject and philosophy. I take up the first of these festive prelections that comes to my hand: it is a good specimen of the class, and will sufficiently illustrate what I mean. It is an address by Helmholtz, delivered in celebration of the founding of the Berlin University, and deals with *Die Thatsachen in der Wahrnehmung*. Let me quote one passage from the summing up: "The causal law is, in reality, a law given *a priori*, a transcendental law. To prove it from experience is impossible; for experience cannot advance a step, as we have seen, without employing inductive reasoning, that is to say, without the causal law. Moreover, from what we have already experienced—even if we could certainly say that everything observed so far has happened according to law—we could only inductively infer, i.e., by assuming the causal law, that the causal law would be valid in the future also." After a little declamation and a verse or two from Goethe, Helmholtz goes on: "In what to me has always seemed the most essential advance in Kant's philosophy, we remain still at the level of his system. In this wise I have frequently in my previous works taken occasion to emphasize the agreement of the newer sense-physiology with the teaching of Kant, but without, of course, intending to swear by the *verba magistri* in every detail." The whole address, in short, is little more than Kant assimilated and turned into Helmholtz. This class of literature bristles with references and choice quotations for philosophers of 'our present level,' to use Helmholtz's phrase. But if philosophy has not advanced, how comes it that scientific men, when they feel the deeper thirst, find their well of waters only in these latest springs? And how is it, when they want to blaspheme, that they fall back either on the crudities of some earlier philosophers or on the extravagances of Hegel or Schelling?

But now, although a dispassionate consideration might soon satisfy any open-minded inquirer that philosophy does move on, there are two or three reasons why it seems to have accomplished very much less than it really has. First, all unsolved and perhaps insoluble problems of any generality fall to the province of philosophy. Some of them go back to that nebulous beginning of all knowledge from which, as I have suggested, the sciences, like planets, have separated and condensed into definite form, and round which they still revolve. All the ultimate questions; all the antinomies, theoretical and practical; the relations of Thought to Being, of the Finite to the Infinite, the One to the Many; the crowd of unanalysed conceptions and uncriticized assumptions of everyday thought and conduct—these all belong to philosophy. It is something even to put them in order, reduce their number, show that some questions are at bottom absurd, and not only cannot be answered but need never be asked; to determine the definite issues within which the solution must lie, and so forth. But, even were all this done, the ultimate difficulties would still remain. Complete knowledge is an ideal; if we regard it as attainable it is infinitely far off. Now, when we boast of the advance of science, we measure the distance we have come, which is finite, so that future advances are comparable with it. But when we despair of philosophy we think of the distance we have to go, which is infinite, and must always remain so, unless, indeed, our rate of advance itself becomes infinite; that is, unless intellectual discursion should some day give place to intellectual intuition.

Another reason why philosophy is apt to appear practically stationary is that, as already hinted, any

ground it does win from the void and shapeless infinite
is ceded sooner or later to science; or if no science
already exists to which it could be logically assigned,
then a fresh science is constituted for the purpose. In
this way, mainly, Logic and Psychology have arisen,
and by such accessions from philosophy they are from
time to time extended. And in this way, too, Epistemology, or the science of knowledge generally, has arisen,
and, as I venture, spite of the heresy, to think, has
attained a large measure of independence. Just as
most of the old Natural Philosophy has become the
Natural Sciences, so much of the old Moral Philosophy
has become the Moral Sciences. Philosophy proper
still remains as the 'leader' or main growing-point of
the whole tree of knowledge, and so regarded seems
as inchoate and nascent as in the days of Thales or
Pythagoras.

But now, in one respect at any rate, I think, we are
bound to admit that philosophy in the stricter sense
might have made more progress than it has. Perhaps
it is an inherent infirmity, perhaps it is essential
strength; at any rate it is true of most philosophers
that they attempt everything. *Aut Caesar aut nullus* is
the philosopher's legend. In this spirit he sets to work
himself: in this spirit he judges most of his predecessors.
No doubt eclecticism in philosophy is the feeblest thing
of all: rhapsodies and centos are absolute absurdities
here. But it is one thing to take pieces out of different
speculative systems: it is quite another to recognize and
formulate a truth that has been found out before.
A comparison of a History of Philosophy such as that
of Erdmann or Zeller with such a History of Sciences
as Whewell's or Dühring's would illustrate what I mean.
In the history of science we observe continually that
the propounder of a wrong theory has nevertheless
ascertained some important law; as Newton, for ex-

ample, ascertained the laws of the refractive dispersion of light, although his corpuscular theory as to the nature of light itself is false and has been overthrown. The law is remembered: the theory is forgotten. Now, in philosophy, as it seems to me, there are similar instances; but here it is the fashion, as the Germans say, to swill out the child along with the bath (*das Kind mit dem Bade ausschütten*). Locke and Hume, we are told, were sensationalists; Descartes and Leibniz were rationalists; and the insufficiency of both these theories of knowledge being made apparent, the only interest of the historian is to treat them as 'moments' in the general development of philosophy. It is not held to be necessary definitely to single out and emphasize the particular truths enounced by thinkers whose speculative standpoint has been superseded. The Dualism of Descartes and the Occasionalism to which it led; the problems of Substance and Cause, as propounded by Locke and Hume respectively; Hume's resolution of all the objects of human inquiry into two kinds—to wit, Relations of Ideas and Matters of Fact; Leibniz's principles of Sufficient Reason and of Continuity,—these may serve as instances comparable in importance with the special laws of nature which the historians of science record. Now I would make bold to maintain that philosophy should have its *monumenta rerum gestarum*: its history should not give the impression of a series of failures—each thinker in succession being handled in accordance with the maxim, *Falsus in uno, falsus in omnibus*. Science treated after this fashion would scarcely fare better: but it never is so treated. The positive results, be they large or small, isolated laws or wide-reaching principles, are what the historian of science puts foremost. And whether it would serve all the purposes of a history of philosophy or not, something of the same kind is at least a desideratum there.

But anyone who should attempt to supply this want
would be at once confronted with a difficulty; though
the difficulty would be the amplest justification of his
enterprise. He would find the same thing, essentially,
said over and over again with accidental differences of
statement, due merely to its place and purpose in the
speculation of each particular thinker. In science, when
a truth is made out it is definitely formulated and receives a name; there is Snell's Law, Boyle's Law,
Avogadro's Law, Ballot's Law, and so forth. But in the
whole region of philosophy, with the partial exception
of Logic, there seem to be no rights and no rule. Philosophy has no nomenclature and no terminology. Every
giant and every pigmy states and misstates and restates
much as he wills: even babes and sucklings rush abroad
brandishing the Infinite and the Absolute with infinite
ignorance and absolute conceit. If there is anything
fixable, why do we not fix it? If any of our conceptions admit of definition, why are they not defined?
Such *axiomata media* of philosophy might gain or lose
in comparative importance as time went on; but that
is true equally of science, which still insists on precision
as far as it goes. It is no uncommon thing—it is rather
the rule—to find philosophers disclaiming any gradual
completion of philosophy: they intend nothing short of
das All auf einem Male. Thus not only the conceited
Descartes concludes his *Principia* with the statement
"that there is no phenomenon of nature whose explanation has been omitted in this treatise," but even
"that most modest and retiring of mortals," dear old
Immanuel Kant, while characterizing philosophy on
the lines of Descartes as 'dogmatic swill' (*dogmatische
Gewäsche*), is still persuaded that metaphysics, which
on his view is the one science that can confidently
reckon on permanence and completeness, has attained
its goal in the *Critique of the Pure Reason.* Of this much

he assures us at the end of his *Prolegomena*, and in the preface to the *Metaphysical Foundations of the Natural Sciences* he again expresses the belief that this absolute completeness of metaphysics generally has enabled him to exhaust the special metaphysics of the material world. Of the still greater extravagance of those who came after him, I forbear to speak. Alas! the best of men are but men at the best. It is not given to the human intellect ever to soar: it can only climb. There are wide differences between science and philosophy, of course; but the truism just now urged in defence of philosophy against its vilifiers from the side of science, if allowed at all, must be allowed to cut both ways. If all departments of knowledge have much in common, since Mind, the most important factor in knowledge, is the only factor that is the same in all; then, while we may expect philosophy to progress as well as science, yet—if it claim to be knowledge—it cannot do more than progress. And, certainly, it would advance more rapidly and with more ease if the positions already attained were definitely set down and named.

But this leads us naturally to consider for a moment the present state of philosophy. There has been no philosophy in England since Hume, says one; and none anywhere since Hegel, says another. 'Back to Kant' is the recent cry in Germany, and I have known some in England who have cried 'Back to Reid.' But in truth I very much question if there has been any harking back at all. Systems of philosophy are no longer the fashion, certainly. But there have never been so many competent experts—as we say nowadays —at work on philosophical questions as there are at present; and never has philosophical literature multiplied at such an amazing pace. The great bulk of this literature falls into one or other of two divisions—historical criticisms or monographs on special points—

such as Geometrical Axioms, the notion of Experience, the Relation of Body and Mind, and so forth. And even the historical studies which form the first division are mainly confined to special lines of thought—a history of the doctrine of Categories, the various forms of Idealism—or to special thinkers and the development of their doctrines. So that we may say generally that philosophical activity has entered upon a new phase; system-makers have given place to specialists. As in science, so in philosophy, ours is the age of monographs. Many are the Jeremiahs with a speculative turn who lament this state of things as an unequivocal sign of degeneracy and disaster; and nobody will maintain that it is an unmixed good. But then what is? Certainly not the *Panlogismus* of fifty years ago. The history of philosophy is full of reactions; and one might fairly say not only that the present state of things is one of these, but that it is a reaction caused chiefly by that exuberant system-making of which the Hegelian philosophy is the crown and climax. This is very impressively put by one bred and born in the school of Hegel, I mean by the venerable Edward Zeller—first in a once famous lecture on "The Plan and Problem of the Theory of Knowledge," and afterwards in his *History of German Philosophy*. Referring at the end of the *History* to the movement in question, as one in which the rapid succession of comprehensive systems left speculation exhausted and forced at length to heed the demand for proofs, Zeller remarks: "On the one hand the flagrant contradiction in which their results stood when confronted with the empirical sciences shook the faith in philosophical systems first of those outside and finally of their own adherents. On the other hand, this state of things gave energy to the endeavour so to modify the principles and methods of philosophy, the materials of the empirical sciences being freely used for the purpose, as to eliminate such contradictions once and for all." Then, in the concluding paragraph, having previously characterized German philosophy from Leibniz to Hegel as an almost unbroken Idealism, he continues: "In Hegel's *a priori* construction of the universe this Idealism celebrated its systematic consummation. The stagnation of philosophical productivity which commenced at Hegel's death, the gradual dissolution of the leading schools, the distraction and uncertainty which possessed everybody, plainly showed that the turning-point had come; and when, hand in hand with the decline of philosophical activity, there came work the most diverse and most varied in the region of the empirical sciences, especially the natural sciences, it was thereby clearly indicated that the new philosophy must enter into closer relation with these sciences, that she must avail herself of their results and their procedure, and must supplement her former all too exclusive Idealism by means of a sound Realism."

It is above twenty-five years ago since Zeller abandoned the Hegelian standard. The assimilation of philosophy and science which he foretold has well begun, in proof whereof is this continual production of monographs. Some fifteen years later the periodical known as *The Quarterly Journal for Scientific Philosophy* was set afoot, and the best of the younger philosophy of Germany comes to light through its pages. Here thinkers of such repute as Paulsen, Siebeck, Benno Erdmann, Göring, Wundt and many others have given in their adherence to the position that—to adapt a dictum of Kant's—philosophy without science is empty and science without philosophy is blind.

But let no one suppose that Zeller or any of those I have mentioned intends for a moment that the sublime speculations of a Spinoza or a Hegel are to remain now

and henceforth meaningless or useless. The point is
that they do not belong to the problems of philosophy
in the present. A vast gulf has disclosed itself between
the knowledge so far attained and any Absolute Idealism
that can claim to be more than a hope or a faith.
Many a lofty mountain that appears to have an unbroken contour from base to summit, when we view it
as a whole and from afar, discloses, as soon as the
actual ascent begins, minor eminences and intervening
valleys innumerable. Then, for those who can only
climb, true progress requires that they lose sight for a
time, perhaps for a very long time, of the final goal;
and quite possibly the really highest peak may turn
out later to be one not at first descried at all. So the
matter stands with philosophy: to-day we are really
further on and have no call to hark back; albeit the
prospect immediately before us is not the grand panorama seen as in a vision by those who went before. It
may be objected that on this view it is impossible to
draw any line between philosophy and science. If this
means that there is, or at any rate should be, continuity between the two, it must be granted. But it
must not be taken to mean that philosophy is itself but
a science. Philosophy on any view endeavours to make
our knowledge and our practice as a whole intelligible.
It is no more a part of the sciences than life is a member
of the body; in like manner it is no more separable
from the sciences than life from vital organs.

Philosophers, then, may not be poets, and cannot be
seers. Ideas are indeed their sole province, but only
such ideas as deal straight with facts. There is a famous
saying of Fichte's—"Tell me of what sort a man is,
and I will tell you what philosophy he will choose."
Such language would be ridiculous applied to science.
Fancy saying that the kind of geology—I will not say
geometry—that a man chooses depends on the sort of

man he is. Fichte's words are full of truth and have deep and important practical bearings, but what they refer to is not scientific philosophy. No, the philosophy which, as I think, has most promise about it now is one that is content to submit to limits in return for stability. There are many alternative theories concerning matter, mind, the past, the future—in short, concerning the universe generally—between which at present our existing knowledge does not enable us to decide. Such are of the nature of hypotheses, and, pending some critical settlement, cannot be accounted actual constituents of philosophy. Take, for example, the alternatives of Monism and Monadism: the one offers us unity by way of substance, the other offers us unity by way of organization. Subjective preferences may incline A to the one and B to the other; but anything like a decision, which shall command assent, whether or not, is out of the question. If it were not, we should not have such continual vacillation between the two, even in our own time. Scientific philosophy has to remain in suspense here much as I imagine scientific physics has to remain in suspense concerning the question whether matter is to be regarded as homogeneous and continuous or heterogeneous and discontinuous.

But some may here object that this is Positivism and not Philosophy. Are we to believe, it may be asked, that the settlement of the ultimate questions of philosophy depends on the ascertainment of fresh facts: is philosophy to depend on measurement as well as science? Not at all; the business of philosophy is with ideas,—that everyone must allow. To be sure, the accumulation of fresh empirical particulars does entail from time to time the emergence of new ideas of philosophic import: take the so-called metageometry, or the theory of natural selection, as instances. Still, what I

especially would urge is, that we have not yet sufficiently cleared up and connected the ideas we have;
and that, till this is done, such ultimate questions as
that between monadism and monism have to wait.
What philosophy seems to want—as I suggested earlier
—is *axiomata media*, middle principles; and it is because
the supply of this want is at length widely recognized
as our immediate business that I venture to think
philosophy is still strong, though no longer startling.

But, now, what of the future? Is philosophy to remain for ever, or not? Who can tell? In the earlier
days of our race, when habits of thought at once geo-
centric and anthropocentric had never been, as now,
so rudely disturbed, an answer would have been forthcoming confidently enough. But it is one thing to
believe that the world is reasonable, and quite another
to expect oneself to see its reasonableness. The first is
an implicit postulate of all philosophical inquiry—nay,
of all science whatever. But even if the world be
thoroughly intelligible, it may be that the human race
can never understand it. Our intellects may be for
ever too finite and too fallible, even if we recognize the
limitation to the phenomenal on which Kant insisted.
Or it may, indeed, very well be the case that with such
limitation a satisfactory *rationale* of the universe is essentially a contradiction. And if so, what then? Might it
not happen that the human mind will at length cease
to ask questions which have baffled it so long? A complete adjustment to environment and conditions would,
in fact, seem to involve the eventual atrophy and disappearance of a propensity that has never been satisfied. Something of this sort is the opinion of thinkers
of the stamp of Comte and Spencer.

Against this death of philosophy from inanition, we
should, of course, urge—as I have just now been attempting—that philosophy *has* progressed; and, further,

that if the sciences advance indefinitely, there will always be work for philosophers to do. But to this last remark there is a possible rejoinder that deserves some consideration. The indefinite advance of science may be, so to say, asymptotic: though it should never actually come to a standstill, it may yet, as regards those first-rate generalizations that open up new vistas for philosophy, reach what will be practically a stationary state. Reverting to a simile I used just now: if the science-finger of the clock of knowledge comes almost to rest, must not the philosophy-finger do so much more? And yet it does not follow, for several reasons; one of which will bring more directly before us another side of philosophy, so far only incidentally mentioned.

It does not follow, we may first observe, because, even if the number or extent of our scientific principles is limited, there is still an opening for continuous advance in the co-ordination and rationalization of those principles. A man is inferior in size to a whale, though really its superior in organization. It is this peculiar *quality* of knowledge as a unified whole, largely (though not entirely) distinct from quantity, which is, at least, one special concern of philosophy. The same material may have very different forms: an ounce of protoplasm, organized as a jelly-fish, and passively drifting with the tide, though it be alive, is a very different form of life from the lark, soaring and "singing in the blinding sky." Still, we must admit that the quality I have attempted to describe is not wholly independent of quantity. Looked at as a mere question of possible combinations, it is clear that, with a finite number of terms, there is but a limited number of possibilities, and the best of these might be reached in time. Then we should have the final and triumphant philosophy: the last and best surviving its inferior compeers—

surviving them, but embodying in itself all the partial truths they contained; the paragon of philosophies, as man is commonly accounted the paragon of animals, exhibiting in himself the essential excellence of all animated nature. At first, the thought of *the* philosophy thus attained at length is a grateful one; but it is not so for long. As G. H. Lewes has somewhere said, "Mankind alternately seeks and shuns finality." And it is plain that the conception of a partial experience of the whole vast sum of things, however completely that experience is classified and transmuted into philosophy, is unsatisfactory, if not—as I just now hinted—contradictory. Either *the* philosophy must be coextensive with being, or knowledge is not to be the prime source of its sufficiency. It must depend for its perfection on something besides theory; and, as we all know, philosophy does also take account of the questions: What ought I to do? and What may I hope for?

Now it is, more especially, this inclusion of the practical and religious elements that forbids us to think that philosophy (if it does not disappear altogether, as the Positivists teach) must assume a final form, supposing the complement of scientific laws humanly ascertainable is ever made up. It is often alleged, as a grievous shortcoming of Locke, that he is content to say our knowledge is sufficient for our practical needs. For my part, I venture to think that his fault lay not so much in the principle he here assumed, viz., that knowledge is subordinate to practice: it lay rather in his ignoring the fact that our knowledge is, after all, *not* sufficient for our practical needs. The earthquake of Lisbon, the cholera bacillus, the dissipation of energy, are all strictly and emphatically cases of natural law: they suggest no theoretical difficulties as such. A theoretical philosophy, which justified pessimism—so far as we could regard it abstractly *as* theory—might satisfy the claims of knowledge as fully as one that justified optimism. We cannot insist on omniscience as essential to a perfect philosophy, but it is essential that such a philosophy should satisfy our moral and religious nature. We may even go further, and say that, were our moral reason satisfied, we could acquiesce in a finite knowledge, which would not satisfy our merely intellectual nature, abstractly considered. This, by itself, knows no measure: it is only in ethics that we voluntarily impose a mean.

When we try to take stock of the world of life, and observe the relation between experience and action, we see at every stage that action is in advance of experience: all things that live seem to learn by doing. A spirit of hopeful adventure appears to possess everything: I might say a spirit of faith. The whole story of evolution is typified in Abraham, the father of the faithful, who "went out, not knowing whither he went." Lungs were not first acquired by water-creatures who then proceeded to live on land: birds were not reptiles that first got wings and then began to fly. The function leads to the structure rather than the structure to the function. The world is full of efforts justified only by the results. There was nothing, we will say, in past experience to justify the first attempts at living on land or moving through the air; *also there was nothing absolutely to forbid it.* The attempt was made, and practice brought perfection. With a new sphere of life came new experiences and fresh enterprises. Say what we will, the practical man *will* reason back from consequences, and not merely forwards from premises.

If we cannot have omniscience then, what we want is a philosophy that shall justify faith—justify it in the only way in which it can be justified by giving it room. So far, at least, one must agree with Kant in the

famous passage in the Preface to his first *Critique*, ending
with the words: "I must remove *knowledge* in order to
get room for *faith*." But, as I have attempted briefly
to suggest, practice may enlarge our theoretical horizon;
and this in a twofold way: it may lead into new worlds,
and secure new powers. Knowledge that we could
never attain, remaining what we are, may be attainable in consequence of higher powers and a higher life,
which we may morally achieve. All seems to turn then
upon whether our existing knowledge, with such theoretical philosophy as it makes possible, leaves this room
for faith, and so for growth.

Assuming this room left, two opposite speculative
hypotheses present themselves, which I must be content
to designate as the religious and the non-religious.
Neither, from the nature of the case, can logically refute and silence the other. It is here, by the way, that
those words of Fichte I referred to just now are in point.
The future of philosophy depends on the issue between
these opposite hypotheses; and what I would suggest
is that that issue will in turn depend on the practical
results to which the two lead. It will be a case of the
survival of the fittest. Mankind seems bent on making
the experiment perhaps on a great scale. In ignorance
of the future of the race, we cannot, on theoretic
grounds, forecast the future of philosophy.

III

THE DIFFICULTIES OF PHILOSOPHY

" CARE has been taken that the trees shall not grow up to heaven." So we may render a familiar German proverb often pointed against human enterprises that obviously require superhuman powers, and particularly often turned against philosophy. As the tree grows beyond a certain height a sort of law of diminishing return begins to assert itself: the sap ascends more and more slowly and the strains upon the timber near the breaking-point. At length, though the tree may keep on growing, it gets no higher. What the limit is depends on the tree: the giant Sequoias of California overtop our tallest pines before they even shew a branch. But all trees alike reach a height beyond which the forces against them exceed all the forces they can muster in their favour. So the best of men are but men at the best. Though philosophy be the consummation of human striving in the direction of knowledge, yet the inevitable limitations of our powers must ever leave us *striving*, vainly reaching toward heights which are there but to which we can never attain.

Such is the parable that may serve as a text for the series of remarks that I have the honour to submit to you to-night. It may be said that the parable is not altogether apt, or can at best apply only to a very individualistic view of human nature. Though the possible achievements of any given thinker may have limits that are humble and definite enough, yet still knowledge may grow from more to more indefinitely; because in the pursuit of it individuals combine their forces and thus the highest attainments of one generation form the heritage, and serve as the starting-point, of the next. No doubt there is truth at the bottom of this objection; but it is a truth very liable to over-statement. It may hold almost literally of knowledge regarded extensively, but it has only a very qualified application to knowledge, intensively regarded; to wisdom if I may so say. Ten observers may go to and fro and increase the store of facts known at ten times the rate of one; but ten councillors do not increase wisdom tenfold. And such extra wisdom as a multitude of councillors may bring must be attributed in part at least to the greater probability of finding the one wise man among the many. Since then we cannot equate quantity with quality, surface with height, solitary genius with mediocre multitude, there is a sense in which what is beyond the capacity of the ablest indi-viduals must, it is said, be beyond attainment by the race. And—as we know—those who hold this view are fond of appealing to history to shew the futility of that striving for higher knowledge which we call philo-sophy. The main questions, it is said, are few in number: every possible answer has been given and refuted in turn: and twenty centuries of philosophic failure to resolve the mystery of existence may surely be held to prove that knowledge that springs from earth can never pierce to heaven.

I do not propose now to traverse this endeavour to deduce the hopelessness of philosophy from its past history. Whatever the ultimate fate of philosophy may be, at least no one competently acquainted with its history would maintain that it has reached the stationary state as yet. But there is no denying that philosophers have accomplished vastly less than they at-tempted; nor that the positions reached are quite other than those at first consciously aimed at. We certainly are still without a theory of being, though this has been the goal of speculation from the first, but we know much more about knowledge than we did and much more about our own ignorance. The difficulties of philosophy are no doubt unique. Let us try to realize some of them.

It has often seemed to me that an instructive comparison might be drawn—though perhaps you will think it far-fetched—between philosophical inquiries and certain quantitative physical problems that involve extreme precision. To draw a straight line, to measure off a yard in length, to determine a given angle, to weigh a given parcel of matter, are operations that anybody can repeat with inexpensive apparatus many times in an hour and yet without an error of one per cent. But to do any of these things with any great exactness would require a special place, costly and complicated instruments, and might occupy a trained expert for weeks, months or even years. Take for example the case of a chemist weighing with such fineness as to indicate a difference of one part in seven millions —which is said to have been done[1]. Such an undertaking is like a siege: it has to be led up to by a series of preliminaries involving many other operations of precision. The beams of his balance have to be accurately graduated; the level position of the balance ascertained, the angles of oscillation indicated and microscopically noted; temperature, moisture, barometric pressure must all be likewise carefully measured and taken into account—in short where extreme precision is essential, things ordinarily regarded as independent and distinct turn out to be mutually implicated to an extent of which the ordinary operator has no conception. Now it seems to me to define with philosophical exactness and precision the meaning of concepts such as knowledge, substance, cause or change is a similarly

[1] Cp. W. S. Jevons, *The Principles of Science*, 2nd ed., p. 304.

tough and expensive job. I suppose it would be a moderate estimate to say that the civilized world spent half a million pounds sterling in the course of last century solely to ascertain the length of a single line—I mean our distance from the sun. And in the next century when two transits of Venus will occur again, I have no doubt, our successors will expend a much larger sum in order to fix this distance still more exactly. Well, I doubt if the true and proper meaning of being and becoming can be settled for less cash than that!

Consider for a moment the notion of change and the extent of its implications. First with regard to time. Are we to define change by means of time or time by means of change? In as far as we only come to know of time in experiencing changes it might be assumed that changes are the reality and time but the abstract of change. If there were no change, it would seem meaningless to talk of time, just as it would be meaningless to talk of the poles if the earth were at rest. But it is at least equally evident that change cannot be *thought* without time and it might therefore be assumed that time as the more abstract is logically the more fundamental. We seem to have a sort of antinomy; the thesis being that time presupposes change and the antithesis that change presupposes time.

Again with regard to the subject of change, what world-old problems at once present themselves! What is it precisely that undergoes change, and what is the real nature of these changes? The answers to these questions will be widely different according as we take the standpoint of Parmenides, or Spinoza, or Herbart on the one hand or that of Heraclitus, or Leibniz, or Hegel on the other. How are we to define a substance if it is now one thing now another? and yet if we exclude change from substances how are we to do justice to experience which forces the fact of change upon us? Yet again science is continually resolving what at first sight appear to be changes in the objects about us into altered relations between the elements of which such natural objects are said to be composed. And so the logician with his notion of essences, and the physicist with his notion of atoms, both seek to extrude change from any part or lot in the substantial as such: and both seek to confine all changes to the external relations or accidents of things. But if we consider change primarily from a psychological rather than from a logical or physical point of view we come upon the facts of self-determination and immanent activity. Change seems essential to consciousness and here mechanical explanations are no longer available, while in voluntary effort and attention we seem to see the notion of substance lost in that of purposeful efficiency.

This brings us to the relation of change to cause, and here again the implications are very intricate. Many of you, no doubt, are acquainted with Herbart's classic discussion of this relation, the complement in several respects of the still more famous discussion by Hume. According to Herbart the notion of change leads to a trilemma. Change either has a cause or it has not: if it have a cause, it is either an external cause or an internal; if no cause, then we have absolute becoming. He proceeds to argue at length that no one of the three is thinkable. The difficulties besetting the conception of transeunt action or external causation are familiar enough. They do not press upon modern science, because a better methodology has enabled it to leave them quietly on one side. As regards knowledge as a whole this exclusion marks an important advance: it is one more case of that division of labour that pertains to the higher and more specialized organizations of human industry. But, nevertheless, the problem is outstanding and still to solve: how and in what respects the being of one thing can affect the being of another. To suppose that no such problem exists would be to commit a blunder like that of the city urchin living wholly among shops, who believes in the baker and the milkman, but not in the farmer with his herds and his wheat. Some of the sciences proceed deductively: others have to be content with induction. In the one case cause is eliminated altogether: in the other, it would scarcely be going too far to say that it is practically supplanted by the notion of law. But if instead of merely ascertaining uniformities whether of co-existence or sequence we venture to ask the old and perhaps scientifically foolish question, how one thing, *A*, produces a change in another thing, *B*? we find that no one has yet answered the question as it stands. Either our notion of thing has to be altered or some *tertium quid* has to be introduced, or the reality of transeunt action is denied altogether; in other words, either the plurality of things is unreal or the Deity intervenes, or there is pre-established harmony, etc., etc.

As regards internal change and immanent causes equal difficulties beset the question: Where and how does a thing change itself? The question is pertinent only in the psychical sphere; the supposed inertia of matter renders such an inquiry unmeaning concerning physical things. The typical case for such an investigation is that of deliberate choice as when a man resolves to change his character, and the mere mention of it will at once call up to your minds perennial controversies, theological, philosophical, psychological, which it would be tedious even to name.

In fact, the difficulties that beset both forms of cause have driven speculative thinkers again and again to the notion of absolute becoming or uncaused change;

this is the alternative by which it is sought to escape
the infinite regress of contingent causes in the case of
physical changes; and by which Kant, for example,
saved the freedom of the will from such contingencies.
Here Cause is swallowed up in Change, and permanent
being in perpetual becoming. But this inversion brings
out a new difficulty that in turn discloses the implications of the notion of change in yet other directions.
It is the general difficulty, as Locke put it, of "adjusting a standing measure to a growing bulk," in this
case of applying a fixed system of discrete notions, such
as thought furnishes, to a real world in which, as
Heraclitus maintained, πάντα ῥεῖ καὶ οὐδὲν μένει. Logic
and ontology, if there be any ontology, are at conflict.
Everything is and everything is not: the real is a synthesis of contradictories. It was by no accident that
Heraclitus and Hegel in elevating becoming seemed
to dethrone logic, and to resolve being equally with
non-being into unreals, that is, into abstractions.

But I have spent an inordinate time on what is intended after all only as an illustration. What I want
to make clear is the appalling amount of mutual implication there is among our ultimate notions; and the
corresponding difficulty of all philosophical inquiry.
The common maxims on which we are wont to rely
when confronted by tasks that seem insuperable—
"Take one thing at a time," "Divide and conquer"—
here appear to fail us. Yet it was to such maxims that
Descartes mainly trusted. Two out of the four rules in
the famous *Discourse on Method*, with which he may be
said to have inaugurated modern philosophy, are but
a resetting of those old saws. His second rule you will
remember, is thus stated. "To divide each of the difficulties under examination into as many parts as
possible, and as might be necessary for its adequate
solution." His third runs: "To conduct my thoughts

in such order that, by commencing with objects the simplest and easiest to know, I might ascend by little and little, and as it were, step by step, to the knowledge of the more complex; assigning in thought a certain order even to those objects which in their own nature do not stand in a relation of antecedence and sequence." Now there is an assumption underlying these two rules of method which I will ask you to consider for a moment—I mean the assumption that knowledge is a sort of Porphyrean tree unfolding continuously in logical fashion from some single, simple root-concept. It is quite a question whether this assumption is true, especially in the sense in which formal logicians understand it; and even it be ever so true of the ideal, it is a further question whether it furnishes a practicable method of systematizing such isolated knowledges as we have.

No doubt for a particular science that has reached the deductive stage it is possible and advantageous to observe such rules of method as the Cartesians and the Port Royalists framed, to divide, as the latter propose "every genus into all its species, every whole into all its parts, and every difficulty into all its cases."[1] But my point is that among those ultimate conceptions which underlie all knowledge, no such 'natural order' as that which Descartes and Pascal assumed has been discovered: rather each seems to involve all and all to involve each. In place of advancing along a series of concepts increasing in complexity, we seem condemned to move round an inevitable circle both in proof and definition, and our attempted analyses of such concepts seem to yield not greater simplicity and clearness, but only greater vagueness and obscurity. They remind us of the attempt of the tyro with his microscope: when an object is shewn him in focus, he tries to see more

[1] *Port Royal Logic*, p. 347.

by bringing the object-lens still nearer: the object is enlarged indeed, but *pro tanto* loses in definiteness. Perhaps the philosophers who have done most to bring this melancholy experience home to us are the dogmatists, like Descartes and Spinoza, who make the most formal attempts at regular deductive procedure.

But a glance at the history of philosophy is equally convincing in another way. The mutual implications of God and the World, of the One and the Many, of Matter and Form, of Subject and Object, Thought and Thing have frustrated every attempt to put one before the other as well as every attempt to take one without the other. Spinoza's rigorous monism is scarcely more deserving of the name of an Acosmism, which Hegel gave it, because it reduced the world to nothing, than Leibniz's continuous system of monads deserves the name of Atheism, because it has logically no place for God except as a *monas monadum*. The one-sidedness of Fichte's subjective idealism, which Schelling proposed to sum up in the proposition: Ego is all, has its counterpart one-sidedness in his own identity-philosophy which he sums up in the converse proposition: All is Ego. But when we look at philosophies that are not thus one-sided we find a dualism that is quite as troublesome. Thus one historian of philosophy charges Descartes with having chopped the world in two with a hatchet, and Schelling taunted Hegel with 'the ugly broad ditch' he had to leap in passing from his Absolute Idea to Nature.

This brings me to notice a very common phrase or rather set of phrases in frequent use among philosohpical writers. I mean Standpoint, Aspect, Orientation and others based on the analogy of the terrestrial or celestial observer. This analogy reveals fresh difficulties that beset the philosopher or shews the old ones in a new light. It is a common thing, especially

10-2

nowadays when philosophers—for the most part—are modest, to represent philosophy as systematizing and unifying the partial and isolated surveys of the several special sciences. When astronomers or geographers confer together in order to combine their several separate observations, their task is in the main an easy one because of the sameness and continuity of space and time respectively; and yet the simplification secured is great. The heavenly bodies we call planets because of their mazy wanderings as seen from the standpoint of the earth are shewn to revolve regularly in the same direction and almost in the same plane when referred to the standpoint of the sun. In order, e.g., to assign the measured surveys of two islands belonging say to different hemispheres to their exact geographical position, methods of orientation are required for which the ordinary surveyor has neither the instruments nor the knowledge; but what he cannot do the astronomer does for him and shews the whole to which those parts belong.

How stands it with philosophy which undertakes to perform these offices for the separate sciences, replacing their relative standpoints by one absolute standpoint, and connecting their *disjecta membra* into one living, organized whole? If I were specially addressing students of science it would be my chief concern, were it possible, to convince them that such work is necessary to complete their own. The great majority of men of science are too little interested in these wider questions to care to formulate a view as to the relations and connexions of their own respective domains. They seem unconsciously to assume that each science has nothing to do but to extend till it touches its neighbours. Psychology will join on to physiology, physiology to chemistry, chemistry to physics, and physics to mathematics. So Comte tells us all science is measurement; and Tyndall, more like a seer than a savant, discerned in matter "the promise and potency of every form and quality of life."

Such foolish optimism is largely sustained by the fact that while it is always some one's business to expound what is known, it is no one's business to attempt the thankless task of estimating or exhibiting the vast seas and gulfs of ignorance that divide these sporadic isles of knowledge. I refer not to the impossibility of being aware of ignorance that is absolute and complete, an inability which may be said to set a limit to our ignorance as much as to our knowledge: I am thinking rather of the many difficulties that prevent us from realizing at all adequately the ignorance we know we have. To do our ignorance justice we ought to devote whole shelves in our libraries to blank volumes that might be filled. But ignorance is barred all direct representation; and so ignorance ignored begets error and confusion. We are all familiar with the cartographer's device for economizing blank space by tucking in the unhappy Orkneys and Shetlands for example, reduced in scale, within the gaping void of the Moray Frith. Doubtless school inspectors could tell us something of the error to which this economic suppression of mere vacuity has led. And the like happens in scientific exposition from neglecting to leave conjectural spaces for ignorance.

But again, closely connected with this minimizing the magnitude of the stupendous ignorances that stretch between science and science, is the further assumption that separate sciences will grow in due course into a single philosophy. The orbis scientiarum, it is taken for granted, is as much a unity as the orbis terrarum, only its terrae incognitae want exploring. Such self-sufficiency on the part of science is usually due to a want of reflection, but Mr Herbert Spencer in what he is pleased to call his Synthetic Philosophy deliberately maintains that philosophy is constituted by "the *fusion*" of all the sciences into a whole, is nothing but "the final product of that process which begins with a mere colligation of crude observations, goes on establishing propositions that are broader and more separated from particular cases and ends in universal propositions. . . . Science is partially unified knowledge, Philosophy is completely-unified knowledge." This is positivism wearing a cloak. I dare not say it is the wolf in sheep's clothing, that would imply fear on one side and malice on the other. Let us say then it is a certain more harmless animal more nobly disguised. It would not, I think, take you long to find Mr Spencer's fusion of the sciences to be their utter confusion.

What is wrong with Mr Spencer's philosophy I suspect is, that it is not philosophy at all, but poetry. Had he but taken as his motto the saying of Heraclitus, πόλεμος πατὴρ πάντων, and written in blank verse, we might have had a moving, evolutionary epic, full of striking *aperçus*. That the leading conceptions in the poem should illustrate the general mutation of all things, and evolve into their contraries, would offend no one, and enable the synthesis to proceed triumphantly to the final "transfiguration" of that realism from which it set out. His philosophy consists in a whole series of 'equivocal generations,' to use Kant's phrase, the change of category, if I may so say, being covered by 'continuities' of sundry sorts. Let me cite instances: 1. Given the conservation of mass and energy, and we have generated all the variety of physical events. 2. Given certain hypothetical molecules of great complexity and they will yield reactions "varying little by little into those called vital." 3. Given an unbroken succession of impressions in an organism, and "there must arise a consciousness." 4. Given "that our states of consciousness segregate into two independent aggregates," and we shall have not the fission of one consciousness into two, but "the mystery of a consciousness of something that is yet out of consciousness," a dualism of Ego and non-Ego. 5. Then, given "the impression of resistance," and there will be "nascent consciousness of force," furnishing a principle of continuity for each of these correlatives, Ego and non-Ego. 6. Equating the Absolute with the Non-relative, i.e., the contrary of the Relative with its contradictory, then a consciousness divested of all relativity will give us the Absolute, as "the Power manifested behind all manifestations, inner and outer." 7. Given our inability "to suppress consciousness" any further, and its persistence will constitute an immediate experience of the permanence of this manifested Power, *alias* Unknowable Reality. So we return to that quantitative constancy of Matter and Force with which the 'Knowable' provisionally began.

From such ground it is impossible to legitimate the categories of Unity, Substance, Cause, End, which, of course, Mr Spencer freely uses, and, in fact, never accounts for. From such a ground, too, it is impossible to shew that the world is rational; and Mr Spencer gives no signs of even understanding that there is such a problem. The only unity his philosophy discloses is that of the Purely Indeterminate, and in this *asylum ignorantiae*, with 'unconscious pleasantry,' as it has been well said, he invites science and religion to dwell together and be at peace[1].

Now I take this so-called philosophy of Mr Spencer's, synthesizing his so-called Matter and so-called Spirit, as helping to prove that philosophy is *not* science

[1] The two preceding paragraphs appear also in the author's article, 'A Reply to Mr Herbert Spencer,' *Fortnightly Review*, March 1900, pp. 474, 476.—Ed.

pushed a stage further, and can never consist of a scientific generalization puffed out till it is so vague and empty that science can know it and use it no longer. Neither conservation of energy, nor natural selection, nor continuous evolution will enable us rationally to synthesize and interpret the experience of which they are but a part. But, as you remember, we came across the Spencerian system in connexion with the question of philosophic standpoints and I proposed to turn it to account as illustrating the difficulties of philosophic orientation.

The moral of all this then is not that Mr Spencer was not a man of parts—he was certainly that: the moral is that to keep steadfast to one point of view is in philosophy, especially in what we might call constructive philosophy, enormously difficult. The alterations of standpoint from that of individual percipience to that of common intelligence, from the *ordo ad nos* to *ordo ad universum*, the varying use of such terms as reality and object, the entire absence of definite meaning in such a phrase as 'relativity of knowledge,' have led to vacillations enough in other thinkers whose meaning from page to page is incomparably less intelligible. But clear as he is in style and detail, I doubt if there has ever been a thinker before as proud of his philosophic congruities and as full of philosophical incongruity.

But the mistakes that with him are so glaring are to be found also in philosophers of a finer mould. We might call them the natural infirmities of naked thinking. Now when we fail to see with our naked eyes we betake ourselves to artificial aids; in fact we have such helps for all our senses: not only microscopes and telescopes, but microphones and telephones, thermometers, galvanometers and what not. Can we not artificially fortify our understandings as well as our senses? The fact is we actually do avail ourselves of intellectual instruments of various sorts in different fields of intellectual work; the symbols of quantities and operations in mathematics, of elements and their combinations in chemistry are instances. The like may be said of certain methods of induction and classification, whence the appropriateness of Aristotle's[1] and Bacon's notion of an Organon. Even sciences that are without such instrumentalities have at least a counter-vailing advantage in the fact that they deal with sensible things in the concrete or with sensible relations of such things. Physiology and botany have their own terminology and nomenclature, every term in which can be attached like a label—so to say—to the facts denoted. But philosophy can never put its conceptions in evidence either by sensible intuition or by ideal construction after the manner of mathematics. It has to depend on natural language alone, just where this is most faulty. One of the most impressive lessons of modern psychology has consisted in pointing out the part that language plays in constituting a common world for intelligents and enabling the individual thinker conceptually to transcend the limits of his own immediate experience. But now it is a very startling and a very humbling truth that there are limits to this community, to this self-transcendence that language makes possible, and that philosophical speculation often oversteps these limits. I suppose if we were to follow the fashion of the hour and collect votes for the three greatest philosophers, the three would be Plato, Spinoza and Hegel. They impress us the most because of the sublimity and daring of their speculation, but if we ask the historian of philosophy we should find, I expect, that these are the three who have divided expositors the most.

[1] Though, to be sure, Aristotle did not himself use the term.

Two questions then arise: Could not philosophy have
a fixed terminology and nomenclature and further
could it not have symbols and a calculus that would
facilitate philosophic investigations? It is well known
that Leibniz held that both of these are possible, and
busied himself with schemes for a philosophical language and a philosophical calculus for fifty years or
more. If we had such instruments, he conceived "there
would be no more occasion for disputes between two
philosophers than between two accountants. It would
suffice for them to take pen in hand, to sit down to
their tables and to say to each other, 'Let us calcu-
late.'" Of course Leibniz was well aware that mathematicians relied quite as much on their special axioms
as on clear and definite symbols, but it was part of his
dream to ascertain the elementary truths or categories
which should be the general axioms of all knowledge
and "the wondrous harmony of which," he said,
"would stir our souls more than the most exquisite
music." That dream seems destined long to remain a
dream. In 1714 Leibniz now an old man and near his
end expresses his regret that he had not a few young
and helpful men to aid him in working out the details
so as to complete his scheme: in 1724 the man was born
who in what he called the Amphiboly of Reflective
Concepts shewed the fundamental flaw in Leibniz's
intellectual system of the world. But there is no reason
why the fate of the larger scheme should entail the fate
of the less. At least a trial is due to a project conceived
at the beginning and cherished to the end of a long
intellectual life by the man who perfected perhaps the
most wonderful intellectual instrument we possess—I
mean the differential calculus.

I confess for my own part to having expected something helpful from recent developments of symbolic
logic and particularly the so-called logic of relatives

But even a slight acquaintance with these algorithmics has convinced me of my mistake. It is true Boole has devoted a long chapter to an analysis of a portion of Clarke on the Being and Attributes of God and of a portion of Spinoza's Ethics, casting the premises into a series of equations and calculating, as Leibniz would have said, the conclusion they yield. In this way, for example, he shews very effectively that the premises from which Clarke thought to establish the proposition "Something has existed from eternity" yield no conclusion at all. Now I quite believe that facility in symbolic logic on Boole's lines is an admirable drill for a young philosopher, and I know from personal experience that men well versed in it are very helpful or very formidable critics. But I am by no means sure that a logical organon of a less formal kind is unattainable; and it was certainly something of this less formal kind that Leibniz intended by his *Characteristica univer-salis.* He imagined a system of signs or characters so devised that a faulty combination of concepts would be at once as evident to all who were decently versed in this grammar of philosophy, as, for example, faulty equations are evident to a physicist when their dimensions do not coincide. Leibniz himself failed in all his attempts to construct this instrument and probably failed, as I have said, because he mistook the nature of sensible intuition and its place in knowledge. I believe he would certainly have worked out something of importance if, instead of trying to depict ultimate notions by signs like Egyptian hieroglyphics or Chinese characters, he had sought to indicate some of the implications of such notions and their relations to each other.

However complex his equations in other respects, a physicist knows that they cannot be right unless their dimensions agree, much as a schoolboy knows his sum is wrong if he finds the actual contents of a vessel to be x square feet or y inches linear. With the help of such a philosophical calculus it might be easy to write out Mr Spencer's Synthetic Philosophy as nonsense in half a dozen lines, and Mr Spencer himself might have been led to turn his wonderful scientific imagination to better account. If the implication of relation were always attached to knowledge, we should not talk of a knowledge of things *per se* unless we meant to identify knowing and being: perhaps we should scarcely talk of things *per se* at all or find that, whether used in the singular or the plural, this notion is tantamount to the entirely indeterminate. Similarly we might find the Unconditioned not to exclude all relations but to include them all. As a mathematician knows that from n independent equations he cannot determine more than n unknown quantities it might be possible, if we had a philosophical calculus, to see by inspection to what extent our data were independent and what was the utmost that could be deduced from them. We should not confound matter with bodies for example, or minds with mind-stuff; nor suppose that teleological or ethical categories could be deduced from mechanical ones, because terms like rhythm, equality, integration, differentiation and others, with which Mr Spencer conjures, have metaphorical applications.

But now I can imagine two distinct objections occur to you which may be dealt with together. It may be said: no calculus can be a substitute for intelligence, or it may be said: we don't need a philosophical grammar to exhibit such barbarisms as some of Mr Spencer's. I agree to both; an abacus is as useless to idiots as spectacles to the blind; but to those who have sense and sight these instruments may be the means of saving labour and gaining power. It is only in the region of finite resources that economizing expedients can have either a place or a purpose. Every improvement of method and technique has been followed at once by the ascertainment of new truths both in mathematics and in the experimental sciences. So it would be in philosophy: better instruments, i.e., a better terminology and a better organon than that of ordinary logic, would make that easy which is now difficult and that possible which is now impossible.

Indeed I think it could be argued that one of the great difficulties in the way of philosophy has been the apparent perfection and completeness of the Aristotelian logic: these have secured it from essential change so long—checking development as much as they checked decay—that some of us had come to regard it as not only the alpha but the omega of philosophical grammar. But at length there are signs that the inevitable fate of all things human awaits even this. First of all psychology has disallowed it: it is neither an account of the thinking process nor an idealizing of that process. Then symbolic logic has laid hands upon it and shewn that syllogistic, at all events, and whatever belongs to that are but parts of a much larger whole, special cases of a more general theory of relations. Meanwhile the distinction that Kant drew between formal logic and transcendental logic has led to the mapping out of a vast and important field of philosophical inquiry scarcely dreamt of before—I mean Theory of Knowledge or Epistemology in the modern sense. But even this is by no means an even field: some of it is on a much higher plane, nearer the thin air of abstract speculation than the rest, which under names such as principles of science, methodology or higher logic, connects itself more closely with the actual sciences. The opening out of this new department of philosophy illustrates, by the way, the difficulty to which I just now referred, of realizing gaps till they cease to be altogether gaps. What an awful blank our biological contemporaries would feel for instance, if the results of Darwinism and recent embryology were blotted out and only the questions they answer remained! Yet Ray and Cuvier and Buffon were practically unaware of that same blank. So it may be with our successors as compared with ourselves in respect of their theory of knowledge.

Now I think it is the want of continuity thus revealed to us that best explains the many failures and confusions of philosophy in the past: it is this total absence of anything worth the name of epistemology in his scheme that has made Mr Spencer such a will-o'-the-wisp. Or, putting it another way, I think we may say that—however ambitious the problems philosophers' have attempted—the chief positive results attained have been additions to the theory of knowledge; and those have achieved most who have addressed themselves most directly to this. Hence the high place we must give to Aristotle, Locke, Hume and Kant. The great mistake made, as I have already hinted, was to try to begin at the beginning; and yet, it may be said, where is there a philosophical maxim if this is not one? Yes, but we must remember that beginning at the beginning is really beginning at what for us is the end and the wrong end, i.e., at what is farthest away. For the plain fact is here we are in the middle; and, however we may deceive ourselves, we can begin only where we are, and can at best but try to get to the beginning. There is no science that has not been inductive or analytic before it was deductive or synthetic —and that earlier heuristic or exploratory stage is the harder of the two. For philosophy it consists, as Kant practically maintained, in an analysis of fundamental concepts; and it is from this point of view that the difficulties on which I have specially dwelt are most apparent. Knowledge is a living thing and growing still, and the difficulties of anatomizing it and determining its various structures and functions are at least as great as are such inquiries into other living things. Subjective and objective elements are blended in all our categories. There is for us no absolute standpoint to which every truth can be referred any more than there is for us an absolute fixed point in space or in time from which positions and dates can be reckoned. Any practicable unification of knowledge must be immanent not transcendent. At this we can begin and it opens up to the critically minded, the thinker who is neither sceptical nor dogmatic, a field of indefinite extent. While there is this work to do we may confidently say that philosophy may still grow though it may never reach to heaven. We may conclude in the words of Goethe: "Der Mensch ist nicht geboren die Probleme der Welt zu lösen, wohl aber zu suchen wo das Problem angeht und sich sodann in der Grenze der Begreiflichen zu halten."[1]

[1] Quoted by Riehl, *Philosophie der Gegenwart*, 3rd ed., p. 179.

IV

THE PRESENT TREND OF
PHILOSOPHICAL SPECULATION

At the opening of a new century it is natural and fitting first to take a retrospective survey of the past and then to attempt a forecast of the future. Such revisions and previsions of most aspects of human thought and activity have been abundant of late, but I do not happen to have come across any dealing specially with philosophy. However, I am certainly not going to waste your time with surmises as to the precise form which the philosophy of the twentieth century will actually assume. As elsewhere so here, the unexpected is what we have to expect. Factors that we cannot foresee are sure to intervene and more or less belie our anticipations. Some people are hopeful that the century may see philosophy dead, and are scarcely disposed to give it decent burial. Well, if philosophy should die, a good many other things that we ought to value will follow it to the grave. It is true, as Novalis said, that philosophy "can bake no bread" and it may be uncertain whether—as he added—"she can procure for us God, Freedom and Immortality." But at any rate it is certain that philosophy has flourished most among the foremost races, and most in the periods of their greatest progress: it has been the vocation of some of the world's best men, and it has maintained ideals of which even religion has more than once lost sight. Among the unlikely things that the century has in store I do not think the extinction of philosophy is one: the signs of the times which suggest such a possibility—that "things are in the saddle and ride mankind"—are just those that thoughtful men deplore and deprecate. For my part then I will repeat the words of Schiller:

Welche wohl bleibt von allen Philosophien? Ich weiss nicht.
Aber die Philosophie, hoff' ich, soll ewig bleiben.

But, though we do not know what will happen in philosophy in the future, we can by tracing its course in the century that has closed discern at any rate *some* of the problems that are likely to be prominent in the speculations of the century that has now begun. What the solutions the new century will offer may be is another matter.

Such preliminary review of the recent past of philosophy may fittingly begin with the general remark that the course of philosophy has been characterized throughout by crises or reactions. In this respect a trivial, though I think an apt, comparison suggests itself. The strenuous idler who seeks to construct (say) a magic square, after repeated failures on one tack, will probably betake himself to its precise contrary: unsuccessful working outwards from the centre he tries working inwards from the sides. So it has been with the efforts of philosophy to systematize the universe: the unmanageable *residuum* of one method of speculation becomes the *fundamentum* of the next. With the latest of these reactions we may start. From 1794 (the date of Fichte's *Grundlage der gesammten Wissenschaftslehre*) till 1831 (the date of Hegel's death) the philosophical world was dazzled by the appearance in quick succession of the three most daring flights of so-called 'pure thought' that it has yet seen. By the middle of the century the last and greatest of these, the Panlogismus of Hegel—as the Germans call it—had come hopelessly to grief. What is known as the disruption of the Hegelian school was by that time complete. And now began the reaction. A couplet of Goethe's became the watchword of the new movement:

Willst du ins Unendliche schreiten
Geh nur im Endlichen nach allen Seiten.

Foiled in its attempt to fly in a vacuum, Philosophy so far from regarding experience as a hindrance to its progress, now proclaims experience to be the one means of its advance: in fact it no longer believes in a reality that is not experience in some sense or other. One consequence of this reaction has been a striking *rapprochement* between philosophy and science. Science no doubt *at first* held aloof coldly and contemptuously, preferring her own home-spun philosophy, if she had to have any at all. This it was thought could be guaranteed as genuinely empirical, founded on facts, and clear of all 'idealistic romancing.'

Hence the outburst of materialism in Germany in the fifties and sixties. The state of scientific opinion in Germany at this time is evident from the fact, that at the famous scientific Congress held at Göttingen in 1854 (when the physiologist, Rudolph Wagner, was to have defended the theory of a soul, but failed to attend through illness—or, as his opponents said, through fear) "among the five hundred persons present, not one single voice was raised in favour of the spiritualistic philosophy."[1] Wagner, however, published his views before the end of the year and so began the famous *Materialismusstreit*. Everybody has at least heard of Büchner's *Kraft und Stoff*, which appeared in 1855 in connexion with this controversy, ran rapidly through seven or eight editions and was translated into the chief languages of Europe. But before the seventies the tide of materialism began to ebb. Lange's *History of Materialism*, a book widely read in the scientific world, and

[1] *Deutsches Museum*, quoted by G. H. Lewes, *Hist.* II. 649.

other works of the so-called Neo-Kantian School revealed the serious defects, the bad metaphysics, that
had lain undetected beneath the rash but plausible
generalizations of the physical realists. Distinguished
men of science such as Virchow, Helmholtz, Kirchhoff,
Du Bois-Reymond and many more, also combined in
various ways to discredit these flimsy speculations, and
joined in the cry: 'Back to Kant.' And from 1865,
when Liebmann first raised that cry, the Kantian
idealism, we may fairly say, has been paramount.
Since the disruption of the Hegelian School, philosophy
has been largely—I might say mainly—occupied with
the theory of knowledge. In this work men of science
have taken, as time went on, an ever increasing share.
Foremost among them was Helmholtz, though several
left science altogether and devoted themselves exclusively to philosophy: as, for example, Lotze, Fechner,
Wundt, Mach, and now Boltzmann and Ostwald. Here
again, in Germany at least, Kant's influence has been
superior to all others.

But in England, till recently, the dominant philosophies have been those of Hume and Berkeley, as presented by John Stuart Mill: the one divested of its
scepticism, the other of its theological polemics, and
both together transformed into a so-called psychological theory of matter and mind, which is essentially
idealistic, and yet preposterously empirical. At least
one Englishman eminent in the scientific roll of the
century shewed a lifelong interest in this philosophy—
I mean Huxley of course. Berkeley's contentions
(1) that what we "call matter and motion are known
to us only as forms of consciousness" and (2) that
"consciousness apart from a thinking mind is a contradiction in terms" he admits to be irrefragable.
"And therefore," he adds, "if I were obliged to choose
between absolute materialism and absolute idealism,

I should feel compelled to accept the latter alternative." But he denied the obligation so to choose,
and dubbed himself an agnostic. The most that experience warranted was, he thought, the assertion that
matter and mind are correlative aspects of the Unknowable. This is the agnostic monism that Spencer
has expounded at length and towards which Mill more
or less inclined. It is still in high favour throughout
the scientific world. Even as it stands, professedly
neutral, it indicates a certain approximation towards
the idealism or spiritualism—as I should prefer to say
—which philosophy has ever tended to maintain,
and tended to maintain the more decidedly the more
it has reflected on epistemological problems. Agnostic
monism at least meets such philosophy half way: in so
far, that is to say, as this monism definitely abandons
materialism. But neutrality that depends on an exact
balance of ignorances is a very unstable thing. It would
be easy to cite passages from Mill, Spencer, and Huxley
which imply that reality belongs primarily to the
spiritual side. Again the crude Pampsychism of Zöllner,
Clifford, Haeckel and Ostwald, and generally more or
less countenanced by scientific speculators nowadays—is
a sort of idealism, though often of a rather crude kind.

On the whole then, I think, we may say that Philosophy in the present day shews a decidedly idealistic
tendency—a tendency, however, due not to speculation
of the 'high priori' kind, but resulting from reflection
on experience as a whole. Our terminology is unhappily not very precise. The term idealism, though
it has the sanction of long usage, is ambiguous: in fact,
as Sidgwick said in the last lecture he ever wrote, its
use in current English thought has become quite in-
tolerable. There are many really very different philosophies to which it is indifferently applied. But there
has been but one thoroughgoing idealism, the so-called

absolute idealism of Hegel, in which reality is regarded as a logical or dialectical process of evolution. And even this we might call a one-sided spiritualism inasmuch as it makes thinking activity the only reality— ideas, said Hegel, have hands and feet—and it is accordingly not unfrequently called Intellectualism. The philosophy of Schopenhauer might in like manner be described as another one-sided spiritualism, in which not Thought but Will is the ultimate reality, and it is therefore often styled Voluntarism, Volitionism or Ethelism. By spiritualism without qualification then we should mean the doctrine that only conscious, i.e., thinking, feeling and willing beings are real. In this sense Berkeley, Leibniz, Fichte and Lotze were spiritualists. The only point we have now to emphasize is that on which all forms of spiritualism alike insist, viz., that matter, or—more generally—that nature, is to be regarded as dependent on, or as the manifestation of spirit. "*Nature* is the *existence* of things so far as that is determined according to universal laws."[1] Such is Kant's definition. If then we find anything that is wholly explicable by universal laws, devoid therefore of all spontaneity, self-direction or initiative, that thing has no being for itself: it is but a product or manifestation of spirit. On the other hand, whatever we find not wholly inert, not absolutely determined from without, that is something for itself, is so far conscious or spiritual. Of course we are here giving a wider meaning than is usual to the term spiritual. But its antithesis to Naturalism, which regards Nature as supreme and consciousness in all its forms as a product of nature, will make the meaning of spiritualism clear.

Another characteristic of the philosophic speculation of our time is the tendency to place the volitional or practical side of Spiritualism foremost. To Kant's

[1] *Prolegomena*, § 14.

insistence on what he called the primacy of the Practical Reason we may trace this tendency back: in Schopenhauer's *Die Welt ist an sich Wille* it runs into one-sided extravagance, the pendant, as we have seen, to the equally one-sided extravagance of Hegel's *Die Welt ist an sich Idee*. But the dominant philosophy of the day is led to emphasize the practical side of reality, not as the result of abstract speculation about knowing and being, but again as the result of reflection on experience in the concrete and as a whole. Conscious life is everywhere and always active life: not mere aimless energy, but directed energy, *conatus* as Spinoza called it. The good is for it the *raison d'être par excellence*, and final causes become the fundamental causes. "The true beginning of Metaphysics lies in Ethics" said Lotze in concluding his earliest philosophical work. Referring to this *dictum* in concluding his latest he says: "I admit that the expression was not exact: but I still feel certain of being on the right track when I seek in that which *ought* to be the ground of that which *is*."[1] Perhaps I may be allowed to quote my own way of stating the same position from the psychological standpoint: "Looking broadly at the progress of life, as it ascends through the animal kingdom and onwards through the history of man, it seems safe to say that knowledge is always a means to ends, is never an end by itself—till at length it becomes interesting and satisfying in itself. Psychologically, then, the sole function of perception and intellection is to guide action and to subserve volition—more generally, to promote self-conservation and betterment. Knowledge, from this point of view, may even be regarded as the joint product of natural selection and subjective selection: it emerges tainted with —as some may think—but, at all events, permeated by, a teleological colouring."[2]

[1] *Metaphysic*, last page.
[2] *Encyclopaedia Britannica*, 10th ed., art. 'Psychology,' p. 56.

The reaction from the intellectual bias which restricted the fundamental problems of philosophy to
questions of knowing and being has taken in America
a very pronounced form, called by its advocates Prag-
matism. "Thought in movement," says William James
in his recent Gifford Lectures, "has for its only conceivable motive the attainment of belief, or thought at
rest. Only when our thought about a subject has found
its rest in belief can our action on the subject firmly
and safely begin. Beliefs, in short, are rules for action;
and the whole function of thinking is but one step in
the production of active habits....To develop a
thought's meaning we need therefore only determine
what conduct it is fitted to produce; that conduct is
for us its sole significance; and the tangible fact at the
root of all our thought-distinctions is that there is no
one of them so fine as to consist in anything but a
possible difference in practice....Our conception of
these practical consequences is for us the whole of our
conception of the object, so far as that conception has
positive significance at all."[1] Or as a brilliant and
rash young Oxford philosopher still more succinctly
puts this new position: "Whatever knowledge cannot
be rendered somehow useful cannot be esteemed
real."[2]

I pass to a third characteristic of modern philosophic
thought, closely related to the last, that has become
increasingly marked of late, and again one resulting
from reflection upon experience as a concrete whole,
viz., the recognition of the supreme importance of
history. As compared with the nineteenth century the
eighteenth—though it produced great historians—was
a century devoid of historic sense. Its speculations concerning the origin of society, of language, of religion
shew this. Lessing's *Erziehung des Menschengeschlechtes*

[1] *Varieties of Religious Experience*, p. 444.
[2] Schiller, *Mind*, N.S., XI, 215.

appeared in 1780 and Herder's *Ideen zur Philosophie der Geschichte* in 1784—not much over a century ago, that is to say; and yet how antiquated, when compared with the present modes of thought, they now appear. Even so Lessing is said to have prepared the way for Hegel's *Philosophy of History*, perhaps the most fruitful of Hegel's works; and the attempt has been made again and again to prove Herder an important forerunner of Darwin. Nevertheless Schiller's idea—adopted by Hegel—of the world's history as its day of judgment (*Die Weltgeschichte ist das Weltgericht*) and Darwin's ideas of the struggle for existence and survival of the fittest are all ideas wholly foreign to the spirit of the eighteenth century *Aufklärung*.

The historical method belongs then mainly to the nineteenth century, and there we find it claiming to have 'invaded and transformed all departments of thought.' "A belief in the Historical Method," said Sidgwick at the outset of a polemic against it, "is the most widely and strongly entertained philosophical conviction at the present day." It is the existence of this conviction that I wish to emphasize: the precise scope of the historical method and its relation to other methods does not so much concern us. The recognition of the supreme importance of history which the historical method implies is transforming philosophy at all events, turning it aside from "Naturalism's desert on the one hand and the barren summits of the Absolute on the other."[1]

The division of knowledge into science and history, and its corollary, that history as unscientific has no interest for the philosopher, have been accepted commonplaces since the dawn of modern thought. But this position is due to a natural confusion which has only gradually become apparent and the conse-

[1] W. James, *Mind*, N.S., xii, 93.

quences of which we are only now beginning to appreciate—I mean the confusion of reason with reasoning, *ratio* with *ratiocinatio*. Mathematics was the paragon of the sciences and was regarded as built up entirely by rigorous deduction from exact definitions and self-evident axioms. The goal of every science was then to be able to proceed *more geometrico*. Descartes believed that philosophy could be treated in this fashion, and Spinoza—as everybody knows—actually made the attempt. "I shall consider human actions and desires," he said, "in exactly the same manner, as though I were concerned with lines, planes and solids."[1] Physics succeeded before long in partially reaching the deductive level, and was known henceforth as Natural Philosophy. The proximate aim of the other natural sciences was then to become branches of physics. In pursuance of this end it was sought to reduce psychology to physiology, physiology to chemistry, chemistry to physics. And undoubtedly such efforts have resulted in a great extension, nay, they have resulted also in a great unification of scientific knowledge.

But obviously such knowledge can deal only with general conceptions and universal laws. It must ignore the historical as merely concrete and particular and as implying irreversible processes. Accordingly Bacon excluded all history, natural as well as civil, from science in his *Globus intellectualis*; and Hobbes did the same, on the ground that history was mere *experientia* and not *ratiocinatio*. We find even Schopenhauer saying: "The true philosophy of history consists in discerning that in spite of all these endless changes and their hurly-burly (*Wirrwarr*) one yet has always only the same identical and unalterable essence before one." The historical in other words was regarded as without ultimate reality or significance. But meanwhile even

[1] *Eth*. iii, pref.

among natural phenomena the residue of the particular and contingent from which science had extracted
its universal and changeless laws began to disclose not
a hurly-burly of facts and events but that historical
continuity which we now call evolution; and to-day
we hear not only of geological and biological evolution
but of chemical evolution and stellar evolution. At the
same time the gap between psychology and history in
the stricter sense was filled by the new science of sociology, including comparative philology, comparative
mythology, etc., and a 'social medium' was seen to be
essential to the development of man as a rational and
moral being. On the other hand, comparative psychology has helped to connect man on the sentient and
instinctive side with the animal world.

When we attempt to formulate a definitive interpretation of this vast and continuous evolutional procession
that the nineteenth century has revealed to us, the
difficulties become appalling and are perhaps insuperable. But at least we are certain that it has a meaning,
that it is teleological; and accordingly in dealing with
it we apply a wholly new set of categories, of which
science, as distinct from history, knows nothing—I
mean of course, the categories of worth or value. These
conceptions hold an important place in the philosophy
of Herbart and Lotze, from whom I have already
quoted. In the last few years the whole subject, known
as the theory of Worth, or Axiology, has been systematically worked out and is assuredly to be counted as
one among the factors that make for idealism. It is
interesting to see modern philosophy coming round to
the position taken long ago by Plato in his *Republic*.
To say that the good-in-itself is the ultimate ground
of all reality is but to say that final causes are the
supreme causes. Nevertheless we may hold that science
has done right in agreeing with Bacon that in *its*

domain final causes are but vestal virgins, altogether unfruitful. It is methodologically false and, in fact, impossible to combine results obtained from two disparate points of view. You cannot, for example, explain how a machine works by guessing at what it was meant to do. This is the lesson so impressively taught by Kant's *Critique of Judgment.*

But the situation is altered entirely when, bringing the scientific and the historical into relation, we seek to estimate their value. The one gives us mechanism, the other gives us meaning, though it be a meaning that we but inadequately grasp. To use the imagery that Goethe has made current—the one takes the loom of nature to pieces, the other spreads out the living garment that it weaves before us: or to use another figure less poetical but equally apt—the one gives us mere letterpress and the other literature. To determine the mechanism of nature we must systematically ascertain coexistences and sequences, resemblances and differences, and from these data advance by abstraction and generalization to universal laws. This process we call reasoning. To understand the meaning of nature this process is unavailing or, at least, insufficient: here reason or spiritual insight is indispensable. I shall not attempt to define reason or philosophy as distinct from reasoning or science. It may suffice to cite the old distinction: the one asks Why, the other asks only How. Hence philosophy is not a mere extension of science, as Spencer and the positivists maintain. That amounted to saying, and has come indeed to mean, that there is no distinct place for philosophy at all. But grant that we are impelled to ask Why, grant that we do see meaning, and not merely law, in things; then the supreme importance of history becomes clear. And when we reflect in this sense on experience as a whole it is equally clear that the meaning, the life, in the universe stands out as fundamental, the mechanism becomes only secondary, nay, in the end it is taken up into the life and meaning. For we cannot suppose that that priority of matter and mechanism for finite minds, which seem to live and work only by this means, is an absolute priority: somewhere this dualism of matter and mind must end. Such at any rate is the conviction of idealism. Let me on this point quote Lotze once more: "It is a true saying that God has ordered all things by measure and number; but he ordered not measure and number but what deserved or needed to have them; not a meaningless, essenceless reality only fitted to support mathematical relations and give some sort of concreteness to abstract numbers. On the contrary the meaning of the world is what comes first and that is not merely something subordinated to a pre-existing order: rather from it alone arises the need of such order and the form in which it is realised. All those laws which we include under the common term mechanical...all these persist, not by their own authority as a groundless destiny to which concrete reality is compelled to bow. They are—humanly expressed—only the final consequences which for the sake of what it wills, the living and active meaning of the world has laid at the foundation of particular realities as a command embracing them all."[1]

These words of Lotze's bring us to a new point, for they raise the question: what is the relation of God or the Supreme Reality to these particular realities, which interact according to a system of law and order which he sustains? In other words we are brought face to face with the old and formidable problem of the One and the Many. Can we predicate veritable reality of both, can we say that both are really in some sense free

[1] Lotze, *Metaphysic*, Eng. tr., p. 535.

and for themselves? Or if we maintain this reality for
the Many does not the One become a fictitious, merely
all-inclusive unity or totality; are we not pantheists?
If we maintain it of the One does not the reality of the
Many become illusory, merely phenomenal? This, it
has been said, will be the philosophical problem of the
twentieth century. Let us see how the century is ap-
proaching it. With such a problem much depends on
the side from which we begin. The nineteenth century
on the whole, I think, began with the Absolute. Its
latest attempt by that subtle Doctor, F. H. Bradley in
his *Appearance and Reality*, probably the ablest philosophical work that has appeared in English during the
last fifty years, might be characterized as Hegelianism
turned sceptical: hence it has been facetiously described as the Disappearance of Reality. For Mr
Bradley the real is one; the self we take to be real is
but a phenomenal adjective, and when regarded as
real becomes 'riddled with contradictions.' The "alleged independence" of the Many, in which we empirically believe, he declares, "is no fact...the plurality sinks to become merely an integral aspect in a
single substantial unity, and the reals have vanished."[1]
Nevertheless Mr Bradley prophesies: "Monadism, on
the whole, will increase and will add to the difficulties
which already exist."[2] The first half of this forecast
at least is true. A decided reaction has set in against
this Absolutism—often confusedly called monism—
which Mr Bradley defends; and Pluralism is now to the
fore. And there it is likely to remain so long as philosophy elects to start from, and to stand by, experience
as conscious life, and to regard that life as directed to
self-realization. For unless human freedom is a reality
and not a mere appearance, unless we have power on
our own act and on the world, what basis of fact have

[1] *Appearance and Reality*, p. 143. [2] *Ibid.*, p. 118, *fin.*

we from which to ascend to a Supreme Reality of a spiritual kind at all? Surely in such a case the universe lapses back into a mechanism, and Naturalism is right.

But now come the difficulties of setting the Many over against the One. A free agent, a differentiation of the Absolute that is logically as essential to the reality of the absolute as its unity is, cannot, it is said, be created: the Many then are eternal. In two recent books—Howison's *Limits of Evolution* (1901) and McTaggart's *Studies in the Hegelian Cosmology* (same year)—this position is maintained *à outrance*; though McTaggart imagines that he is still expounding Hegel, while Howison is an avowed pluralist, both of course being spiritualists. "This Pluralism," says Howison, "held in union by reason, this World of Spirits, is thus the genuine Unmoved One that moves all things. Not the solitary God, but the whole World of Spirits including God, and united through recognition of Him, is the real 'Prime Mover.'...Its oneness is not that of a single inflexible Unit, leaving no room for freedom in the many, (no room) for a many that is really many; but is the oneness...of spontaneous cooperation, in which every member from inner initiative, from native contemplation of the same Ideal, joins in moving all things changeable towards the common goal....This movement is what we have in these days learned to call the process of Evolution."[1] And again: "The circle of self-thinking spirits indeed has God for its central Light, the Cynosure of all their eyes: *he* is if *they* are, *they* are if *he* is; but the relation is freely mutual, and he only exists as *primus inter pares*, in a circle eternal and indissoluble."[2] Howison allows himself to talk of creation, but creation with him is, equally with regeneration, analogous to what certain theologians call synergism: God is not its efficient but its final cause. God is

[1] *Limits of Evolution*, pref., p. xv.   [2] *Ibid.*, p. 359.

the Creator simply as being "the impersonated Ideal of every mind."[1] As this Ideal, he is indeed central and determining, and therefore real and the measure of all other reality."[2] For Dr McTaggart God is not even the *Monas monadum* he becomes for Howison. The Absolute is spiritual, but it is not personal, has neither cognition nor volition. Its unity is for its differentiations, which are persons, but they are not for it. To illustrate this relation of the Absolute to finite spirits, Dr McTaggart instances that of a College to its fellows, but adds: "of course the Absolute is a far more perfect unity than a College."[3] In its final determination the Absolute for him is Love: knowledge and volition disappear swallowed up in this, not only the highest reality in the universe but the sole reality. But it is not love of God. "For love is of persons, and God, as we have seen," says Dr McTaggart, "is a unity of persons, but not a personal unity."[4]

It may be that speculations such as those of Howison, and still more those of Dr McTaggart, are at the mercy of every critic who will seriously examine them. But they do not stand alone; I have referred to them at length as being extreme instances of a reaction that is very widespread—a reaction, which even if it should constructively fail—as Bradley foretells—will at least profoundly modify any absolutism that arises after it. Wundt in Germany, Renouvier in France and James in America have advanced pluralistic views—to say nothing of the 'anarchic individualism,' as it has been called, of that very self-centred individual, Prof. Lutoslawski. Renouvier applies the principle of relativity to the idea of the Absolute in a very rigorous fashion. God is neither definable nor even thinkable except in relation to the world, which nevertheless he

[1] *Ibid.*, pref., p. xiv.   [2] *Ibid.*, pref., p. xvi.
[3] *Hegelian Cosmology*, p. 58.   [4] *Ibid.*, p. 289.

is supposed to have created. He is consequently finite, being limited by the personality and freedom of the monads, and upon these entirely rests the existence of evil. Renouvier was an important figure among the increasing number of earnest men who are striving for the moral regeneration of France, and William James is, in many respects, his disciple. But James carries pluralism to even greater lengths. He recognizes no pre-established harmony as Renouvier does, and even doubts whether religious experience either warrants or requires more than polytheism: all that is needed, he thinks, is "the belief that beyond each man and in a fashion continuous with him there exists a larger power which is friendly to him and to his ideals."[1] And James roundly asserts that "the truth is too great for any one actual mind, even though that mind be dubbed 'the Absolute,' to know the whole of it. The facts and worths of life need many cognizers to take them in."[2] "Radical empiricism," he says again, à propos of a book to which I will next refer, "thus leads to the assumption of a collectivism of personal lives (which may be of any grade of complication, and superhuman or infrahuman as well as human) variously cognitive of each other, variously conative and impulsive, genuinely evolving and changing by effort and trial, and by their interaction and cumulative achievements making up the world."[3] The book reviewed is a volume of eight essays by Oxford lecturers, entitled *Personal Idealism*—a name by which Pluralism is sometimes described. The book is avowedly published as representing 'a tendency in contemporary thinking.' A word or two from the preface may be worth quoting: "Personality," it begins, "one would have supposed ought never to have needed special advocacy in this self-

[1] *Varieties of Religious Experience*, p. 525.
[2] *Talks to Teachers*, pref., p. v.   [3] *Mind*, N.S., XII, 97.

assertive country of ours. And yet by some of the leading thinkers of our day it has been neglected; while by others it has been bitterly attacked. What makes its vindication the more urgent is that attacks have come from two different sides. One adversary tells each of us: You are a transitory result of physical processes; and the other: You are an unreal appearance of the Absolute. Naturalism and Absolutism, antagonistic as they seem to be, combine in assuring us that personality is an illusion. Naturalism and Absolutism are the adversaries against whom the personal idealist has to strive."..."The two points in respect of which Absolutism tends to be most unsatisfactory are, first, its way of criticizing human experience, not from the standpoint of human experience, but from the visionary and impracticable standpoint of an absolute experience; and secondly, its refusal to recognize adequately the volitional side of human nature"—remarks obviously directed against Bradley.

The last essay, by Dr Rashdall, is entitled *Personality, Human and Divine*. Dr Rashdall moves as one that walks on eggs. But in one or two places he seems to put his foot down somewhat more firmly. "Do you say that all this makes God finite?" he asks. "Be it so, if you will. Everything that is real is in that sense finite. God is certainly limited by all other beings in the Universe, that is to say, by other selves, in so far as He is not those selves. He is not limited, as I hold, by anything which does not ultimately proceed from His own Nature or Will or Power. That power is doubtless limited, and in the frank recognition of this limitation of power lies the only solution of the problem of Evil which does not either destroy the goodness of God or destroy moral distinctions altogether."[1] And again: "The indisposition to admit that souls have an

[1] *Personal Idealism*, p. 390.

existence which is not merged in that of God, seems to arise largely from the fact that philosophers have imposed upon themselves and others by the trick of simply assuming (without proof) an identity between God and the philosophical 'Absolute,' and then arguing that if any of the attributes ascribed by theology or religion or common-sense to God are inconsistent with what is implied in the conception of 'the Absolute' no such being as the God of religion can exist. Personality is undoubtedly inconsistent with the idea of the Absolute or Infinite Being, and therefore it is assumed that God is not personal. The arguments of Idealism really, as it seems to me, go to prove that over and above our souls there does exist such a Being as theologians. . . have commonly understood by God. The Absolute, therefore, if we must have a phrase which might well be dispensed with, consists of God and the souls, including, of course, all that God and those souls know or experience."[1]

On another tendency of contemporary philosophy I can only say a word: it is as we have seen closely connected with the last—I mean the treatment of the problem of evil. The easy optimism of Leibniz's *Theodicée* is wholly a thing of the past. In the nineteenth century we have had two pessimistic philosophies; and the question Is life worth living? has been seriously discussed. The twentieth century bids fair to be neither optimistic nor pessimistic. To say that evil does not exist for the Absolute, that, as Mr Bradley puts it, "all discord as such disappears if the harmony is made wide enough,"[2] is not likely for many reasons to content it, till Absolutism and Quietism are in vogue again. But that good comes of evil and a good that can only be understood from a higher standpoint—*that* history and evolution seem to teach. A faith that good may

[1] *Personal Idealism*, p. 392.   [2] *Appearance and Reality*, p. 202.

eventually triumph is then possible: the fact that evil, physical and moral alike, can be diminished by struggle and effort is certain; the fact that physical and moral good alike can be increased by struggle and effort is equally certain. Hence the doctrine of *Weltverbesserung* as the Germans say: the doctrine to which George Eliot, I believe, gave the name of Meliorism. Quite apart from religious considerations this faith in progress is widely held and shapes the life and conduct of thousands who subscribe to no religious creed. Yet this faith based on evolution and history is affecting religious conceptions in two or three ways. First what we might call religious pessimism—the theory that nature, and men as natural, are bad, the religious conviction that we associate with Puritanism and Calvinism, is surely succumbing to a healthy worldliness. Again the Christian virtue of meekness, turning the other cheek—in a word—non-resistance, is likely, in spite of Tolstoi, to be at least materially transformed.

One other point already referred to—the relation of God to evil. If God is not—for whatever reason—absolutely omnipotent, then, to quote the words of John Stuart Mill, "one elevated feeling is possible which is not open to those who believe in the omnipotence of the good principle in the universe, the feeling of helping God—of requiting the good he has given by a voluntary co-operation which he, not being omnipotent, really needs, and by which a somewhat nearer approach may be made to the fulfilment of his purposes."[1] Speaking generally and in conclusion, then, we may say that the spiritualistic and practical tendencies of philosophy at the present time are bringing it into close relations with religion: its theory of knowledge is one that leaves, as Kant said, "room for faith." Whether the result will be a remoulding of Christianity or a new religion time alone can shew.

[1] *Three Essays on Religion*, p. 256.

V

PHILOSOPHICAL ORIENTATION AND
SCIENTIFIC STANDPOINTS

ITHIN the last few months the civilized world
has been united in commemorating the distinguished philosopher whose life ended at
Königsberg a hundred years ago, but whose thoughts
have been active and fruitful throughout the century
that has closed and bid fair to continue their influence
in the century that has now begun. In a short article,
written in 1786, entitled: *Was heisst: sich im Denken
orientiren?* Kant has provided us with a good starting-
point for our present discussion.

Sich orientieren, to orientate oneself or find one's bearings, means, says Kant, "in the literal sense of the
words, from a given quarter of the globe, one of the
four into which we divide the horizon, to fix the rest,
in other words, to determine which is the east. If I see
the sun in the sky and know that it is now noon, then
I know how to find the south, west, north and east.
For this purpose however one thing is indispensable,
a 'feeling' of difference within myself as subject, the
difference namely between the right hand and the left.
Without this, being in the west, say, I should not know
whether to locate the south on the right or on the left.
And if by miracle all the stars were to reverse their
courses, retaining their relative positions, the astronomer attending only to what he sees and neglecting
what he 'feels' would unavoidably lose his bearings."
In order, then, to orientation in the literal sense, geographical orientation, two factors are necessary, the
objective data, the sun or the pole-star as seen, and the

subjective sense of difference between right and left. Now for Kant's question: "What does orientation in thought mean?"—philosophical orientation, as we may call it. Though our answer to this question, the answer most commonly given nowadays, is in the main that which Kant gave, it will be best to deal with it independently. If the analogy between spatial and speculative (or philosophical) orientation is to hold we must determine what there is in the latter corresponding to the objective factor, and what to the subjective factor, in the former.

The objective factor, the horizon for philosophy, is the circle of the positive sciences. It is said that science is the exact measurement of phenomena, and again that it is their methodical description, their systematic classification. But phenomenon is a doubly relative term. Things *per se* we may talk of, but phenomena *per se* are impossible. An appearance must be not only an appearance *of* some one, it must be also an appearance *for* some one. *Wie viel Schein, so viel Hindeutung aufs Sein,* said Herbart: the phenomenal everywhere intimates an adequate reality, and not only a reality adequate to its production but a reality adequate to its perception. An astronomer cannot produce an eclipse nor can a worm perceive one. The existence of phenomena, then, implies a double activity, a certain *rapport* between giver and receiver. This fact we recognize when we describe experience as the interaction of Ego and non-Ego; and we may follow Leibniz in saying that between the two there is a correspondence such that the more advanced the Ego, the wider its horizon, the more varied the data of its experience: every Ego or subject 'mirrors' the same universe, but each from its own point of view. The data of science, then, answer to the human horizon. But in calling itself positive, science intends expressly to confine itself to these data, and to leave the real implications of Ego and non-Ego—which such data presuppose—entirely aside; in other words, science ignores altogether what we call philosophical orientation. This is no defect in science as such, but it is a limitation, the inevitable consequence of that division of labour which the successful prosecution of research in so wide a field entails upon the narrow mind of man. It is only when the limitation is forgotten—as unhappily it often is—that we find men of science losing their bearings and drifting towards philosophic nihilism. In the beginning it was only phenomena, in the end it is only illusion. To use terms that Kant has made current—only however to express a distinction that goes back even to Plato—science is wholly the affair of the understanding, or reasoning; it is reason—a very different matter—that enables us to orientate ourselves.

Reason, then, is the subjective factor which, by its theoretical and practical demands, helps us to determine our ποῦ στῶ and to find our bearings. The concrete world in which we live and move and have our being is not a museum arranged in classes and compartments: sorted and dissected in this fashion, we can never discern its meaning or interpret our place and purpose in it. Life is the supreme fact in this world and the good is its supreme idea, the end and aim of that activity which all living things display. The greatest names in philosophy—Plato, Aristotle, Spinoza, Kant, Hegel—are on this point at one; and the common thought of mankind, which has no conscious philosophy at all, here agrees with them. For we have all to face life and the world as a whole, and are supremely concerned about practical issues. But science, which is bent only on ascertaining what it calls the ultimate elements and the fundamental processes of things, treats them—as Hegel quaintly put it—as if it were peeling off the coats of an onion. It disintegrates and takes to pieces, and then is apt to labour under the delusion that the world after this analysis still remains for us as it was, is still the living concrete reality and not so many lifeless abstractions. The error lies in forgetting that analysis is only one-half the process and that the main point is the re-union and interpretation of what has been divided. And it is when analysis never gets beyond the stage of division that Goethe's words are true:

> Encheiresin Naturae, nennt's die Chemie;
> Spottet ihrer selbst, und weiss nicht, wie:
> Hat die Theile in ihrer Hand,
> Fehlt leider nur das geistige Band.

But though analysis be only half the process, not the main point but only a preliminary, it is nevertheless an essential one. We may have the parts in our hand without the spiritual tie that makes them a living whole, but we cannot have this articulate whole without the several members of which it is to consist. Or in the language of Kant's metaphor, with which we began, we cannot find our bearings in a vacuum devoid of objective contents any more than we can find them without reference to ourselves. Philosophy cannot dispense with science nor can science, however complete, render philosophy superfluous. The whole indeed is nothing without the parts, but it is always more than the bare sum of them, most of all more when these *disjecta membra* attain to life and meaning. Obvious as this is now to all of us, its truth was ignored at first when philosophy essayed to read off the meaning of the world before it had learnt either to spell or to construe. Nowadays we are familiar with the opposite extreme, when to the many that say, "Who will shew us the good?" some A B C of physics or physiology, some

Grammar of Science is presented, as if letters were the same as literature and a knowledge of the parts of speech sufficient for the interpretation of the so-called riddle of the universe. Philosophy, then, cannot begin at the beginning as "a metaphysic without assumptions" and by a royal road demonstrate *a priori* what is the reality and what the meaning that underlie appearances. But the sciences which decipher and classify these phenomenal data from a hundred diverse standpoints are still further from beginning at the beginning, nor can they carry us on to the end, and without any philosophic orientation reveal to us the living and active meaning, the spiritual tie, that unifies them all.

Still it is not my purpose to offer any remarks on the central ideas of Philosophy—the true, the beautiful, and the good in their relation to the soul, the world, and God. It is in respect of these that it is said that philosophy begins where science ends. But there is a humbler function of Philosophy in which it has simply to criticize the fundamental concepts of the sciences themselves. In other words, before we attempt to orientate ourselves to the whole of experience, we recognize nowadays the desirability of orientating the diverse standpoints of the several sciences to each other. In a big national survey it is found that—after the several trigonometrical figures have been made consistent, each for itself—a further so-called 'final reduction' is requisite before all these figures can be adjusted to each other so as to make one consistent whole. This final reduction is not obtained by further surveying, but by reasoning applied to the surveys already attained. The department of philosophy known nowadays as Epistemology, or the Higher Logic, has an office analogous to this final reduction to perform for the partial surveys of the sciences. The latest historian of science, Dr Theodore Merz, in his *History of*

European Thought in the Nineteenth Century, treats in succession of the astronomical, the atomic, the mechanical, the physical, the morphological, the genetic, the vitalistic, the psychophysical, and the statistical views of nature. Even when these several views have been mutually adjusted and combined, there remains, as we have already seen, the final and supreme problem of *interpreting* the whole, which they merely *present*. But as they stand, some turn out to be incompatible with others: contradictions emerge, and therefore there must be error somewhere; and as we are willing to concede that it does not lie in the special concepts of any given science, we infer that it must lie in some mistake as to the relation of their several standpoints to each other. The first business of philosophy, then, is to reduce these to a consistent orientation.

This conflict of the sciences, this "strife among the faculties" as Kant called it, has, I understand, occupied your society during the past year, and I gather that I am invited to the honourable but not very enviable task of reviewing the situation in ignorance of the results of your deliberations. The special topics with which we are to deal are the relation of the 'inorganic world' to the 'organic world' and the relation of the 'world within' to the 'world without.' I propose to start with the last so far as it involves the problem of adjusting the sciences that deal with matter and those that deal with mind, and then to pass to the problem of adjusting the sciences of matter and the sciences of life. We have no direct concern with the details of any of these sciences: what chiefly interests us are their distinctive categories and the relations of these on the one hand to our own minds and on the other to our experience as a whole.

The several sciences of matter, the physical sciences, have each their special concepts and methods, but the

so-called pure science of dynamics is assumed to be
ideally applicable to them all. Their aim is to substitute its fundamental categories in the place of their
own special concepts as derived from sensible experience, and also to advance their own more or less
inductive methods to the deductive stage to which
dynamics has already attained. In pursuit of this ideal
they all alike seek to describe qualities in terms of
quantity, to replace the varieties of material objects by
geometrical configuration of mass-points, and to represent the diverse states and changes of those objects
by the positions and motions of such mass-points. Now
there are several possible forms of dynamics, equally
self-consistent and internally coherent, just as there are
several possible geometries and algebras. But in all
forms of dynamics it is assumed that mass-points,
whether they constitute discrete atoms or a continuous
ether, are ingenerable, indestructible, and inert. Hence
it follows that the positions and motions of each and all
are rigorously concatenated; so that from a knowledge
of all of them at one time[1] the positions and motions
at any other time—whether past or future—can be
exactly calculated.

In the organization of the sciences pertaining to the
physical standpoint thus briefly sketched, three sorts of
knowledge are concerned:—particular percepts, empirical generalizations, and mathematical constructions; or in the language of English philosophy:—the
present testimony of our senses or the records of our
memory, inductive probabilities, and the universal and
non-temporal demonstrations of the exact sciences. The
first and last are certain, but the first, as Locke taught,
can only assure us of particular realities here and now,
and the last, as Hume said, though "they ever retain
their certainty and evidence, are without dependence

[1] 'One time,' but such that 'positions and motions' are given in it.

on what is anywhere existent in the universe."[1] The several laws of nature belong entirely to the second class: they are not presented matters-of-fact and they are not necessary relations of ideas; they occupy a peculiar position between the two. They start from and rest on sensible experiences, but in systematizing and unifying these data or 'facts' we are said to apply the 'ideas' or principles of the abstract sciences, which are independent of concrete experiences. It is important now to note that every form of pure dynamics is wholly abstract and exact: it is altogether ideal in Hume's sense, 'without dependence on what is anywhere existent in the universe'; as is evident on a glance at any accredited text-book. Pure dynamics is concerned only with absolute time, absolute space, absolute motion: it recognizes no qualities, no substances, no causes, no laws: its fundamental concepts or principles are not given but defined; in the language of Locke they are not ectypal but archetypal, and the whole procedure is rigidly deductive. It is obvious that the special sciences which are supposed to keep in touch with sensible reality and to proceed by methods of observation and experiment can never without a complete breach of continuity advance into this ideal domain. Facts never sublimate into pure ideas, nor inductive probability into deductive proof. Now what —in view of this undeniable gap between the ideal and the real—is meant by applying abstract science to concrete experiences? Supposing a particular geometry or dynamics does not 'apply,' it may become useless to the physicist dealing with this world: in fact non-Euclidean geometry and non-Newtonian dynamics do not at present interest him; but that does not affect their intrinsic truth. What then is the significance of a dynamical system that does apply?

[1] *Essays*, ed. Green and Grose, ii, 22.

To this question two different answers are given by the two different schools into which on this issue physicists are now divided. The one we may fairly call the physical realists—since they dub their opponents nominalists—and the other we may allow to be physical conceptualists or symbolists. The first are metaphysicians in spite of themselves. For them the structure built on the Newtonian laws of motion is verily Natural Philosophy, as it was long called; it discloses the reality that lies beyond or 'behind what we can see and feel.' For the second that structure is but a mathematical scheme, whose sole use, in the now famous words of Kirchhoff, is "to describe in the exactest and simplest manner such motions as occur in nature." Here, applicability means only utility, economy: one aspect of facts, the processes of nature as quantitative, are to be described in manageable and comprehensive formulæ; but there, applicability means revelation: nature *is* a mechanism. Of course if the realists are right, the symbolists are right too, in so far as the greater includes the less; if nature verily is a mechanism it may surely be described as one. *But the converse is not true.* The most we know is the descriptive applicability, and from this the real identification of nature with our ideal scheme does not follow. Even mechanical *description* is not adequate to nature as a whole, but only to one aspect of it. The like holds, of course, of arithmetical and geometrical description; these have a still wider range though they are still more inadequate. To the attempts of the Pythagoreans to make number the ultimately real, and of Plato to connect the five elements—earth, water, air, fire, ether—with the five regular solids, the mechanical theory of the physical realist is a fitting sequel[1]; and what an ancient scholiast said of Plato could be said of him—κατεμαθη-

[1] Cp. Lasswitz, *Geschichte der Atomistik*, pp. 53 f.

ματικεύσατο τὴν φύσιν—he reduces nature to a mathematical abstraction.

But leaving abstract ideas and returning to the actual phenomena with which the physicist is confronted, we find that he can never discern, much less ear-mark, anything resembling mass-points. He can only apply his tentative mechanical specification to statistical results, and his confidence as to the ultimate basis of these cannot be compared with, say, the anthropologist's knowledge that his 'mean or average man' is a concept based on tables relating to real men. Moreover the moral statistician knows that real men are distinguished by idiosyncrasies of character, and are actuated by motives, which find no place in his abstract concept of the average man: in other words he describes certain aspects of society in mathematical fashion, well knowing that his description tells him nothing of the real factors at work in the making of history. The physicist is in a worse position. At best, nature, if a mechanism at all, is a concealed mechanism; so that his problem is an inverse one, and the chances of his particular specification being correct are infinitesimally small. And since this must hold of every particular specification, he must for ever face the possibility that he is wrong in assuming that nature is really and fundamentally a mechanism at all. Happily science nowadays—science, I mean, that minds its own business and keeps to its standpoint—finding indeed that 'all things are ordered by measure and number' and therefore so far amenable to mathematical description and statistical treatment, yet does not confuse its quantitative symbols and 'mental pictures' with the phenomena so far described —to say nothing of any reality behind them. On the contrary to render its descriptive scheme as simple and comprehensive as possible, science is ever revising its hypothetical mechanism and giving to its working-

models a more and more abstract and ideal form,
thereby rendering their symbolic and conceptual character ever increasingly evident. There is no question
of its utility as a working hypothesis, for it works; but
it has worked better the more abstract and ideal it has
become, the farther it has advanced from all semblance
of concrete reality.

But scientific beliefs, like fashions, have a way of
spreading downwards, and so physical realism, though
it has passed its heyday among the scientific classes,
still flourishes among the unscientific masses. Perhaps
it would be truer to say that while its scientific substance has practically vanished, its metaphysical shadow
still hangs over us like a pall. It is what is now commonly called Naturalism. Let us recall the question
that interests us. We are confronted by the theory of
nature as a mechanism, and we ask: What is the relation of this theory, on the one hand, to ourselves as
consciously active, and, on the other, to the perceptual
world with which we are practically concerned? There
are two distinct answers. If we perpetuate the oldest
and naïvest of metaphysical blunders—we might call
it the metaphysical fallacy *par excellence*—in other words,
if we regard abstract ideas as concrete things and then
take the standpoint of the theory itself as the primary
and absolute one, we have the answer of Naturalism.

Orientating in such wise from this standpoint, life
and mind, humanity and the whole course of human
history and experience, are declared to be but secondary and 'collateral products,' mere epiphenomena or
incidental scintillations in the working of the soulless,
ruthless, meaningless wheels which we call the laws of
nature, but might equally well call the mills of Fate.
These wheels grind slowly and grind exceeding small;
working together neither for righteousness nor against
it, they compel us forever to banish from all regions of

human thought what we have been wont to call spirit and spontaneity. These wheels were rolling on before we with all our hearts' desires came flickering on the scene, they roll on now unconcerned by our impotent presence, and they will still roll on, when we with all our hopes and fears are extinguished forever. Such is the creed of Naturalism. If on the other hand we begin where alone, as I say, we can truly *begin*, here and now with ourselves and our actual experience as historical fact, we may reach the answer of Epistemology, which the views of the physical symbolist adumbrate. This is what I call philosophical orientation. We have now to consider it in more detail.

Laws of nature I have said are neither presented realities nor necessities of thought. How then do we get to this knowledge of laws, and what does it imply? This is Kant's problem: science, we allow, is not directly concerned with it, but Naturalism by fore-stalment renders it null and void. It is really a long story and the very barest outline must here suffice. We start then, as said, with the tangible, visible, sonorous world, in all its qualitative diversity of particular things and events; but we do not start as passive and in-different spectators of all this ceaseless change. We have definite wants and corresponding impulses, and a certain primitive credulity leads us to expect again what we have experienced before. We are round men or square men, and only as we succeed in occupying appropriate holes do we find our expectations justified and make a career. A fish out of water has ordinarily no chance of learning that nature is uniform, though it makes a beginning in such knowledge while it remains in its native element. So in an appropriate environ-ment we acquire familiarities and facilities, experiences and expertnesses, in other words habits, whereby sub-ject and object, Ego and non-Ego, fit like hand and glove. This is the new philosophy of clothes, which Naturalism turns inside out. Man, it has been said, is the measure of all things—for man. And he measures them largely by finding if they fit him, and he advances chiefly by making them fit, that is by growing himself. Such advance is a series of ventures, a continual struggle: experiments are made first to meet practical needs, and finally to satisfy curiosity, which at bottom is a practical need. So we are told Necessity is the mother of invention, and War or Struggle the father of all things, leaving only the fittest to survive. But throughout we are anthropomorphic: *practically* the fittest for us is what suits us best, and *theoretically* it is what has most analogy with what we are and know already. We find other men, other living things, form an important part of our environment, and their doings we have to reckon with; in the light of these facts we interpret the rest as far as we can. Put more abstractly, this amounts to saying that our entire organon of real categories—substance, cause, and end—are anthropomorphic, projections of ourselves. And as these categories form an organic unity within—as we are active subjects with definite aims—we assume that everywhere in the phenomenal world without we have directly or indirectly the manifestation of such subjects. So far as this fundamental postulate, this demand of reason, is verified, the world is intelligible, and no farther.

But on one supposition and one only are the uniformities which we significantly call 'laws' so many verifications of the intelligibility of things, and that is that—though the laws be inviolable—the knowledge of them can be intelligently turned to account. Now we have just seen that it was precisely through our practical endeavours to turn things to account that their laws were discovered; for laws, it must be remembered, are not themselves realities. Moreover as our knowledge of nature's laws has increased, our power to control and direct things has increased; and what hinders our further advance is not 'the tightening grasp of law,' but our outstanding ignorance of it. And why should this progress ever stop? "The heavens declare the glory of Newton and Laplace!" was the boast of science a century ago, and many have been the wonderful inventions and discoveries to which their methods have led since. Yet when rigorously pursued, those methods, we are now assured, shew Newton, Laplace, and us, their humbler brethren, to be mere impotent puppets, having percepts, thoughts, feelings and volitions, indeed, but only as fatally predetermined concomitants of that illimitable mechanism, the workings of which Laplace and Newton were able to an infinitesimal extent to foretell. "But if those conclusions are true," the exponent of Naturalism may rejoin, "and if still progress has already been made, why should not the progress go on: after all what difference does it make?"

If those conclusions are true, if we are verily but conscious automata, I reply, then the ground is cut away from the mechanical theory on which they are based: in reducing man and his experience to the epiphenomenal, Naturalism refutes itself. In the first place I must ask you specially to note that we do not at the outset *know* that we are conscious automata. On the contrary, as I have been urging, we appear to ourselves—to say the least—as spontaneously active both in our thinking and in our doing. We are immediately conscious of limits, but not of impotence. The doctrine of conscious automatism is a conclusion, and a conclusion opposed to common sense: we have therefore good grounds for suspecting its premises. And surely enough in these we find the concept of causal efficiency playing an odd *rôle*. Supposing himself to be occupying a standpoint aloof alike from the mechanism that he takes to underlie phenomena and from the mind to which these phenomena pertain, the naturalist[1] attributes to the former a real efficiency while declaring the efficiency of the latter to be altogether spurious and illusory. Surely this is emulating the feat of the rustic who sawed off the very branch on which he sat! What warrant is there for the application of this concept of efficiency without, if its internal source is wholly fallacious? The fact is that the naturalist forgets the essential implication of his standpoint. His position is really comparable to the solipsist; is in fact, as we shall see, its psychophysical counterpart. The most he can safely conclude is that other people are only automata. The solipsist does not say: There is no transcending individual experience and therefore I am only a modification of your consciousness. And all the naturalist should say is: I have ascertained by careful experiment and calculation that all nature is a mechanism, and, as for me your body is only a part of this mechanism, I am forced to conclude that you are at most a conscious automaton. And with that opinion of us we may safely leave him, and continue as he does to make use of the concept of causal efficiency but declining to apply it to an abstract scheme to which it is wholly foreign.

But even when we reject the theory of conscious automatism as only a vague and ill-disguised form of materialism, the manifold absurdities of which are now coming to be universally recognized, there remains a position hardly less extravagant to be considered. I refer to what is known as the theory of psychophysical

---

[1] The older naturalists went thus far, but not the modern naturalists, who profess to know nothing of efficiency of any sort. Still, in making the psychical epiphenomenal, they make it dependent.

parallelism. In one possible sense of the words such parallelism is a fact beyond all question: in so far, namely, as there is the closest and most intimate correspondence between mind processes and brain processes, between *psychoses* and *neuroses*, as we say nowadays. But correspondence does not necessarily exclude reciprocal action; and both biology and psychology proceed entirely on the assumption that such mutual interaction is regular and continuous. Nor is there a single known fact at variance with this assumption; whilst without it the vital distinction of *sensory* impression and *motor* response becomes meaningless for psychology, and all intelligible connexion between life and mind is gone. Nevertheless the truth of psychoneural correspondence so understood is absolutely denied by the theory of psychophysical parallelism that we have now to examine.

This too is a consequence of accepting the mechanical view of nature not simply as a working hypothesis, valid within its limits, but as a complete presentation of the fully-orbed reality; and once again we have the *prima facie* facts of experience discredited on *a priori* grounds: we have Naturalism contradicting science through a faulty orientation and confusion of standpoints. The very phrase psychophysical parallelism is itself evidence of such confusion. We should never have heard of a parallelism between the psychical and the physical, but for the intervention of the organism between the individual experient and the inorganic world. Here in the psychoneural correspondence just referred to we do indeed find a parallelism that goes some way towards justifying the familiar comparison of the one series to the sounds a reader utters, and of the other to the letters that he sees. To qualitative differences on the one side there are answering qualitative differences on the other: to simplicity

or complexity in the first, there is an equivalent simplicity or complexity in the second. In this wise psy-
chosis and neurosis, functions of mind and functions
of brain, may up to a certain point be said to be concomitant, keeping time and rising and falling together.
But if we resolve the neuron or structural unit of brain
into untold millions of mass-points, there is no longer
any assignable correspondence between the motions of
these and distinguishable experiences or 'states of
mind'; less correspondence even than there would be
between printed characters and the sounds they signify,
when these are decomposed into atmospheric waves.
Over against the enormous wealth of qualitative diversity in the one, the other presents only a quantitative
monotony of the extremest type. The only hope of
reinstating the parallelism that has vanished lies in
pulverizing mind to psychical dust, so to say, and from
this, the logical outcome of psychophysical parallelism,
some of the exponents of naturalism do not shrink.
There is nothing like courage: it has rid the world of
many wild theories.

Though psychoneural parallelism or correspondence
is a fact, psychophysical parallelism is, then, plainly a
misnomer. Of parallel lines we can say two things.
They never meet, and they consist of corresponding
points. But it is only in respect to the first of these
properties that my experience and mass motions have
any analogy with parallels; in this respect they are on
a par with say a book of dates and a book of logarithms;
and the simile of parallels is no more appropriate in
the one case than it is in the other. At bottom, psychophysical parallelism affirms only the old dualism of
matter and mind, but affirms it with new emphasis,
because, for the mechanical theory, matter is divested
of every vestige of quality, and nothing left of its substance save quantitative constants, or of its causality

save dynamic equations. But for the old dualism to which common thought and language are adjusted, the interaction of each conscious subject with its objective environment was a fact, though the intervening psychophysical process—in common however with all other cases of transeunt action—was a mystery. So far all causal laws are occasional laws. Yet Naturalism, which is no whit better off, denies this basal fact of experience, not because the *modus operandi* in psychophysical processes is inexplicable, but solely because such a process cannot be mechanical, and is therefore necessarily non-existent for its standpoint. This is very much as if a blind man should say there were no such things as colours because he could not feel them; and his argument would be sound enough, if touch were the only sense there was, and blindness therefore no limitation. And in any case touch and sight are mutually exclusive and only brought into relation by the conscious subject, who can both see and feel. The dualism of matter and mind is of this sort, only that instead of two mutually exclusive concretes we have two mutually exclusive abstracts. Till in both cases we transcend these severally disparate standpoints there can be no talk of orientating them, and therefore no statement involving both can be intelligible; not even the assertion that both exist at all. And that is all that psychophysical parallelism in the mouth of the naturalist comes to. He essays to describe your organism and your environment—as they are for him—in mechanical terms. You tell him that—for you—all experience consists in transactions with the physical or outer world which he thus describes, and like the blind man who hears of colours he replies that of such transactions he has no knowledge; that is to say, from his standpoint, they are non-existent.

Mutatis mutandis, we get a like reply from those

psychologists who essay to describe this experience as consisting wholly of 'ideas' or subjective modifications, and who therefore also preach psychophysical parallelism. If the naturalist and such a psychologist then proceed to regard their several standpoints as final and complete, in other words to orientate from these, the one is led to conscious automatism and the other to solipsism, as I have already said. Short of this the two standpoints are simply unrelated; and that is all that psychophysical parallelism means till we betake ourselves to Epistemology, within whose wider purview both are immanent. Then we find how far two halves are from making a whole; we see that the psychology of dualism ends in shutting itself *in*, and the physics of dualism in shutting itself *out*, by an imaginary sundering of the one world of experience into two worlds that are alike devoid of reality.

At this point some representative of Naturalism will be inclined to ask: Are we then to assume that energy is not a reality? And no doubt he will be ready to press the familiar arguments for psychophysical dualism which the principle known as the conservation of energy is supposed to warrant. Let us take these points in turn. If the qualities we perceive in our environment and the changes in it which common sense attributes to human purposes and plans are, as we are told, so many transformations of energy, we have no reason, so far, to question its reality. Energy, then, means for us "the life and activity of the physical universe," to quote the words of a distinguished physicist; and to find the best possible *modus vivendi* within it, we may add, is then the practical meaning of all experience. But further, if our percepts are without assignable psychical antecedents—so that we do not look to psychology, say, for an account of the weather—and if our acts are without assignable physical antecedents

—so that we do not ask physics to forecast conduct—
how can we imagine an impassable gulf to separate this
one world of experience into two and leave both real?
But what if the conservation of energy gives us no
choice? Well then I am afraid even that principle is
doomed: but let us see.

Leaving aside the question as to the supposed impossibility of matter affecting mind as only a clumsy
and left-handed way of raising the problem of external
perception, it will suffice to examine the alleged impossibility of mind acting on matter, and first on the
assumption that such action implies the introduction
of energy. The principle of the conservation of energy
appears in three forms, and in each, energy has a
different meaning: (1) as an inductive generalization
founded on experiment, (2) as a deduction from the
mechanical theory, and (3) as a metaphysical first-
principle. (i) At the empirical level, from the standpoint of the new science of Energetics, that is to say,
there are many forms of energy, and no attempt is
made to get behind their phenomenal diversity to the
underlying reality common to them all. Experimentally all that is ascertained is that the total energy of
a finite and isolated material system is constant: it can,
then, only be increased from without. But an influx
from the psychical side, however determined, would be
an increase from without; and no physicist, I imagine,
will be bold enough to attempt to *prove* that such influx
—which conflicts with nothing that is experimentally
ascertained—is in fact impossible. (ii) For the mechanical theory, energy is not a phenomenon but a
conception involved in the motion and configuration
of a system of mass-points connected according to the
classical dynamics of Newton and his successors. Now,
making the very large assumption that this theory is
adequate to describe all the changes in the external

world so far as it is left to itself, it is certain that it must
fail to describe its actual course whenever mind intervenes. But surely it was devised solely to describe the
world as left to itself: its fundamental assumption is
only that all *matter* is inert, not that everything is. The
only ground then, so far, for denying that mind can
affect a given material system as another material
system might do, is that in that case, and so far, the
world cannot be regarded as dead. In other words, it
is a question of fact, and the question is begged to save
a theory. I think it important to observe that physicists
are the last people to do anything so outrageous: in
our own time Helmholtz, Kelvin, Maxwell—to mention but three great names—have expressly repudiated
such extravagance. But I should like to quote a sentence from one who might perhaps have eclipsed them
all had he not been snatched from us in his early prime
—I mean Heinrich Hertz, to whose researches wireless
telegraphy is due. In his latest work he proposed to
include the principles of mechanics in a single fundamental law. In a system of bodies which conforms to
this law, "there is," he says, "neither any new motion
nor any cause of new motion, but only the continuance
of the previous motion in a given simple manner. If
we were to extend the law to the whole of nature," he
continues, "we should offend against a feeling which
is sound and natural. It is therefore prudent to limit
the probable validity of the law to inanimate systems.
This amounts to the statement that the law, applied
to (organic or living beings), forms an improbable
hypothesis."[1] (iii) But now, beyond experimental
facts, beyond mechanical ideals, we are pulled up at
length by what at bottom is a metaphysical principle.
The energy of the universe, say the naturalistic philosophers, is constant and allows of no increase: it is

[1] *Principles of Mechanics*, § 320.

impossible therefore for mind to add to it. But that is only true, if mind is included in it, for expressed in this form the statement ceases to be physical or even material. It amounts simply to the old Lucretian doctrine: *Ex nihilo nihil fit: in nihilum nil posse reverti.* Robert Mayer, who is perhaps best entitled to be called the founder of the principle of energy, expressly falls back on this metaphysical doctrine: Joule and Colding, his immediate successors—to say nothing of Herbert Spencer—were equally speculative. But, as Prof. Poincaré, the *doyen* of modern mathematicians, has said: "If one wishes to enounce the principle in all its generality, applying it to the universe, one sees it, so to say, vanish and only this is left: There is something which remains constant."[1]

So far we have proceeded on the less favourable assumption that mind must be able to evoke energy in order to control the motions of matter. But change of direction without work is certainly possible within a mechanical system, and there are many physicists who maintain that such guidance by mind is also conceivable. Be this as it may, it is at least certain that we are active beings and somehow control the movement of these bodies we are said to animate. No facts are more immediately certain than these, and there is nothing in our actual experience that contradicts them: from these facts—as we here clearly see—are derived the abstract concepts on the strength of which Naturalism, by a grievous misapprehension of its own standpoint, attempts to question them. Stationed at the very outskirts of the Knowable and intent only on the quantitative aspects of things, like those fabulous beings of geometrical romance, the inhabitants of Flatland, it finds impassable barriers which have no existence in the fuller dimensions of concrete experience. Orien-

[1] *La Science et l'Hypothèse*, p. 158.

tating from this central position, we may retort upon
Naturalism with the words of Goethe:

> Das Unzulängliche
> Hier wird's Ereigniss:
> Das Unbeschreibliche
> Hier wird's gethan.

Or, again, with the words of Shakespeare: "There are
more things in heaven and earth than are dreamt of
in your philosophy."

Having satisfied ourselves then that mechanism is
not the secret of the universe; that if it is to have any
meaning it must subserve some end; finding everywhere that increased knowledge of nature's laws means
increased control of nature's processes, we accept the
facts of experience in which subject and object interact,
rather than the conclusions of dualism, in which mind
and matter are two alien worlds and all knowledge an
inexplicable mystery. These results make it possible
to deal more briefly with our remaining topic, the relation of the physical sciences to the biological. Can we
describe the living in terms of the lifeless? Naturalism
which has advanced so far beyond the old materialism as to treat mind as epiphenomenal, still claims
life as belonging wholly to the physical domain.
I think we may stake the issue on one point. Comparing the characteristics of the physical world as
modified by mind with its characteristics when left to
itself, let us then decide with which the facts of life,
taken as a whole, accord the better. Starting from an
uninhabited desert and following the advance of civilization from the bare underground caves of the pre-
Adamite to modern cities with their cloud-capped
towers and stately palaces, we note a steady increase
in the number, variety, and complexity of objects and
processes that we call artificial. At first we find only

rudely shaped stones, pointed sticks, hollowed trunks, differing distinctly and yet but slightly from like objects in the desert behind us. As we move on we find rough sun-dried bricks give place to fired pottery of exquisite shapes; coarse wraps of natural fleece or grass exchanged for textile fabrics wrought in wondrous looms. At first we find only natural substances altered in shape and arrangement: at length we have the myriad products of metallurgy and chemistry, such as unaided nature has never formed. Tasks wholly beyond the native strength of many giants, we see in the end performed by machines that a child can control. The moving energies of wind and water, that, left to themselves, would only level down the surface of the earth, are artificially directed or resisted to subserve human ends: and the stores of potential energy in coal, nitrates, and the like, which nature would denude and scatter, are made to work the engines of peace and war. In short, compared with a horde of naked savages whose raw victuals, meagre resources, and defenceless condition afford a life at best but "nasty, brutish, and short," the inhabitants of a modern city are like beings invested with a vastly superior organism living in a re-created and comparatively perfect environment, where through organized division of labour, the products of the highest skill are secured to all with the smallest outlay of effort. Now this metamorphosis of nature by human art and industry, though it exceeds the wildest dreams of Fairyland, is yet throughout natural in so far as no new forces or elements are involved in its several processes and products, and the laws of nature are everywhere observed and obeyed. Yet we know that it is throughout the work of man, not the work of nature; and that it is even contrary to nature, in the sense of requiring ceaseless guidance and control.

Let us next compare the organic world with the inorganic, proceeding as before from the lowest forms of life towards the highest. Taking the amœba as the counterpart of the untutored savage, we find a distinct though comparatively slight difference between its behaviour and that of inanimate particles: in the technical language of physiology, it is irritable and it is automatic. It does not react merely quantitatively and inertly to forces, but qualitatively and purposively to 'stimuli'; its motions are not wholly determined from without, but partly from within. Special organs of sense and movement first appear as we advance to multicellular organisms, and when we reach the higher types of these we find a division of labour, a co-ordination and consensus of members and functions, which has made the analogy between such organisms and a commonwealth so apt and striking. With such increasing complexity there is a corresponding increase in the variety, delicacy, and range of the organism's adjustments to its environment, and again in its control over it. Throughout the organic world we find an inexhaustible diversity of structures and processes equalling or surpassing the inventions of human skill, and all of them, like these, aid in the adaptation and control of the environment and promote the furtherance of life: and they are all of them structures and processes, too, which nowhere occur in the inorganic world outside. Again, contrasting these two so-called 'worlds,' we remark the steady downward trend of the one as opposed to the continuous development and progress of the other—a contrast nowhere more conspicuous than it appears when we compare the dissolution of the dead organism with the building up of the living one.

In all this evolution of life we may allow that no new forces, no new elements are involved, that the laws of

Nature are everywhere observed and obeyed. But is it not also unquestionable that there is present, throughout, a ceaseless guidance and control, such as the works of mind display? And since we find the manifestations of life merging continuously into the manifestations of mind and advancing *pari passu* with these, how can we separate the two? And since on the other hand we find the sharpest contrast between the processes peculiar to this animate world and those characteristic of the inanimate—the one anabolic, the other essentially katabolic, to use the expressive terms of a Cambridge physiologist—how can we possibly identify the two? The naturalist's claim so to do is made on the ground that there is nothing in all the several processes or products of living things that is physically inexplicable. But that is equally true of the processes and products of human skill, and yet we know that here mind is the efficient and formative principle. And it is equally indisputable that physical laws fail to account for life *as a whole*, either in its origin or its progress. Can we then doubt that life, like mind, is an efficient and formative principle, and therefore not a merely physical phenomenon?

We cannot talk of life without implying a living individual and an adapted environment, and also along with these the whole class of teleological categories which they involve. From the physical standpoint which Naturalism takes to be primary such concepts never come into view at all. This, as I have said already, is no defect—quite the contrary—but it is assuredly a limitation. *Ex pede Herculem*: to conjecture the whole statue that shall be adequate to the torso that is given. To solve such a problem in the present case would be to ask, What does all the law and order that science discloses require besides to make it intelligible? But what Naturalism strives to shew is that the fragment is the whole: all there *is* is this mechanical substructure: there is for Naturalism no rational edifice at all. But from the epistemological standpoint we can see not only the fragment but the outline of the whole: we can see not only the limitations of science but also the causes of the mistakes into which Naturalism falls.

VI

AN INTRODUCTION TO PHILOSOPHY

I. What Is Meant by Philosophy

IN general, it may be described as "the thinking consideration of things" (*denkende Betrachtung der Gegenstände*), said Hegel. It is, however, neither the only nor the earliest form of thinking: thinking in the first instance, and still for the most part, is practical or rather instrumental to practice. But thinking is prompted at length by the curiosity which leisure brings: necessity may be the mother of invention but "wonder is the mother of Knowledge" as an end in itself[1]. Science and philosophy are alike in so far as, in both, truth for its own sake is said to be what we pursue. Nevertheless, neither the end nor the motive in the two cases is quite the same. In the sense in which we talk of many sciences we do not talk of many philosophies, and in the sense in which we talk of many philosophies we do not talk of many sciences. There are several sciences, because each has a restricted domain, deals with some special class or aspect of things; whereas in that sense philosophy is one, for it purports to embrace the whole of things. On the other hand, while we recognize only one science of physics or chemistry or biology, we find almost as many philosophical systems as there have been philosophers: all of them striving to present an intelligible *Weltanschauung* or 'synoptic view' of the concrete whole. It might strike one as odd, but for the familiarity of it, that philosophies are often named after their authors, Platonism, Epicureanism, Cartesianism, Spinozism, Hegelianism, etc., while no science

[1] Cf. Aristotle, *Metaphysics*, 982 *b*, 10–27.

ever bears a human name. This difference we may find presently to be due to the fact that philosophy is primarily a personal matter. Science seeks to know the *what* and the *how* of this or that: philosophy seeks to know the *why* or *meaning* of the whole. And meaning in experience varies with the experient: to no two men is the world quite the same.

But much as philosophies have varied, 'the philosophic spirit' has been always essentially the same— the habit of reflecting upon one's stock of knowledges[1] in the hope of unifying them all in one concrete 'intuition' or 'Idea.' And to 'knowledge' here we must give a wide meaning, including whatever is accepted as true, whether actually true or not. Thales did not philosophize the less, because he regarded the magnet as alive; or Plato, because he believed in the preexistence of souls; or Aquinas, because he held the doctrine of transubstantiation; or Schelling, because he believed in *clairvoyance*. Given certain materials— knowledges or what are reputed such—the philosophic habit is a species of mental rumination in which the mind endeavours to elaborate the various items of experience into such form and order as to render them an intelligible and organic whole. It is important, then, to distinguish between the 'informing' or organizing spirit of philosophy and the outcome in a particular instance: for the latter is often so crude and imperfect that we, with our wider knowledge and clearer insight, may fail to see anything in it deserving to be called philosophic at all. Few, we may suppose, nowadays begin the study of early Greek philosophy without feeling this. Most of us found it hard to see

[1] This "term in frequent use by Bacon (and others), though now obsolete should be revived" (Hamilton, *Metaphysics*, I, 57 fin.) —a proposal which Herbert Spencer seconded, and which has moreover the support of French and German usage.

anything but absurdity in the doctrine of Thales for instance, that the principle or ἀρχή of all things is water; or in the doctrine of Anaximenes that all the variety of nature is due to a thickening or thinning of another primeval element, viz., air. Even the more abstract speculation of the Pythagoreans—of whom Aristotle tells us that they regarded number as the essense of all things, and the organization of the universe as but a harmonious system of numbers and their relations—even this will appear as barren and empty from excess of abstraction as the Ionian philosophies seemed crude and confined from defect of it. But very much the same feeling might possess us on observing the earliest attempts at pictorial representation, the rude scratches on mammoth tusks, for example, no more like a man than the conventional diagrams of *Homo sapiens*—full face and profile combined—which school-children draw on their slates. But the point is, both *are* pictures, however bad as likenesses: they are the outcome of the idea of pictorial representation, the result of an artistic purpose. So it was with the earliest attempts at philosophy. Here, too, we must distinguish between the idea and its execution: all the pregnant worth of these primitive essays lay in the idea that there is an ἀρχή or first principle; so that all the diversified plurality of the world may be traced to some fundamental One.

II. Philosophy and Mythology

We may realize the significance of this early philosophy more clearly by contrasting it with the mythology that preceded it. In that imagination was dominant, and there was no tendency to generalize: behind the concrete facts of sense there were only the concrete creations of fancy. "Mythology ran riot in a plurality or multitude of powers which it invoked, and to which

it assigned the government of the universe; but philosophy, on the contrary, aimed at a unity of agency or
causation in all things. (Thus) the very conception of
reducing the diversified exuberance, the infinite plenti-
tude, of nature to the unity of one principle, shewed
a speculative boldness which proved that a new intellectual era was dawning on mankind."[1] Still we
must not forget that unity here implies continuity and
in fact, looking closer, we find a certain continuity even
between mythology and philosophy.

The savage, too, has his metaphysics: as Andrew
Lang has well said, "The chief distinction between his
mode of conceiving the world and ours is his vast extension of the theory of personality. To the savage . . .
all nature was a congeries of animated personalities."[2]
This anthropomorphism, so flagrant in the theogonies
and cosmogonies of polytheism, we still recognize
without difficulty as shaping the literature as well as
the art of religion even in the present day[3]. But the
like is equally true, though less obvious, in the case of
philosophy. Thales for instance not only, according to
Aristotle, connected his doctrine with the ancient myth
that Oceanus was the father of gods and men, but
supposed all things to be full of gods[4]. Even Plato
turned old myths to account and invented several new
ones, if what is deliberately invented by one man may
be called a myth. Altogether, Plato is credited with
some dozen myths of one sort or another[5]. We seem
justified, then, in maintaining the presence of anthropomorphism or 'poetical metaphysics' not only in the
speculation of primitive man but even in those of philo-

---

[1] J. F. Ferrier, *Lectures on Greek Philosophy*, 1875, pp. 40, 41.
[2] Andrew Lang, 'Mythology,' *Ency. Brit.*, 11th ed., XIX, 132.
[3] Cp. Hegel, *Vorlesungen über die Aesthetik*, 1837, II, 13 ff.
[4] *Metaphysics*, 983 a; *De Anima*, I, v, 411 a.
[5] Cp. J. A. Stewart, *The Myths of Plato*, 1905.

sophers down to our own time. But 'dogmatic anthropomorphism,' as Kant called it—which had lingered on both in theology and philosophy, though assuming ever worthier forms as humanity itself advanced—was finally rejected as 'not proven' in Hume's famous *Dialogues Concerning Natural Religion*. Admitting this, Kant nevertheless maintained that 'symbolic anthropomorphism,' an anthropomorphism that is to say, based on analogy, is still necessary as furnishing us with 'regulative Ideas.'[1] But the philosophies of the Absolute that have been in vogue since Kant's day and flourish still, claim—at any rate as 'barely theoretical' —to have eliminated all such analogies.

Granting this and leaving aside for the present the question how far philosophy can be called 'barely theoretical,' we may still point out that the 'real categories'—substance and attribute, cause and effect, end and means—which even these philosophies recognize, are themselves anthropomorphic[2]. But here what philosophy has failed to do, positive science claims to have now done. This brings us to a new point.

III. THE CONNEXION BETWEEN SCIENCE AND PHILOSOPHY

Here again we are reminded that unity implies continuity, and again, in fact, we find it. Philosophy presupposes knowledges, even when it essays to take the royal or *a priori* road; but it does not necessarily presuppose science. In western thought indeed philosophy is comparable to a primitive nebula from which the sciences in a certain order were gradually set loose as satellites.

[1] Cp. his *Prolegomena*, 1783, §§ 57, 58, pp. 173 ff.
[2] Cp. the writer's *Psychological Principles*, 1918, ch. XIII, § 6; and on the question generally, the late F. Paulsen's essay 'Die Zukunftsaufgaben der Philosophie' in *Systematische Philosophie* (edited by P. Hinneberg), 1908, pp. 407 ff.

The need for that division of labour which the advance of knowledge has involved was hardly felt before the sixteenth century. The ancient philosophers in particular were all more or less polymathic: all the general knowledge of their time they knew, and to systematize and extend it was the main business of their lives. But some knowledges took scientific form sooner than others; and there were two sciences in particular —mathematics and logic—which, though developing alongside of philosophy, are really, and were from the first, largely independent of it. This independence they owe to their purely abstract form and exact character which seemed to betoken a certain transcendence, complete freedom, in other words, from all the presuppositions which concrete things imply. In consequence, they have themselves powerfully influenced the course of philosophy down to our own day; for reality without restriction is its theme; and logic and mathematics seem to cover everything and yet, as formal, to depend on nothing. It was this exaltation of the exact sciences that led Greek philosophy to disregard the empirical and historical—a strange outcome of the desire to find the meaning of *things*.

Let us try briefly to note how the philosophic spirit was thus first diverted from thinking about things to thinking about *thoughts*. It is perfectly possible, however, to think about both without inverting their relations. But this is not what happened in Greece, where our western philosophy took its rise. Had civilization begun in England or Holland, for example, where industrial and mercantile interests are so absorbing, the history of this philosophy would have been vastly different from what it is[1]. The *intellectus sibi permissus*,

[1] F. A. Lange thought that even as it was, from the standpoint of Sophists like Protagoras, a development of Knowledge was already possible that would have obviated or short-circuited "the

that wrong way of attaining truth which Bacon exposed, might then not have retarded the progress of
empirical knowledge for two thousand years. As it was,
while the natural sciences were still unborn, the Greek
mind gave birth to what is known as dialectic.

1. *Logic.* Beginning with this we may consider first
the influence on philosophy of logic, which in fact was
the offspring of dialectic. According to Aristotle, dialectic was the invention of the Eleatic philosopher,
Zeno: in fact, however, it seems to have been for him
a necessity of the situation rather than a method deliberately devised. He was bent on refuting the plural-
ists who were his philosophical opponents, and he
developed the contradictions implicit in their doctrines
simply as the most effective way of refuting them.
But his negative results were so imposing that it is no
surprise to find Socrates—and Plato, still more consciously—employing this dialectical method with the
positive aim of eliciting knowledge by turning thought
inwards 'to recollect itself.' In doing so they exerted
an influence on the future of philosophy second to none
beside. Ignorant alike of psychology and philology—
professing, in fact, to know nothing—nevertheless,
Socrates in his endeavour to evoke the meaning or
definition implied in words helped at once to prepare
the logical instrument of knowledge and to prevent its
efficient use. Misconceiving the relation of words to
thoughts and of thoughts to things, Plato, the disciple
whom he inspired, then propounded his famous
'realism'—commonly called the Platonic idealism—
thereby inaugurating a philosophical mythology that
in one form or another lasted on till its consummation

great digression (*Umschwang*) which led the world for thousands
of years into the false path of the Platonic idealism." *Geschichte
des Materialismus*, 3rd ed., 1875, I, 41–43. Cp. J. Herschel, *Preliminary Discourse*, 1838, pp. 105 ff.

in the *Logic* of Hegel[1]. Plato maintained that 'universals' were *entia* prior to and independent of *fientia*, the particulars perceived by sense[2].

More than that, he also maintained that the one way to knowledge of *entia*, to philosophy that is to say, was the dialectical way of immanent logical development: to empirical knowledge no philosophical validity was to be allowed at all. So, from that day to quite modern times, philosophy, as Bacon said, was engrossed with its own *anticipatio mentis* and diverted from the *interpretatio naturae*; while the empirical sciences, so long as they remained under its step-motherly tutelage, scarcely progressed at all. There were, it came to be assumed, two sources of knowledge, reason and sense, and two kinds of knowledge, that of noumena and that of phenomena—to use the old terminology which Kant revived—the one constituting what he at one time called the *mundus intelligibilis*, the other what he called the *mundus sensibilis*. The former had come to be spoken of as the world *sub specie aeternitatis*, beyond not merely time but space as well[3]; this was the world of ideas, where alone according to Plato truth could dwell. The latter was the world of nature, the empirical world of change in space and time: this for Plato was the sublunary abode of passing shadows, the domain of opinion and probability at the best.

After all, it may be said, the intelligible world seen by the light of reason, is surely the world that philosophy should strive to understand; can it be that the

[1] In the preface to the second edition of his *Logic*, written within a week of his death, Hegel himself refers sympathetically to Plato as his forerunner. Cp. p. 13.
[2] Cp. G. Grote's *Aristotle*, 2nd ed., 1880, App. 1, 'The Doctrine of Universals.'
[3] As regards space, however, perhaps all rationalists were not equally clear—Plato, Aristotle, Descartes, Spinoza, and Leibniz, for example, held conflicting views.

pursuit of such knowledge will ever be abandoned? At any rate the dialectical method of attaining it has come to be regarded more and more as delusive and unsubstantial—negatively in consequence of continual crises in the history of philosophy itself, and positively in consequence of the progress of science in spite of it.

The first great crisis in the development of philosophy began at once with Plato's own disciple, Aristotle. Dialectic never meant for Aristotle what it meant for his master. Nevertheless, he improved the imperfect instrument that Socrates and Plato had made out of it. But it is a mistake, although a common one, to identify logic as Aristotle conceived it with the so-called formal logic into which it was ultimately transformed[2]. Aristotle's Logic was no mere instrument (or organon) of that *maieutic* art which Socrates professed; and Aristotle never regarded it as such. It was that, but it was much more[2]. True, he raised the standard against the Platonic realism, but he only modified it: he never broke with it altogether. As Prantl has said, he was still Platonic, and without Plato would be unintelligible. He still admitted the reality of universals; and denied only that they were independently and antecedently real: their reality for him consisted in their embodiment in particulars. On the other hand, even Plato allowed that the particular had a certain semblance of reality, because it participated in or adumbrated a universal.

As regards particulars then, the two philosophers had some common ground; yet their methods were different: Aristotle started where Plato ended, that is

---

[1] Cp. Prantl, *Geschichte der Logik*, I, 135–140.
[2] No sharp line can be drawn between the subject-matter of Aristotle's so-called Logic and that of his metaphysics or 'first philosophy'; nor in fact between this and what he called physics. (Cp. Grote's *Aristotle*, pp. 62, 422.)

to say, with the actual things with which he found himself surrounded. These were either natural or artificial: he began with the latter first of all as the better known, for man had made them. So he came by his famous doctrine of the four causes—the material, the formal, the efficient and the final. But in the case of artifacts, the three latter are connected together in the individual artisan, who for the sake of the *end* devises the *form* and *effects* its embodiment or materialization. In this συνθετόν as Aristotle called it, the form is the determining factor, but the artisan is the indispensable agent or 'moving cause.' But Aristotle left the efficient agent—for a time at all events—out of account, and regarded the universal or form as if it were what Prantl describes as *ein schöpferische Wesensbegriff*, or had itself 'notional causality,' as Grote translates the term. If we stop here, many thinkers have felt that after all Plato's position was the better of the two: for according to that, the 'ideas' were real anyhow; whereas, according to Aristotle, the forms not being real *per se*, but only notional, could surely not effect their own realization. Merely to deny Plato's position did not help him to establish his own; for it is inconceivable how two non-entities can effect the synthesis whereby they become τόδε τί, *hoc aliquid*.

So far, Aristotle's procedure had been primarily analytic. It is, however, only fair to him to say that he did not ignore this further problem concerning the synthesis itself which the particular as compound (σύνολον) implies. Accordingly the correlatives, matter and form, are now supplemented by another pair— bringing the moving cause again upon the scene—viz., potentiality (δύναμις) and actuality or energy (ἐνέργεια). The former correlatives, matter and form, were relevant to the question what the concrete particular is; the latter, potentiality and energy, are concerned in the question how it comes to be. The *venue* is thus completely altered: Aristotle now for a time leaves the domain of 'logic,' to which change and process are altogether foreign, for that of 'physic' or nature[1], where they are always dominant and at home. The new terms, as we have seen, found their clearest exemplification in mankind; for potentiality means power or faculty, as 'latent,' and energy faculty or power, in overt action. Now—since any movement suggests some prior potentiality—we may bring the changes in nature into line with the changes we make.

But potentiality in Greek has another meaning which Aristotle expressly distinguished, viz., possibility. The two meanings are indeed connected, since potentiality as such implies logical possibility; and Aristotle plays fast and loose with the two. "We must not seek a definition of everything," he says, and here "must be content to grasp the analogy."[2] But what is this analogy? The statue is to the marble block as the man actually studying to the man when he is not. But the relation of the statue to the block of marble is the relation of form to matter, while the relation of the man when he is studying to the man when he is not is the relation of energy to potentiality. The man not studying can study if he likes: the process here starts from the faculty. But the shapeless block cannot begin of itself to take on form: the so-called potentiality then is here no faculty; it is just bare possibility—a fact which Aristotle himself brings out when he follows back the notion of matter to its limit. So far as becoming a statue goes, the block can do nothing. But as mere matter, matter as such, is not potential, so pure

---

[1] Etymology, often helpful in revealing conceptual along with lexual roots, may be usefully appealed to here. Cp. φύσις and *natura*.

[2] *Metaphysic*, IX, vi, *init*.

form, form as such, cannot be actual: to be that it
must be real[1].

How then could Aristotle assume any inherent efficiency in form, and yet refuse to recognize the independent 'reality' which Plato attributed to it? This
question still awaits an answer. Meanwhile several of
Aristotle's ablest commentators have pointed out that
his analogy so far from dispensing him from definition
hampers him with contradictions of which he seems
dimly conscious and yet does not seriously face[2]—contradictions so glaring that a well-meant attempt has
recently been made to relieve him of them by attributing all the confusion to his editor[3]. Instead then of
demolishing the Platonic structure, Aristotle only re-
modelled it on the old foundations: he too was still a
'realist' but less thorough than his master and less
consistent. In short, in a case of 'either-or' he was
something of a trimmer.

No wonder, then, that this difference between the
two master minds lingered on for centuries unresolved
by the comparatively feeble thinkers who followed
them: no wonder that Platonists and Aristotelians came
alternately to the fore, till at length it was assumed
that every man must be one or other: no wonder that
the chief gain to philosophy of ages of scholastic
wrangling was only a certain 'precision and analytic
subtlety' of language which the ancients did not

[1] These two pairs of correlatives pre-eminently characteristic
of Aristotle's philosophy have remained fundamental in the terminology of philosophy till our own day without ever being
adequately scrutinized.

[2] Cp. Heyder, *Aristotelische u. Hegel'sche Dialektik*, 1845, I, 181 ff.;
Bonitz, *Aristotle's Metaphysica*, 1849, II, 379, 395, 569; Zeller,
Aristotle, Eng. trans. 1897, pp. 373 ff.; Gompertz, *Greek Thinkers*,
1912, IV, 85 f.

[3] Cp. W. Freytag, *Die Entwicklung der griechischen Erkenntnistheorie
bis Aristotles*, 1905, p. 85.

possess[1]. Words still masked the face of things with a
veil like that of Isis, which—till the modern era—there
was scarcely an attempt to uplift.

2. *Mathematics.* We come now to the influence on
philosophy of the other exact science, that is mathematics. Mathematics is historically the oldest science;
and it is the first that everybody has to *learn*—hence
perhaps its name, commonly attributed to the Pythagoreans. Like logic it is beyond scepticism and beyond
cavil: in this respect it is—conjoined with logic—
science as nothing else is. That it should have influenced the course of philosophy profoundly is therefore
not surprising: it has, in fact, done so; and that in two
ways. First, in respect of *method*—of such influence the
classic instance is that of Spinoza; this, however, which
we may call its epistemological result, does not for the
present concern us. But, secondly, it helped to determine
the *content*, the subject-matter of philosophy, notably in
the case of Plato. This we may call its ontological
result: a remark or two on this seems here in place.

As Plato regarded 'ideas' of which things are only imperfect semblances—so the Pythagoreans regarded the
numbers of the decad and the geometrical forms which
they imagined these to imply. The whole sum of things,
modelled accordingly to the principles of number, was
a cosmos, as Pythagoras is said to have first called it[2].

[1] A gain, however, that has been generally underrated. But
cp. the mottoes at the beginning of Mill's *Logic*.
[2] His discovery of the mathematical proportions of musical
intervals as exhibited in the length of the strings producing them
(1 : 2 for the octave, 2 : 3 for the fifth, 3 : 4 for the fourth) revealed the connexion between number and harmony, which he
boldly generalized and applied in all directions. Regarded in
the light of number not only was there a 'music of the spheres'
beyond our sensible ken, but the very chaos of sense itself became
a cosmos. Shall we with Bacon call this a *superstitio crassa*; or,
reminded of Galileo watching the swinging lamp and Newton
the falling apple, shall we call it 'a flash of genius'?

Indeed, the similarity between 'ideas' as Socrates had led him to conceive them and 'numbers' as conceived by the Pythagoreans it was—some have supposed—that finally led Plato to his so-called realism. At any rate he eventually included the Pythagorean theory within his own. So the two so-called 'rational sciences' seem to be enthroned as presenting the essence of all things; and Hegel's *dictum*, "all that is real is rational" to have been anticipated. Yet, in fact, the true meaning of reason was thereby only obscured. But of this later. Meanwhile the important point is this syncretism of Plato and Pythagoras, of logical form and mathematical form, which claimed to be in one respect the last truth of things; as if indeed God, as Plato said, "always geometrizes." So we are led naturally from mathematics to physics, where mathematics is 'applied.'

3. *Physics.* Here Plato's *Timaeus* has an interest for us that is unique; since, as Grote remarked, it is "the earliest physical theory that has come down to us in the words of its author." Having elsewhere expounded his philosophy of what always is and has no becoming —the world of ideas or forms—he here attempts to face the problems of the sensible world with all its bewildering multiplicity of transient appearances, where, as Heraclitus maintained, all is flux. Certainty is no longer possible, but problems are there none the less. *Wie viel Schein, so viel Hindeutung aufs Sein,* said Herbart; and Plato, unable to deny this implication of being in the phenomenal world, as the Eleatics affected to do, casts about to determine wherein this implication or *Hindeutung* lies. What he required was, so to say, a mediating term between *Sein* and *Schein,* the eternal world of ideas (or *entia*) and the endless diversity of the world of fleeting show (or *fientia*). With such a clue the Pythagoreans provided him through mathematics. The sensible world was rational just so far as "God

had ordered all things in it by measure and number,"
as Lotze said.

There was, however, a still older physical theory that
bore considerable resemblance to the theory of Plato's
Timaeus, viz., the atomic theory of Democritus, a man
whom Plato never mentions and is said to have detested.
According to Democritus the world of the naïve man
is to be explained by the configurations and motions of
innumerable, invisible and unchangeable elements
variously aggregated or combined in the sensible
objects which are all that he actually perceives[1]. This
Democritean world, though unmistakeably implied in
Plato's *Timaeus*, was there so smothered by the myths
and fanciful conjectures with which it was overlaid
that it could never have been taken for genuinely
Platonic doctrine, even if Plato himself had treated it
quite seriously. In fact, however, he allowed that
imaginary world building was at best a pastime; but
one permissible enough when dealing with what after
all were only probabilities[2]. But the rejection by
Democritus of all teleology marked off his philosophy
as essentially mechanical, that is as materialistic:
whereas the corner-stone of all Plato's thinking, the
idea of the Good as the alpha and omega of his cosmos,
defined his philosophy as through and through spiritualistic in intent. Again, Aristotle's entire rejection
of atomism—the chief defect of his physics—and his
own strenuous advocacy of teleology, conjoined with
Plato's, sufficed to arrest the steady development of
mechanical theories till comparatively modern times
—to the great detriment of science, it is needless to say[3].

[1] These elements or atoms Democritus oddly enough also spoke
of as σχήματα or ἰδέαι.

[2] Cp. *Timaeus*, 59 c.

[3] The use of the term *physicus*, which long prevailed to denote
not a physicist, but a *medicus* or physician, as we still call one who
prescribes 'physic,' is a curious confirmation of this fact.

Nevertheless, during all this long period Democritean revivals, so to call them, occurred at irregular intervals[1] till Newton's *Principia* led back to atomism as one of the problems involved in what he called natural philosophy. But it was a problem which he himself did nothing to solve. He too was content to deal with the *phenomena* of nature according to mechanical, i.e., mathematical principles, leaving philosophy strictly so-called entirely aside[2].

4. *Psychology.* The sharp distinction between matter and mind, though now a commonplace, is nevertheless quite a modern acquisition. In the crude anthropomorphism of primitive man, as we have already noted, everything is animated. At the same time, the etymology of such words as ψυχή, *anima*, πνεῦμα, spirit, clearly shews that mind was regarded as but a subtler form of matter: while objects were personified, subjects were reified. In short, the Cartesian dualism, round which so many of our problems nowadays revolve, was at first unknown.

Even for Aristotle, with whom empirical psychology as a science is supposed to have begun, ψυχή answers more nearly to life in a wide sense than to the subjective factor in experience, as now commonly understood. Like the modern biologist, Aristotle contemplates living organisms as advancing from the purely physiological functions of plants at one extreme to the purely intellectual functions of man at the other. Again he differs from the modern materialist only in the use he makes of his *Machtspruch*—as a German might call it—his famous doctrine of the four causes,

---

[1] As chief in this catena Epicurus and Lucretius may be mentioned, and then, skipping the darkness of the Middle Ages, Giordano Bruno, Galileo and Descartes. (Cp. Lasswitz, *Geschichte der Atomistik*, 1890.)

[2] Cp. *Prin.*, Bk. III, *init.*

that is to say. The term ψυχή for him connotes formal, efficient and final, but *not* material, cause. In so far as cause implies efficiency, and that surely is its primary meaning, matter is neither a cause nor yet an effect. How what according to Aristotle is in itself so entirely negative, can have any part in the wonderful series of definite transformations which in his *De Anima* it is said to undergo, he appears never to have thought of inquiring. However, so long as the organism is concerned —when, that is to say, sense-data are in any way involved—the account given is physiological or rather, strictly speaking, physical. But on reaching intellection, as a faculty, Aristotle's definition of ψυχή gives out; for intellection, he maintained, has no bodily organ. Soul instead of being the form of the living body becomes something—or perhaps we should say is replaced by something—essentially disparate from the living body. So Aristotle seems to end where Descartes began, but only by traversing the wide gulf between matter and mind.

For Plato this rational soul was the real soul and immortal, its temporary connexion with the body being not a help but a hindrance. So he perhaps might, on account of his semi-mythical speculations, be called the father of 'rational psychology'; but that is not science.

For empirical psychology, on the other hand, which aims at being scientific, he had, as has been well said, only a step-motherly regard[1]. His handling of sense-data and whatever is connected with them is more crudely physical than that of Aristotle, as a reference to *Timaeus*, where mainly they are dealt with, would suffice to shew.

5. *Epistemology.* As regards physics and psychology, then, the two main divisions of empirical science, we find that little or no progress was made till they

[1] Cp. J. I. Beare, *Greek Theories of Cognition*, 1906, p. 42.

succeeded in liberating themselves from the thraldom of philosophy—to the great advantage of themselves and of it. In the wake of this advance the discussion of questions as to the validity and the limits of knowledge, which had long been debated in a more or less inchoate fashion, at length began to take shape as an independent theory of knowledge or epistemology. This science is often called the propædeutic of philosophy, since it is now recognized as an indispensable preliminary of philosophy in the stricter sense: the two, however, must obviously be closely connected.

IV. THE RELATION OF PHILOSOPHY TO HISTORY

History is still frequently and at first was universally regarded as outside the circle of the sciences, and so, as beneath the notice of philosophy. All historical knowledges were merely empirical—confined to 'the that' (τὸ ὅτι) but never explaining 'the what' (τί ἐστι) or 'the why' (διότι) of things. "Aristotle therefore calls his empirical work on animals, *History of Animals*; Theophrastus, his empirical work on plants, *History of Plants*; Pliny, his empirical book on nature in general, *Natural History*."[1]

Similarly Bacon regarded history, both natural and civil, as non-scientific, because it pertains to memory and not to reason[2]; and Hobbes, because "such knowledge is but experience, or authority, and not ratiocination."[3] Locke and Hume relegated historical knowledge to the region of unphilosophical probability exposed to the devouring tooth of time, from which certain knowledge 'depending on the agreement or disagreement of ideas' is free[4]. Kant too distinguishes

[1] Hamilton, *Metaphysics*, I, 56.
[2] *Advancement of Learning*, II; *De Augmentis*, II, i.
[3] *Computation of Logic*, I, 8.
[4] Locke, *Essay*, IV, xv; Hume, *Treatise*, I, iii, 13.

historical knowledge as *cognitio ex datis* from rational knowledge as *cognitio ex principiis*, and Schopenhauer contrasts history, confined to particulars, as ever crawling along on the bare ground of experience, while the genuine sciences, embracing universals, soar above it[1]. Finally, Dr Bosanquet has recently told us that "History is a hybrid form of experience, incapable of any considerable degree of 'being or trueness'."[2]

On the one side were principles, reasoning and 'law'; on the other particulars, conjecture and 'chance'; there we could know and predict, here we must wait and can only rarely foresee. In a word, even when narrating facts and not telling 'stories,' history was too like the hurly-burly that Schopenhauer had called it, to engage the attention of philosophers. Not till the eighteenth century was nearing its close do we find a philosophy of History beginning to take its place beside the long standing philosophies of Nature and of Mind. But once in being the progress of this latter-day philosophy was rapid: by the middle of the nineteenth century the new 'historical method' was already invading and transforming all departments of thought; and before the century closed, a very competent observer pronounced "a belief in this method" to be "the most widely and strongly entertained philosophical conviction" of the day[3].

'Nature's *routine*,' its perfection viewed statically as a closed mechanism, has had in fact to yield in importance to the continual '*novelty*' which the world viewed historically presents. Here it is the open possibilities for development which *der Trieb der Perfectibilität*, the striving for betterment, as Hegel called it,

---

[1] *Welt als Wille u. s. w.*, Bd. II, ch. 38.
[2] *Individuality and Value*, 1912, p. 78.
[3] Cp. H. Sidgwick on the Historical Method, *Mind*, 1886, p. 203.

involves, that are being continually realized[1]. In short, what history presents is what we nowadays call *epigenesis*, or creative synthesis. So far then as the historical extends, not chance indeed but certainly contingency, enters into the very heart of things—the contingency, that is to say, of the actions of one free agent, relatively to those of others, all alike bent on self-conservation and animated by some idea of the Good. Here first we reach the standpoint whence at length we can see that the world has a meaning which we can understand; whereas from the standpoint of a philosophy of nature alone it has none: only when regarded as subservient to mind does nature become intelligible. Here then— and this above all, it is important to remember—the *entia* are not Platonic ideas but living agents, and the *fientia* are not primarily phenomena, but the actual deeds of such agents. How far this historical domain extends, we have no means of empirically deciding. It remains an open question whether there are any *entia* devoid altogether of that striving which characterizes life. This is one side of the things which philosophy has to consider.

[1] Hegel, *Philosophie der Geschichte*, 1837, p. 51.

VII

MECHANISM AND MORALS

THE WORLD OF SCIENCE AND THE WORLD OF HISTORY

I PROPOSE to invite attention to some of the problems that arise when we try to correlate and to harmonize two very different views of the one world in which we live and to which we belong—namely, the scientific and the historical.

It is precisely the complete disparity between the two that prevents these problems from obtruding themselves. We may indeed adjust our mental vision to each in turn, as we may at one time look through a telescope and at another through a microscope; but to focus both at once seems a hopeless undertaking, and the diversity of our interests and pursuits for the most part precludes the attempt. Hence most people, even cultivated people, pass their time without ever realizing the serious contradictions that the two seem to involve, and therefore without feeling any need to reach a higher standpoint, from which these differences can be mediated and reconciled.

Both science and history start confronted by that exhaustless variety of ceaseless change which we immediately perceive. Science working, so to say, outwards, has, since its dawn in the ancient cities of Ionia, been seeking to find the ἀρχή or first principle of all this bewildering diversity: at length it claims to have succeeded—subject to one gigantic assumption—in replacing by one fell stroke the whole qualitative panorama of the concrete world by what we are wont to call mechanism—matter in motion. The assumption is that everything qualitative in the world is our private affair, 'subjective modification,' and everything quantitative wholly objective and independent of us. Apart from their presentation to sentient beings like ourselves, the things we are supposed to see and hear and by our muscular efforts to move, are but a mazy dance of physical points, undulating, oscillating, seemingly attracting and repelling each other, but all without a shade of those accidental deviations, those *clinamena* which for Epicurus meant so much. True, it is from this manifold of qualitative presentations that science must start, true that only by means of them can it experiment and verify; nevertheless it holds them to be only subjective symbols of the one objective world of matter and motion; and only so far as these symbols can be translated into their mechanical equivalents will it allow that real knowledge is attained.

But it is at once obvious and undeniable that such knowledge must consist primarily of numerical formulæ or so-called 'laws': facts, on the other hand, which are the primary concern of history are only of interest as exemplifications of these. The apple which fell opportunely at the feet of one philosopher and set him thinking, and the tortoise dropped inopportunely on the head of another, bringing his reveries to a close, are for science but indifferent illustrations of the law of falling bodies. Individuals again, though they are essential factors in history, have but a very insecure and provisional place in the world of science, where matter is conceived as indefinitely divisible or as a differentiation, more or less permanent, of a primordial ether. On the other hand unity, or rather continuity, of a very simple but very rigorous kind is ever present: I cannot wipe my shoes without disturbing the rest of the planet and setting up ethereal radiations that extend indefinitely outwards into space. This thorough-

going continuity gives a special character to the scientific concept of causation. It is not merely that every
so-called cause is in turn an effect, but cause and effect
are in all cases equal, consisting solely in a transformation of a definite quantity of energy and its transference
from one inert mass to another. And since the total
mass and total energy of the physical world are held
to be constant and the world itself continuous, the total
change beginning at any one instant is perfectly definite, a case of so-called 'least action' or unguided
action. This initial change, it is held, admits of adequate expression in a single vast differential equation.
At the beginning of the last century, Laplace, it is well
known, assumed that science is capable of approxi-
mating without limit to a knowledge of this equation:
at the beginning of this, his successors rather admit the
improbability of ever knowing precisely a single term
of it. Nevertheless the belief in the equation still abides.
As Prof. Poincaré has recently expressed it: "The
fundamental notion of physical law for us...is that of
a constant relation between the phenomenon of to-day
and that of to-morrow; in a word, it is a differential
equation." But he continues: "The universe is a
machine, much more complicated than all those of
industry, and of which almost all the parts are profoundly hidden from us: but in observing the movements of those that we can see, we are able, aiding
ourselves by the principle of the conservation of energy,
to draw conclusions which remain true whatever may
be the details of the invisible mechanism which animates
them."[1] The world of science then is still a world of
mechanism as much as ever, invariable in its ultimate
constituents and absolutely determined in all its movements. Given its state at any moment, then all its
previous equally with all its subsequent movements are

[1] *Monist*, xv, 3.

calculable. Always equally simple or equally complicated, its continuous changes of configuration give no
hint of either progress or meaning. To be sure, if it is
finite, a time will come when, to senses such as ours, it
will seem to have stopped, but "after years, whose
number it would take millions of figures to write,"
says Poincaré, "it will begin to move again"—and
apparently to move backwards.

Turning now to the world of history, we find that
facts, individuals, purpose and meaning, progress or
decline—all that we miss in the world of mechanism—
are the essential elements of which it is composed. It
may be that not all facts and not all individuals are
accounted important, but such as are chiefly significant
are so, not as starting-points for wide inductions, steps
towards a knowledge of universal laws, but as salient
features in a living picture, every trait in which is really
unique. The things and events that claim its first attention are not natural phenomena—these are merely the
scenery—but the *dramatis personae* themselves and their
acts and deeds. Acts and deeds imply causation of
course, but not a causation to be expressed in dynamical equations or deduced as a necessary consequence
of what has happened in the physical world already.
It is rather a causation determined by regard for the
future, a causation springing from individual motives
and individual preferences: spontaneity and purpose
are of its essence; but of such causation science knows
nothing. Purpose carries with it the notion of good or
worth, the supreme category in the world of history.
Even natural things and events are appraised by this
standard, for they are still regarded in the qualitative
concreteness of actual perception, not as science conceives them. And when we enlarge the range of history
and contemplate nature in its progressive development,
it is still as a world of concrete things and events that

we regard it, the meaning and purpose of which we
seek to understand. Final causes, though useless to
reveal the *modus operandi* of its processes, still cannot be
wholly eliminated, unless indeed we can content ourselves with calculations and measurements merely. So
we talk of struggles for existence, survival of the fittest:
we see life pass from lower to higher forms, and see
mind controlling nature ever more and more as the
centuries move on. Above all, in the world of history
we distinguish between what is and what ought to be;
whereas in the world of science what is and what must
be are one and the same. This, the supreme contrast
between mechanism and morals, discloses in the historical world a far more complex and intimate unity
than the merely quantitative continuity of the mechanical world, with its abstract categories of space,
time, and mass, can possibly shew. For the ideal of
moral order supposes a community of free persons,
severally distinct and peculiar, but all co-operating for
a supreme end. I cannot perform your duty nor you
mine: as little may I ignore your rights or you mine.
In a word, the moral order at once relates each to all
and all to each. And in the light of this moral order
the meaning or purpose of natural objects is so far
understood as such objects prove to be the instruments
and the medium—the scenery and properties, as I just
now said—of the real history. Indeed, from this teleological standpoint it would seem that natural objects
can only be completely understood if we regard them
as ultimately either subordinate individuals with some
initiative—at least the striving or *conatus* towards self-
preservation and well-being—or as merely the acts and
utterances of other agents: in a word, in this historical
world we can recognize only individual agents and
their manifestations. Things which do not act, we
should say, are themselves but the products of beings

that do. There may be no such inactive things at all, and this was Leibniz's view; but if there are such they are the manifestations of mind, as Berkeley held. What is nothing for itself is nothing in itself. (We shall have to return to these alternatives later on.)

With differences so profound, it is no wonder that these two worlds should seem absolutely disparate and distinct. It is, however, nowadays at length allowed that such an ultimate dualism is out of the question. And, as we have seen, both science and history set out from the same world of actual experience, but they proceed in diametrically opposite ways; the one outwards, the other inwards. The one goes in search of a general abstract framework amenable to exact mathematical treatment, the other in search of concrete meaning in the light of the notions of purpose and end, of worth and good. At length the one finds a unity in terms of matter and motion, the other in terms of life and mind. But when these two are again confronted there arises what Kant has called antinomies: what is essential according to the one view is impossible according to the other. The very fact of these antinomies is, by the way, evidence that both views claim to present the same world, as I have just said.

I propose to consider but one of these antinomies, that most obviously suggested by the outline just given. Mechanism is conceived as fixed and, so to say, fatally determined: morals imply guidance and control, the choice beforehand of what shall happen. In the historical world to be forewarned is to be forearmed; and over and over again the very knowledge that science furnishes of what in "the natural course of things" will inevitably happen, is the means of averting such an issue. Here the arts follow in the wake of science, and to their 'applications' of science we owe such artificial products as, say, dynamite, telephones, stoneless fruits, etc.; nay, the very apparatus and instruments indispensable to scientific investigation are instances of such contrivance. The existence of artefacts, it is contended, is not explicable by an appeal to merely natural causes. Still, at bottom they are but particular collocations of matter, continuously connected with the total collocation, and the mechanical theory of the world never pretends to explain parts in isolation from the whole. But, keeping the whole steadily in view, it maintains that not only the artefact, but the artificer himself, belongs to this mechanism: not his so-called acts and deeds alone, but his every thought and feeling, it is contended, are physically conditioned. With this contention, which science deliberately makes, the antinomy becomes acute. And now what of the solution?

Kant's solution, as every student of philosophy knows, depended on distinguishing between the phenomenal and the noumenal, between the empirical objects to which scientific knowledge is confined and the scientifically unknown objects beyond, the 'transcendental' objects, which the objects of experience necessarily imply. This implication science allows, not merely by its constant use of the term 'phenomenon,' but often expressly by the avowal that it does not know, and probably never will know, what matter really is. It may be well for clearness' sake to illustrate this implication of the phenomenal by an example. I take a straight rod notched in the middle, and, placing it slantwise in a vessel, fill up the vessel with water to the level of the notch: at that point the rod now seems bent, and the immersed half to be shorter. I can readily ascertain, say by touch, that there is no change in the rod, but I cannot assume that nothing has really happened. There must be some reality behind the appearance. In the particular case the position of the rod in two different refracting media—air and water—

is what we call, relatively, the reality, in comparison with which its bending and shortening are but appearance. But in the case of the world of science appearance is all we certainly have, the absolute reality is problematic. This, at any rate, was Kant's position, and substantially too it is the position of those numerous physicists who avow their ignorance as to what matter in itself really is. The law and order of phenomenal events are certain, the interpretation of this law and order as due to an underlying mechanism is hypothetical. Or, to put it otherwise: phenomenally the course of the world may appear determined throughout by dead mechanical necessity, but possibly it is really determined by the spontaneous purpose of living agents. In that case science and history would not actually *contradict* each other: the one would describe only the phenomenal concatenation of events, the other their several real determinants.

But of course there is nothing in the world of science itself to suggest any such notion as that of free agency. This belongs entirely to the world of history. The solution of the antinomy then which Kant offers us amounts to saying that possibly the world of history is the reality of which the world of science is the appearance. To this science may demur, demanding evidence that morals are not phenomenal as well as mechanism, and maintaining in the meantime that both must be taken as appearances of an unknowable reality that is neither matter nor mind. It may even turn the tables and contend that material mechanism is the reality of which mental life is only the appearance. This last is the doctrine we know as materialism; the second we may call agnostic monism, a doctrine much in vogue among scientific men in our time; the first, which the study of history and morals naturally suggests, we may call spiritualism or idealism. We have then a sort of triangular duel between the three. Let us see how it works out.

The materialist position need not detain us long. The doctrine, no doubt, has the prestige of antiquity, but the older notions of matter were very hazy. Thinkers, like Descartes, who attained precise ideas concerning it, in so far as they held that matter is metaphysically real, held also that a like metaphysical reality pertains to mind. They were, that is to say, dualists. But two centuries of vain efforts philosophically to digest the old leaven of dualism have led the successors of the older materialists at any rate as far as the agnostic monism with which Spencer and Huxley have familiarized us. The first serious question then is this—Can we stop there: can we regard the facts of mind as like the facts of matter, as phenomenal? We have noticed already one implication of the term 'phenomenon,' which science invariably admits; there is however another, which it as invariably ignores. A phenomenon or appearance must not only be the appearance of something, but it must be also an appearance for someone: literally, to appear it must be perceived, and to be perceived there must be a percipient. Such a percipient is one of the spontaneous agents of the historical world: it is—*primâ facie*, at all events—active and selective even in perception, interested in some phenomena, esteeming them good or bad; indifferent to others; and responding to the presence of those that affect it by appropriate actions. And now the question is: Can we say that this conscious subject and its varying activity in varying situations are in turn but phenomena; and that the notions of spontaneity, worth, purpose, 'ought,' and end, are but a hypothetical scheme to describe such phenomena, the reality behind which may be wholly different? If the conscious subject and his deeds are phenomena, then they must be phenomena for some one; but for whom? Certainly not for any other percipient. Herein lies the most striking difference between the facts of mind and the facts of what we call the external world. These are accessible to many percipients, and it is, by the way, this common property which we all have in the phenomena of the external world that misleads science into ignoring the second implication of the term 'phenomenon' just now referred to, viz., that some percipient is indispensable: what is common to all is confused with what is independent of all. No one has followed Leibniz in maintaining that percipients (his nomads) are without windows through which to look out on this common world, but at least he was right in maintaining that they have no windows by which another can look in. So then, if I, as a centre of experience and activity am a phenomenon at all, I must be that phenomenon to myself. But surely such a supposition is a flagrant contradiction; for the last-mentioned relation which the term 'phenomenon' implies, disappears absolutely when both percipient and percept are identified: the appearance cannot appear to itself, or the eye be nothing but what it sees. What then of self-consciousness? it may perhaps be replied. Well, but it is precisely at this stage that the distinction becomes first of all clear and explicit. It is as self-conscious that I know myself as a feeling and acting subject to whom objects appear. It is only as I am here that I am aware of them as there. I am not self-conscious *in vacuo*, but only as confronted by a not-self, and I am never self-conscious save as I am conscious of this duality. Moreover, unless I had somewhere experienced the contrast between appearance and reality, I could never make the distinction: and where is this experience to be gained if not here? It is surely a needless perversity to talk of knowing anything as unknowable, unless we refer to what is in itself absurd; but to call both the subject and the object of experience phenomena, so that all *reality* is absolutely beyond our ken, and yet to proclaim them connected by an un-knowable reality, seems obviously both suicidal and contradictory. For how in the world in such a plight can we ever come to frame the notion of reality at all? Every phenomenon then is connected at the outset to two realities, and one of these at least we know belongs to the historical world, is an individual subject living and acting in the objective environment which science resolves into mechanism. But if we grant the reality of the subjects of experience and also reject absolute dualism, we have reached the spiritualistic position. The objects of experience are now to be regarded as the appearances or manifestations of other subjects, and the physicist's concept of absolutely passive and inert matter as merely a hypothetical fiction or *Hilfs-begriff*, indispensable, it may be, to his purposes of systematic abstract description of what happens, but not as an existing reality.

From this position we may now proceed to inquire how far the proposed solution of our antinomy will actually apply. Can we, we have to ask, conceive such an interaction of spontaneous agents as history presents, taking on the appearance of mechanism? As I started by referring to Kant, I ought perhaps to note that his solution turns on his doctrine that time itself is purely phenomenal and the acts of free agents as real, therefore out of time. It is, of course, quite impossible here to examine this doctrine. The abstract concept of empty time—symbolized as a line along which the present instant, a point dividing past from future, flows in one direction at a constant rate—like other abstracts has, we may allow, no reality. Such a form suffices for mathematical description, and is so far evidence of the

unreality of the whole mechanical scheme. But in the
world of history the fundamental fact is the concrete
experience of change, and by no possibility can we get
this into a present that has position but neither parts
nor magnitude. Nor can we regard all change—as
Kant and so many philosophers have done—as purely
phenomenal and the real as the unchangeable. Such
absence of real change is, in fact, true of the mechanical
world as science conceives it, where nothing happens
but motion of inert particles, themselves always the
same. The individuals of the historical world have
characteristics the diametrical opposites of all this.
They remember the past, they anticipate the future,
and have thus a sense of their own identity—an identity,
however, which would mean nothing if it were but
the stark dead permanence of the physical atom, whose
ceaseless motions are externally determined, but which
itself does nothing and suffers nothing. It is this unity
of self-consciousness that makes the difference between
what etymology identifies, the atoms of the mechanical
world and the individuals of the world of morals; but
then this unity is a unity that implies both diversity of
experiences to be unified, and activity in the unifying.
External determinations, as mechanically understood,
have then no place here: all the objective changes experienced are either the causes or the effects of subjective changes. According to the spiritualistic position, both the doing and the suffering of the historical
or moral world imply free agents.

Concluding then that process, or becoming, belongs
to the real as well as to the phenomenal, we now come
back to our question: Can acts and deeds be really
from within, for the agents, spontaneous; and yet from
without appear as merely externally determined events,
parts of a continuous unbroken mechanical process?
Starting with things as they are to-day and with our-

selves, it is obvious that our freedom of action is limited. As in chess, we may play well or ill, but at least we must comply with the laws of the game; so in the world we have to acknowledge that we can never violate natural laws. But natural laws, we may without absurdity suppose, are not mechanical laws. Still, for the present we have to deal with the contention of science that in point of fact they resemble such. If so, then we are at that stage of the game when all our so-called deeds seem but 'forced moves.' But our position is that this is *only* seeming, and that really they are free. And otherwise, indeed, all our consciousness of initiative and activity would be an illusion, and an inexplicable illusion too. For, as I have said elsewhere, "even the illusion of activity and spontaneity would be certain evidence that activity and spontaneity somehow really exist; and since by common consent they are not found in the physical world, they must be in the moral."[1]

But if the world of minds is verily the real world and mechanism only its outward appearance, we ought, it might be supposed, to be able to see directly how the appearance arises—or at any rate to make some considerable progress towards accounting for it from our knowledge of that world. For we should then be beginning at the beginning with the real causes; whereas the procedure of science has been an inverse one. It has started from the effects, the phenomena, and attempted to find the causes without ever penetrating beneath the phenomenal surface: it has always remained on the outside of things and ignored the inside altogether. Now, between science thus understood and history there are two branches of knowledge to which the name of science is often denied—as it was by Kant, for example—I mean psychology and sociology. The biological sciences again have a somewhat dubious

[1] *Naturalism and Agnosticism*, 2nd ed., II, 49; 4th ed., p. 343.

position, in so far as the facts of life are intimately related on the one hand with mind and on the other with matter. When a place in the hierarchy of science is accorded to them, their range is assumed to be restricted by the sciences which are held to be more fundamental, but which in truth are only more abstract, than themselves. And as biology is expected to accept as final the mechanical interpretation of the world—although there is so far not the remotest prospect of a physical theory of life—so psychology in turn is expected to concur in the deliverances of physiology, although all attempts to deal with mind in terms of brain have so far been futile. But if the real is always concrete the more abstract view of things is, after all, not the more fundamental, and to treat it as such cannot be an ultimately valid procedure. Prompted by reflections of this sort several attempts have been made, and especially of late, to work out the details of the world directly from the standpoint of history and in terms of life and mind, untrammelled by that mechanical scheme which science is wont to regard as 'binding nature fast in fate.' Like the well-known monadology of Leibniz, such theories deny the existence of any but animate and active beings; but they reject altogether the 'pre-established harmony' and absence of reciprocal action in which he believed. They, on the contrary, assume that all the constituent beings of the world, the monads—or souls as we might perhaps say—are linked together in the closest fashion by intercommunication and interdependence; while the only harmony in which they believe is a final harmony, which is the goal, not the starting-point, of history.

We begin then, it is supposed, with a world of compossible conative agents, each ideally limiting each, though possibly for the most part to an imperceptible extent; and further, only in such a way that some action is still possible to all. What is done cannot be wholly undone, and all acts being, of course, definite acts, there is always a determinate though very complex relation between what has become actual and what remains still possible. Some of these possibilities may remain possibilities indefinitely: on the other hand, some former possibilities will be such no longer, while new possibilities may arise which were not possibilities —at least not immediate, imminent, if I might say so —not actual possibilities, before. Such statements are, I fear, too general to be impressive, and yet there is no time even to attempt to fill in the outline. A single illustrative instance, however, may suggest many more. At a certain stage, and along one line in the evolution of the animal kingdom, vertebrates having four limbs appeared: prior to this definite appearance, forms with six or more limbs were, we may suppose, a possibility, since such forms actually occur along some of the earlier invertebrate lines; but after it, though manifold modifications of the four vertebrate limbs arose, their number was fixed once for all. But more germane— an essential point indeed in the theories we are con- sidering—is the appeal to the facts of habit and heredity. All beginnings are hard, as the Germans say; but practice makes perfect: familiarity and expertness can result only from repetition. The more the facts of life are studied, the more clearly the very simplest ad- justments appear as the outcome of random trials and errors, like the child's first attempts to walk or to write. Such adjustments become 'secondarily automatic,' but they were due primarily to spontaneous efforts. So all nature is regarded as plastic and evolving like mind: its routine and uniformity being explained on the analogy of habit and heredity in the individual, of custom and tradition in society; while its variety is

attributed to spontaneity in some form. As the mathematician, C. S. Peirce, puts it: "The one intelligible
theory of the universe is that of objective idealism, that
matter is effete mind, inveterate habits becoming
physical laws."[1] And certainly, as Schelling and
Fechner have urged, we continually find the living
passing over into the lifeless, just as conscious processes
become mechanical reflexes; but we never find the converse process of life arising out of what has ceased to
live. Or, to quote another exponent of these pampsychist theories, Prof. Royce of Harvard: "In (the)
case of Nature in general, as in the case of particular
portions of Nature known as our fellow-men, we are
dealing with the phenomenal signs of a vast conscious
process, whose relation to Time varies vastly, but whose
general characters are the same. From this point of
view, evolution would be a vast series of processes
suggesting to us various degrees and types of conscious
process. These processes, in (the) case of so-called
inorganic matter, are very remote from us . . . (but) all
this finite consciousness shares with ours the character
of being full of fluent processes whose tendency is twofold,—in one direction towards the formation of relatively stable habits of repetition, in the other direction
towards the irrevocable leaving of certain events,
situations, and types of experience behind. I suppose
that this play between the irrevocable and the repeated,
between habit and novelty, between rhythm and the
destruction of rhythm, is everywhere in Nature as it is
in us, something significant, something of interest,
something that means a struggle for ideals."[2] But of
course such views are but genial *aperçus* at the best:
they can never do the work or take the place of science,
and they make no pretence of so doing. Yet the attempt

---

[1] 'The Architecture of Theories,' *Monist*, 1890, I, 170.
[2] Royce, *The World and the Individual*, II, 226.

—looking at the whole world from the historical stand-point—to regard both the uniformity and the develop-ment which it discloses in the light of the uniformity and progress which we find in concrete individuals and societies—this attempt, I say, yields after all a better *Weltanschauung*, a more vivid and adequate view of the world, than we can ever obtain by attempting to re-construct it in terms of the ultimate abstractions reached from a standpoint which leaves all that is concrete, all that has life and meaning, wholly out of sight.

But there is one thing we must not do—if such theories are to have any meaning at all—we must not confuse the two standpoints. Yet this is what common thought and language are continually doing: we talk of a chair or a stone as an individual thing, though it is neither biologically nor physically an individual at all. Nevertheless its physical coherence, which admits of its movement as one whole, leads us to regard it as a 'body,' and our practical interest may lead us to identify and individuate it as, say, the coronation chair or the Rosetta stone. But, on the strength of such popular usage, to think to nonplus the pampsychist by asking how stones or chairs can be alive, is only to betray ignorance and incapacity. He makes no pre-tence of knowing all the types of individual, the whole scale of beings, which the universe contains; but on the analogy of the behaviour, singly and in combina-tion, of those he does know, he seeks to interpret the uniformity and the development which the world as a whole discloses. How far in a particular case of what are called actual laws—say those of chemical action—the results observed are directly due to a Supreme Being, as Berkeley would have said, or to barely sen-tient monads without distinct perception or memory, as Leibniz supposed, as to this he can only conjecture. To be sure, the name pampsychist is usually applied only to those who accept the latter alternative, those who prefer the former being called simply spiritualists or idealists. But the difference between them is not fundamental: their common persuasion is that life and mind are at the bottom of all. Yet, unless the ultimate atoms of chemical theory are comparable to 'manufactured articles,' in being severally exactly alike, as Sir John Herschel and Maxwell believed, the Leibnizian, or pampsychist, seems preferable to the Berkeleian or idealist alternative, inasmuch as it introduces greater continuity and simplicity into our view of the universe. Assuming prime-atoms to be real beings at all, they are, according to the pampsychist, to be regarded as possessing some psychical properties and some individual peculiarities: thus the historical world is the whole world. Of course, such lowly individuals are wholly beyond our reach: no one can, or ever will, ear-mark even a molecule and follow its meanderings. The physicist in his researches here is wholly confined to what we may fairly call statistical methods. But now we know, from the use of these methods in human affairs, that there is nothing in the mechanical regularity of large numbers incompatible with very great diversity in the constitution, character, and motives of the individuals that make up the aggregate. As individual men all differ from the 'average man' of statistical tables, so may the individual monad from the constant atom of the chemical theory. There is then so far nothing in the statistical results of the world of science to exclude, *ab initio*, the pampsychist's interpretation.

On the other hand, the latest results of physical inquiry—the most revolutionary and disquieting that science has known for long—seem to disclose internal processes of change and development in those very atoms that were long regarded as ingenerable and immutable. This appearance of evolution in a domain that was supposed to lie wholly beyond it, coupled with the tremendous advances which this idea has secured to the biologist and the sociologist, go far to justify the boast that the historical method "has invaded and transformed all departments of thought." It is interesting in this connexion to notice that in the support which it lends to pampsychist views the theory of evolution seems likely to have an ultimate effect on science the precise opposite of that which it exercised at first. That was a levelling down, this will be a levelling up. At first it appeared as if man were only to be linked with the ape, now it would seem that the atom, if a reality at all, may be linked with man. Such an application of the principle of continuity in psychology is, after all, as legitimate as its application in physics, to which no one demurs. If the concept of mass-points, bodies without extension, is legitimate, Leibniz's concept of monads without memory, momentary consciousnesses, is equally legitimate. Both alike are limiting notions—an experience without any time-span and a body that occupies no space; and pampsychism identifies the two. The momentary mind will have an elementary body, but it will not be inert.

This brings me to emphasize one characteristic of a world of conative as distinct from inert beings, such as the physicist contemplates. There will be no laws, prior to these agents, making them what they are; but they, being what they are, their action and interaction, will result in uniformity and order. Habit, dexterity, and familiarity do not precede experience, but arise in the course of it: language and custom, social status and obligation, originate and consolidate with the progress of society and are nothing apart from it. On the spiritualistic view then—whether pampsychist or idealist —the agents are first: and law in every sense and evolution are but second. And surely this is the only tenable position. Laws without a lawgiver, intelligible order and no intelligent agents, meaning and purpose before there is aught that feels or strives—a phantom skeleton first which then quickens itself to life and power—is not this unthinkable? Moreover laws are not real forces, but only abstract formulæ. Bodies gravitate no doubt, but not because constrained to do so by an independent law: the law is but a generalization describing their behaviour: to know more about that we must know more about them.

But to return to our antinomy. It seems obvious that the historical world, i.e., the whole world in its concrete reality, with its contrasts of variety and uniformity, progress and routine, invention and imitation, where "the old order changeth, yielding place to new" —can never actually assume even the appearance of such unmitigated necessity as mechanism implies. The distinction of reality and appearance then will not solve the antinomy: in other words, the said mechanism cannot be even phenomenal. The phenomenal is commonly held to involve sense-perception; such, for example, was the doctrine of Kant; but there is no sense-perception in the mechanical scheme of science. Matter is here at length wholly resolved into form, and what we have left is not the perceptible but the conceivable simply. And concepts without percepts—as Kant was fond of saying—are 'empty,' thoughts not facts. The progress of science has in this way unconsciously refuted its own naïve assumption. For long it seemed to be advancing nearer to the empirical reality which sense-perception was held merely to symbolize: in the end it turned out that unawares this reality had somehow been left wholly behind, had slipped away, as it were, between the experimenter's fingers and the mathematician's equations. But science might fairly console itself with the reflection that it had, after all, been doing better than it knew. Setting out in search of matter as that which is alien to mind, it ended by discovering only law and order, which are the sure marks of mind. But the course of events in a world of minds can never be comparable to the running down of an hour-glass, where the path and velocity of every single grain is determined irrevocably by its original position; for in a world of minds there must be continual new beginnings. All that science then could do—even were it complete—would be to enable us to forecast not what the future *will* be, but what it *would* be if present tendencies persisted unmodified; if every agent in the world, that is to say, became fossilized into a creature of habits. Habit, no doubt, is well described as second nature, but the living individuals of history are ever rising "on stepping-stones of their dead selves to higher things"; and this is more and more true the higher in the scale of life they stand.

"The solution of the antinomy then is not to be reached by distinguishing between reality and appearance, but by distinguishing between fact and fiction: that seems to be the outcome of the solution you offer," some representatives of science may say. Well, I admit this seems startlingly like a *reductio ad absurdum*; but provided I may put my own meaning on fiction, it is the only conclusion I can attain. Leibniz made a famous distinction between truths of fact and truths of reason. Now, if fiction is to imply falsehood, then I allow that the fundamental principles of science are not fictions. But whereas the truths of history *are* truths of fact, these truths of science *are not* truths of fact, but only truths of reason. They have the unique distinction of being necessarily *true*; but as facts do not enter into their premises, facts cannot emerge in their conclusion. Hence it is usual to speak of science in this sense as pure or abstract science. All that it tells us about a mechanical world is necessarily true; but it does not and cannot tell us that the actual world is necessarily mechanical. In a word, the application of pure science to the actual world is wholly hypothetical and tentative. So far as nature is routine, *natura naturata* as Spinoza called it—so far, I mean, as it is like wheel-work or mechanism—so far some scheme of pure mechanics will exactly apply; so far, on the other hand, as nature is spontaneous and living, *natura naturans*, so far that scheme, though still as true as ever, ceases to apply at all: its conclusions hold, but its premisses no longer fit the facts. Seeing a child gambolling on a dangerous hill, an Irishman is said to have exclaimed: "If that child were not alive he would certainly be killed," meaning, no doubt, that an inanimate object in the child's place would certainly roll to the bottom. It was really a very profound remark, and its moral is obvious. Yes, the merest common-sense, you will say. Well, I am content to leave it at that.

But it may be worth while to put the case another way. The mechanical scheme is not merely pure, i.e., true, apart from its application to facts, but it is also abstract. As it stands, it is not fact, and even when it describes facts truly it does not describe them adequately: it does not put the real world before us, but only an aspect of it, and to take this for the whole is to mistake the whole seriously—in fact it is precisely in such a mistake that the antinomy lies. And yet the mistake is a very natural as well as a very ancient one: indeed it is itself due to identifying one aspect of knowledge with the whole of it. Science is measurement, Comte used to say, and God always geometrizes, Plato had said long before. Certainly, as regards exactness and precision, mathematical, that is, quantitative knowledge, is the ideal of knowledge. If then our knowledge were perfect and complete, would not this ideal be attained? In that case we should, I suppose, know *how* everything happened, and yet perhaps not understand *why* anything happened. And in fact the positivist ideal of knowledge only allows us to inquire how, and forbids us altogether to ask why. But surely we are not merely cognitive and disinterested spectators of events, but rather interested and effective agents in the strife. It is primarily the end to be attained to which the question *why* is directed, that leads us to concern ourselves with the means which the question *how* discovers. Now it is these higher, so-called teleological, categories which science, as abstract, ignores, but which history, as concrete, mainly contemplates. Mistake and confusion only result when the limitations which the abstract or mechanical aspect of the world inevitably involve are forgotten, as they are only too apt to be. "It is a very deep-seated and perhaps the main defect of modern researches into nature," said Hegel, "that even when other and higher categories than those of mere mechanism are in operation, they still stick obstinately to the mechanical laws; although they thus conflict with the testimony of unbiassed perception, and foreclose the gate to an adequate knowledge of nature."[1] It is this defect that the biological and moral sciences are slowly but surely correcting. For in these sciences "other and higher categories than those of mere mechanism" are indispensable, and by means of these—the notions of end, purpose, value—they help to resolve the antinomy that otherwise arises between the mechanical and the moral. Referring to the progress of the biological sciences, we find even a German physiologist maintaining: *So treibt uns der Mechanismus der Gegenwart dem Vitalismus der Zukunft mit Sicherheit entgegen*[2]. (Thus the

---

[1] *Encyklopädie*, § 195, Wallace's transl., 2nd ed., p. 291.
[2] G. Bunge, *Vitalismus und Mechanismus*, 1886, p. 20.

mechanism of the present is surely impelling us towards the vitalism of the future.) But we may go
further and extend the prophecy. The collapse of
materialism within the last half century, the present
tendency of neutral monism towards the teleological
and away from the mechanical side, of which Haeckel
furnishes a conspicuous example—all this points to the
advent of a spiritualistic interpretation of the world
that culminates in the notion of the Good.

VIII

HEREDITY AND MEMORY

WRITING in the middle of the seventeenth century on 'the efficient cause of the chicken,' William Harvey of Caius College in this university quaintly remarked: "Although it be a known thing subscribed by all . . . that the egge is produced by the cock and henne, and the chicken out of the egge, yet neither the schools of physicians nor Aristotle's discerning brain have disclosed the manner how the seed doth mint and coin the chicken out of the egge." "How much nearer a disclosure," asks a writer who quotes this passage, "are we to-day? . . . On the whole we have (still) to confess that we do not know the secret of development, which is part of the larger secret of life itself."[1]

Now it is commonly taken for granted that on this great problem—the problem of Heredity—psychology can have nothing to say. But I have come at length to think that, provided we look at the world from what I would call a spiritualistic and not from the usual naturalistic standpoint, psychology may shew us that the secret of heredity is to be found in the facts of memory.

But first of all, in accordance with the observation just quoted, it seems desirable to enounce a few general propositions true "of the larger secret of life itself" and applicable also to this particular part of it.

To begin—we find the processes observable in the world around us can all be ranged in one or other of two classes, as either anabolic processes or katabolic—

[1] J. Arthur Thomson, *Heredity*, 1908, p. 416.

to use in a somewhat wider sense the terms of a Cambridge physiologist. The former we take to imply action contrary to, the latter action along the line of, least resistance. The processes of the one order build up: those of the other level down. The one order implies that direction, in the sense of aim or end, which we associate with mind as sensitive and purposive; the other that indifference which we associate with matter as lifeless and inert.

Of such guidance or direction—I would ask you next to note—we have immediate experience only in the case of our own activity, as in building a house or organizing a business. It may well seem rash therefore to attribute such processes as the formation of chlorophyll in a blade of grass or of albumen in a grain of corn to guidance in this sense. But at all events they are processes pertaining exclusively to living organisms, and found nowhere else. If these processes should some day be artificially repeated in a laboratory, as Prof. Schäfer so confidently expects—even this would imply the guidance of the living chemist. But still, it may be asked, what right have we to identify life and mind; what right, for example, to credit plants with souls, as Aristotle did? The right that the principle of continuity gives us. No sharp line can be drawn between plants and animals nor between higher animals and lower.

But here the advocate of Naturalism may intervene. "Continuity is just as complete regarded from below as it is regarded from above," he may urge; "and if so, surely the proper method of investigation is to begin with the simpler and earlier rather than with the later and more complex." Not necessarily, we must reply: all depends—as Plato pointed out long ago—upon where the characters we have to study are clearest and most distinct. In the case of life there can be no doubt that this is where they are the most developed. "It is clear," as G. H. Lewes once said, "that we should never rightly understand vital phenomena were we to begin our study of life by contemplating its simplest manifestations . . . we can only understand the Amoeba and the Polype by a light reflected from the study of Man."[1] Moreover if we begin from the material side we must keep to this side all through: if matter is to explain life at all, it must explain all life. But it is evidently impossible to describe the behaviour of the higher organisms in physical terms. Indeed the ablest physicists recognize that the concepts of physics are inadequate to the description of life even in its lowest forms. We may conclude then, that when, as in the case of life, we are seeking to interpret the meaning of a continuous series we must start where that meaning is clearest, where it is best known and most definite, not where it is least known and most inchoate.

Working in this fashion from ourselves downward, what then, we may now ask, do we find as the irreducible *minimum* which all life implies; and what are the most general characteristics that mark every advance from lower forms to higher? To the first question the answer, I trust, may here suffice that life everywhere implies an individual and an environment. To changes in this environment the individual's behaviour is, or tends to be, so adjusted as to secure its well-being. For—it is worth remarking by the way—throughout the realm of life the category of value, which such terms as well-being and ill-being imply, is relevant, though irrelevant everywhere else. It is this that gives to what we have called guidance or direction its motive and its meaning.

As to the second question—what are the general characteristics of advancing life?—this is on the whole admirably dealt with in Herbert Spencer's Psychology

[1] *Problems of Life and Mind*, 3rd Series, 1879, p. 122.

under the heading *General Synthesis*. Defining life as the adjustment of internal relations to external relations, he shews how, as evolution progresses, this adjustment extends in range both spatially and temporally; how at the same time it increases in speciality and complexity; how separate adjustments are more and more co-ordinated and unified; and so forth. The interval between the palæolithic man, whose world was bounded by his river-valley, who knew little of the past and planned less for the future, who lived from hand to mouth content with raw food and possibly no clothing, who possessed only the rudest implements and had but a cave for his dwelling—the interval, I say, between him and civilized man with his long traditions, fixed laws, innumerable arts and organized division of labour, sufficiently illustrates the character of this progress when already far advanced. The inheritance of the permanent achievements of one generation by the next is obviously the main factor of such social progress: this we may call heredity in the literal sense. But we talk also of heredity as a factor in the biological progress from the *Protista* up to Man; though here the heir and the inheritance can only be distinguished by calling the individual the heir and his organism the inheritance, that is to say by regarding as two what the biologist conceives as one. It is this biological heredity that is our problem.

Before attempting to attack this problem directly there is however still a characteristic of life or experience that we may for a moment consider, which seems to throw some light upon it. Experience I once proposed to define as the process of becoming expert by experiment; and recent elaborate observations[1] of the behaviour of the *Protozoa* shew that these micro-

[1] H. S. Jennings, *Contributions to the Study of the Behaviour of the Lower Organisms*, Washington, 1904.

scopic creatures frequently succeed, as we do, only by way of trial and error. Even plants prove capable to a great extent of accommodating themselves to changes in their environment. All this presupposes a certain plasticity, which in turn implies retentiveness: in other words, just as later generations inherit from earlier generations so later phases of the individual inherit, as it were, from earlier phases. In our own case we get a good deal of insight into this process in what we can observe of the growth of habit. What was originally acquired by a long series of trials and failures, engrossing all our attention, becomes at length 'secondarily automatic'—to use Hartley's now classic phrase. Of this such feats as skating or piano-playing are familiar examples. This mechanization of habit is aptly described in the saying that "use is second nature." It sets attention free for new advances which would else be impossible. So *natura naturata* is the condition of further *natura naturans*. The organism gives us a warrant for the term 'mechanization' in the permanent modification of brain and muscle which the acquisition of new dexterities entails; and *mutatis mutandis*, the same holds true of the knowledge we know so thoroughly that, as Samuel Butler said, we have ceased to know that we know it at all. Now this law of habit we may reasonably regard as exemplified in the life of every individual in the long line of genealogical ascent that connects us with our humblest ancestors, in so far as every permanent advance in the scale of life implies a basis of habit embodied in a structure which has been perfected by practice.

And now, starting from the analogy just noted— namely that habit connects successive phases in the life of one individual as heredity connects successive stages in the development of one race—we may pass at length to our problem. That analogy suggests the possibility of an indefinite advance upwards in the scale of life without the succession of individuals which heredity involves—provided, of course, that a single individual lived sufficiently long and did not grow old.

In place then of the innumerable individuals a certain genealogical ascent has successively entailed, let us imagine one individual accomplishing the whole of it. The final result as regards structure might conceivably be substantially the same, nor need the time required be very different. But there would certainly be one very important difference. For the solitary immortal without ancestry structure would be wholly the result of function. But for the many mortals—who have a racial history as well as a personal history—function would be the result of structure, so far, that is, as the embryonic stage of their existence is concerned. To this stage Haeckel accordingly gave the name of *palingenesis*; because in it the structural acquisitions of our imaginary immortal are recapitulated. But whereas the same level of development might have been attained in approximately the same time in the two cases—that of a single persisting individual and that of a continuous succession of perishing individuals—the recapitulatory process, peculiar to the second case, proves to be vastly more rapid. It took thousands of years, say, to produce the first chicken, but the hen's egg reaches the same level in three weeks. To be sure the recapitulation is not precise and complete in every detail; yet most biologists, I believe, allow that it is very full and substantial. Nevertheless even in the most complex organisms far the greater part of it is accomplished within a year. How may we account for this extraordinary brevity in the repetition of a process that took so long at first? The consideration of this question in the light of our preliminary investigation may lead us towards a solution of our problem.

Let us suppose our imaginary individual, when he had proceeded but a little way in the slow and arduous fashion of a pioneer, to have been set back to the beginning once more, *still however retaining the memory of his former experiences.* "We may be sure," as I have said elsewhere, "that in that case he would make good the ground lost in much less time than he required at first, and also without following all the windings of the tentative route into which his previous inexperience had led him: his route the second time would be routine."[1] So, for example, a man, who had gradually by various improvements adapted a house or a machine to his purposes, would proceed, if either by some accident was destroyed. Let us again suppose that after a while, when a still further advance had been achieved, our imaginary individual had to submit to a like setback once more; and that after a yet further advance the same thing recurred again, and so on indefinitely. The result would clearly be that the latest acquisitions would be the least straightened out, the least automatic and the least fixed. Now we know directly by observation that in like manner the memories and dexterities that are acquired latest are the least engrained and the most likely to fail. And turning from the individual to the race, Darwin has shewn that here it is specific characters, which are acquired later, rather than the generic, upon which they are superposed, that are peculiarly liable to variation.

Now the situation we have supposed closely resembles that of a new complex organism. Though not identical with the old it is nevertheless continuous with it, and it does reproduce the ancestral acquisitions with the less hesitation or variation, the more they have become habitual, secondarily automatic or organized. This no doubt implies—*prima facie,* at least—that

[1] *The Realm of Ends,* 2nd ed., 1912, p. 209.

acquired characters are inherited. But it implies also—*a point too often forgotten*—that we should not expect any clear manifestation of such heredity till the functions that have led to structures have passed far beyond the initial stage where conscious control is essential to their performance.

This doctrine of the inheritance of acquired characters, enounced, I believe, by Aristotle, accepted alike by Lamarck and Darwin, was only seriously called in question some thirty years ago. But so rapidly has opinion swung round, that now the great majority of biologists—and especially of zoologists—reject this hypothesis, as they call it, altogether. If they are right, it is useless attempting to develope further the psychological theory I have been trying to suggest. At this point then we must pause to examine their objections.

First, it is said, neither observation nor experiment has so far yielded any really decisive evidence for the old theory of inheritance. But it is equally true that they furnish no conclusive evidence against it. There are at present no crucial instances either for or against it; but as I have just said, we should not expect that there would be. Even the theory of natural selection was not established in that way: there too the argument depends entirely on cumulative evidence and general considerations. It must be owned that a vast mass of worthless cases of hereditary transmission has been exploded by Weismann and his followers; and this has naturally led to a general distrust of the rest. Yet, as a singularly fair-minded and acute biologist, Delage, maintains, the evidence is still formidable; for as another Lamarckian has said, "transformation . . . acts *as if* the direct action of the environment and the habits of the animal [the parent animal that is to say] were the efficient cause of the change, and any explanation which excludes the direct action of such agencies is confronted by the difficulty of an immense number of the most striking coincidences."[1]

Yes, the Weismannians reply, we allow that appearances all point in the Lamarckian direction, but inasmuch as the *modus operandi* of the transmission is altogether inconceivable, we decline to believe that they are more than appearances. This is their second argument. But as the 'impassioned controversy,' as Delage calls it, has gone on, this argument, it is hardly unfair to say, has changed its form. No process of transmission being conceivable, it is assumed that no such process is possible. In this way the neo-Darwinians relieve themselves of the difficulty there is on their side of proving a negative. But assumption is not argument, and our mere ignorance of the 'how' alone will not justify us in rejecting *primâ facie* evidence. We do not brush aside the facts of gravitation because we are utterly ignorant of the process which they involve.

We certainly are entirely in the dark as to how structural changes in the body of the parent can affect at all the structure of the germ which it nourishes; since the two are anatomically entirely distinct. But it is something to the point to note, as Cope did years ago, that there is at least one case of a very precise connexion between two distinct tissues which is perhaps quite as wonderful as the connexion between body-plasm and germ-plasm and hardly less mysterious—viz., the adjustment of skin-coloration to ground-surface brought about through the organs of sight. Of this the chameleon furnishes the most familiar but not the most impressive instance. I came the other day across an account of some experiments that seem clearly to imply the intervention in some way of consciousness in bringing about this adjustment—an intervention which

[1] Prof. W. B. Scott, *American Journal of Morphology*, 1891, p. 395.

Cope surmised but could not prove. Into a tank of flat fish, whose colour matched its sandy bottom, a number of pebbles of a different colour were introduced. As seen by the fish the mosaic so produced would appear more or less foreshortened; but presently for all that the fish became mottled like the bottom, not as it appeared to them at rest, but as it would appear to an observer looking down from above, like the enemies the fish had to elude. Also it is perhaps noteworthy that there is at least a very intimate connexion one way between body-plasm and germ-plasm, as the extirpation of the reproductive glands shews.

But in the third place not only is the inheritance of acquired characters said to be without specific evidence, not only is it declared inconceivable and so incredible *a priori*, but in what he calls 'germinal continuity' Weismann claims to have found direct and positive proof that it is actually impossible. At the same time he contends that the mingling of ancestral characters in sexual reproduction is sufficient to provide endless variations on which natural selection can work, thus rendering it also needless. Continuity of germ-plasm in some sense is an obvious fact in any case; and Harvey's position, *omne vivum e vivo*, is one that no biologist is concerned practically to deny. What Weismann means by germinal continuity, however, is such an absolute continuity of the germ-plasm as entails its absolute discontinuity from the body-plasm. Let the changes acquired by the parents be what they may, they can, he maintains, make no difference to the offspring. The circular character of the argument is here again apparent. Till the impossibility of the Lamarckian position is proved, germinal continuity or continuity of the germ-plasm may exist, but the absolute isolation of this germ-plasm from the body-plasm is still open to question; and apart from this isolation the Lamarckian position remains tenable. In fact Romanes, who has criticized Weismann at length with much acumen, represents him not as attempting to prove but as simply '*postulating*' the absolute non-inheritance of acquired characters and deducing the absolute continuity of the germ-plasm in his sense from this.

A brief examination of Weismann's main position and a word or two on an important supplementation, to which he was eventually driven, may I trust suffice to bring us round again to the theory of 'organic memories' or 'engrams'[1] to which our preliminary propositions led up. In order to see more clearly the issue raised, we may begin by comparing our imaginary immortal with some mortal double, who has reached the same level of biological development within a few short years. The bodies of both are related to the simplest form of life—the one directly the other indirectly—the one having developed from such a form by continuous interaction with its environment, the other, according to Weismann, having developed from a continuous stock of germ-plasm, entirely cut off from the environment since the unicellular stage. Now in both cases there is an 'immortal' concerned—our imaginary individual in the one case, and Weismann's hypothetical germ-plasm in the other. Also the result attained is in both cases the same; and certainly it is the most wonderful instance we know of what we call an end, a τέλος. The fundamental factors in the one case are (1) the environment, and (2) experience: the latter an essentially positive or teleological factor, since

[1] This theory was first definitely broached by Prof. Ewald Hering in a lecture, *Concerning Memory as a general function of Organized Matter*, delivered at Vienna in 1870. It has recently been revived and developed by Prof. R. Semon of Munich (to whom the word 'engram' is due), in *Die Mneme als erhaltendes Prinzip im Wechsel des organischen Geschehens*, 2te Auf. 1908.

it is always directed towards self-conservation or better-ment. But the factors fundamental in the other case are (1) natural selection, and (2) amphimixis or the periodical blending of two ancestral strands of the immortal germ-substance; and both alike are non-teleological.

Can it be that one and the same end can be reached by such disparate means? Its attainment through ex-perience without natural selection is conceivable: its attainment without experience, by natural selection and fortuitous variation alone, is surely inconceivable. That both experience and natural selection have co-operated seems indeed to be the fact, as Darwin himself at all events assumed. But this co-operation Weismann with Wallace and the rest of the neo-Darwinians denies. And this denial it is that entitles us to say that *dis*continuity, or isolation from the body-plasm, is the essential feature of Weismann's germ-plasm. This germ-plasm persists indeed continuously; but it per-sists, so to say, underground, screened like the sacred queen-bee[1] from all the functioning with the external world which the offsets it periodically throws out dis-charge. Nevertheless it alone—not intercourse with the environment—is supposed to determine their structure. Can the manifold adaptations such structures display and the endlessly diversified series of them—continu-ously advancing in complexity of adaptation—which the evolution of life as a whole displays, can all these, we ask again, be explained from such a standpoint?

Yes, they can, was Weismann's answer: which, how-ever, as I said, he afterwards qualified. Any detailed examination of his theory would require a volume, has in fact occupied many volumes. But the discontinuity just referred to—duly considered—suffices, I think,

[1] An illustration used by Dr Francis Darwin in his Presidential Address to the Brit. Assoc. 1908.

summarily and yet successfully to dispose of it. Let me try to make this clearer. First of all I must ask you to note that, so long as we confine our attention to the unicellular organisms, there is no special problem as to the inheritance of acquired characters, nor in fact as to inheritance at all; for, as Weismann himself has shewn, there is here no natural death, and therefore— strictly speaking—no succession of generations. In his own words, "Natural death occurs only among multi-cellular organisms, the single-celled forms escape it." Referring to the well-known cell-division by which the one individual becomes two, he remarks: "In the division the two portions are equal, neither is the older nor the younger. Thus there arises an unending series of individuals, *each as old as the species itself, each with the power of living on indefinitely, ever dividing but never dying.*"[1]

And now, in the next place, "it should also be borne in mind that," as one of Weismann's ablest supporters has observed, "many of these unicellular organisms . . . are highly differentiated, i.e. [are provided] with great complexity of structure . . . and that many have very definite and interesting modes of behaviour, such as swimming in a spiral, seeking light or avoiding it . . . trying one kind of behaviour after another—functional peculiarities, some of which cannot be described without using psychological terms."[2] Lowly as these forms of life appear when compared with our own, still the enormous diversity to be found among them, their wide range in space and their prodigious antiquity, together suggest that between the highest of them and the very beginnings of life lies a long, long history of "one kind of behaviour after another." In the course of that history functions were mechanized and structures fixed.

All this while the situation is that of our imaginary im-mortal developing by intercourse with its environment,

---

[1] Italics mine.   [2] J. Arthur Thompson, *Heredity*, p. 33.

save that here the immortal is real and not imaginary; and also, instead of remaining solitary, is continually manifolding itself into new individuals who
start equipped with all its acquisitions. All this while
too the whole organism of every individual is in touch
with the environment and every new acquisition is
passed on to all the individuals into which any one is
manifolded. If we like to call this inheritance, then it
is inheritance of acquired characters, and there is no
other. And all this while too there is no ground for
distinguishing between body-plasm and germ-plasm;
unless the cell-nucleus—without which the cell never
divides and which always divides with it—were to be
called germ-plasm on this account.

But now so soon as we advance to the *Metazoa* and
the *Metaphyta*—that is to the multicellular animals and
plants—we are supposed, according to Weismann, to
be suddenly confronted with an absolute discontinuity
of mortal body and immortal germ. The one can no
longer bequeath, the other can no longer inherit.
Surely in such a case what we should naturally expect
would be not the enormous advance from jelly-fish to
mammal, which is what we find, but rather a practically
stationary state. For consider the parallel case of social
progress referred to earlier. The main factor in such
progress we found was heredity. Imagine then, if you
can, what would happen if now from this time forth
every new generation had to begin where the old *began*
and not where it left off; if no single human product
from now onwards outlasted the individual who produced it; if in short all tradition and inheritance were
from henceforth no more. Such a breach of social
continuity between the future and the past would
surely be startling; and yet it is an even greater discontinuity that Weismann seemed to imagine as marking
off the *Protozoa* from the *Metazoa*. The Lamarckian

factor good up to that point has, in his view, been absolutely inoperative beyond it. Natural selection and the blending of ancestral traits, more or less diverse, have henceforth sufficed.

The essentials of this process of amphigony or mixed generation, as Weismann conceived it, are simple enough. Two packs of shuffled cards he has himself suggested as representing the paternal and maternal germ-plasm. Now imagine half of each rejected and a new pack made of the remainders. A portion of this new pack will remain unaltered, though it will grow indefinitely: this portion is the latent germ-plasm that continues undeveloped until the advent of a new generation, when the processes of mixing, shuffling, and reducing division are repeated. From the remaining portion the new individual arises. Any one of the cards would suffice for its complete development, for each corresponds to a single ancestor. But there are many of them, and so a struggle ensues. The card or plasm of one ancestor—a paternal grandmother say—succeeds in shaping the nose: another—perhaps a maternal great-grandfather—provides the mouth, and so on. Though any one of them might conceivably have furnished the whole, it is far more likely that all or most of the pack have a share in it. In all this—the mingling of ancestral plasms, the reducing division, the reversion and atavism—we are, so far, in the region of fact. But when Weismann asks us to regard these ancestral plasms as themselves quite stable, we enter the region of fable. And even in this region, if we try to picture out—not everyday instances of heredity—but the primitive heredity, the link, that is to say, which long ago connected the evolution of mortal multicellular organisms with the wholly distinct evolution of immortal unicellular organisms, we are utterly at a loss to find any resemblance between the two.

No doubt amphimixis is a potent source of congenital variations, and such variations are the indispensable *point d'appui* for natural selection. But what avails that if all possible variations are confined to such unit-characters as the unicellular organisms display? As Henry VIII long ago remarked: "You can't make a silk purse out of a sow's ear," turn it how you will. And how, in view of the stability of germ-plasm and its discontinuity from body-plasm—which, according to Weismann, are maintained throughout multicellular evolution—the higher levels of life were reached is a mystery. For, as Delage has said: "Without the inheritance of acquired characters there can be no new ancestral plasms, and without ancestral plasms more complicated than those of the *Protozoa* there can be none of the superior animals."[1] But Weismann rejects the inheritance of acquired characters and so cuts off the first possibility: also he maintains—or rather began by maintaining—the absolute continuity and isolation of the germ-plasm, and so cut off the second.

Simultaneously with Delage's criticism however—in 1895 that was—Weismann made the complete change of front to which I have just alluded, abandoning—or at least essentially modifying—both his main positions, viz., the stability of germ-plasm and its discontinuity from body-plasm. In the same year, H. F. Osborn[2] had said: "If acquired variations are transmitted there must be some unknown principle in heredity, if they are not transmitted there must be some unknown factor

[1] Yves Delage, *L'Hérédité et les grands Problèmes de la Biologie générale*, 1903, p. 560. But to Prof. Hartog of Cork belongs the credit of first conceiving "cette objection capitale sous la forme du dilemme," as Delage expressly allows. *Op. cit.* p. 559 n. See Prof. Hartog's letter in *Nature*, 1891, vol. xliv, entitled, 'A Difficulty in Weismannism,' pp. 613 f., and a second letter, vol. xlv, pp. 102 f.

[2] In a lecture entitled *The Hereditary Mechanism and the Search for the Unknown Factors of Evolution.*

in evolution." "A perfectly correct conclusion" Weismann at once replied, and set to work to find the new factor by the simple method of extending the range of natural selection to the ultimate constituents of the germ-plasm itself. He supposed that the drama of the world without is here repeated on a minute scale. The determinants or ultimate constituents of the germ-plasm struggle with each other for nutriment. Some at length succumb and the successful survivors are thus 'selected.' So variations arise within the germ itself, followed of course by corresponding variations in the body that they eventually build up. This, his latest theory, the theory of intra-germinal selection, has practically convinced nobody; though it has been hailed by opponents of Darwinism as sounding the knell of the theory of natural selection[1]. Why, even if we allow the propriety of regarding Weismann's hypothetical determinants as organisms struggling for nutriment—and facts seem to be against it[2]—why, even then, it *must* follow that useful and consentient variations will appear just when and where they are wanted, is more than Weismann has seriously attempted to prove; though he confidently asserts that it is so. What is important about his new theory however is the sur-

[1] "With a 'rehabilitation' of natural selection in the real Darwinian meaning and only fair application of the phrase the new theory has nothing whatever to do. It is, much more, a distinct admission of the inadequacy of natural selection to do what has long been claimed for it." Kellogg, *Darwinism to-day*, 1907, p. 199.

[2] "Actual experimentation on the influence of food-supply in development does not bear out the assumption on which the theory of germinal selection rests. Weismann himself gave the larvae of flies...an abnormally small food-supply..., with the only result that the mature individuals were dwarfed; that all their parts were reduced in size, but the actual proportions... were unchanged." Kellogg, *op. cit.* p. 201. But cp. especially Plate, *Die Bedeutung des Darwinischen Selectionsprincipes*, 2te Auf. 1903, pp. 164–70.

render both of the ancestral continuity and also of the somatic discontinuity of the germ-plasm, a surrender that, as Delage and many others have urged, undermines his whole position. In short, while the ground on which was based his direct and positive proof of the impossibility of the inheritance of acquired characters is abandoned, his full and definite admission of the need for some equivalent of that Lamarckian factor remains. We may then now resume our consideration of what I have called the psychological or mnemic theory of heredity. Obviously we must begin from the biological side, for we have no *direct* experience in the matter. Moreover it is not *our* memory, but a so-called organic memory with which we are concerned.

Now if it is once admitted that the body influences the germ-plasm in one way—i.e., by way of nutrition—the possibility of its influence in other ways can hardly be denied. Even the influence in the one way may mean a great deal more than Weismann surmised, may involve not merely quantitative differences but qualitative differences as well. Truly, as Mephistopheles said: "*Blut ist ein ganz besondrer Saft.*" For example, through the blood there circulate certain secretions, called hormones, destined—as our Regius Professor of Medicine has said—"for the fulfilment of physiological equilibrium." "Thus," as he goes on to say, "the reciprocity of the various organs, maintained throughout the divisions of physiological labour, is not merely a mechanical stability, it is also a mutual equilibration in functions incessantly at work on chemical levels, and on those levels of still higher complexity which seem to rise as far beyond chemistry as chemistry beyond physics[1].

[1] Sir T. Clifford Allbutt, *Ency. Brit.*, vol. xviii, art. Medicine, pp. 57 f.

But now the most striking instance of the equilibration of its functions that an organism displays is that
which brings about the adjustment of internal relations
to external relations. In this adjustment indeed we
may say, as I have already urged, that life essentially
consists. But this adjustment in the higher organisms,
where the characteristics of life are most distinct, is
directed and sustained by a nervous system. Now to
this system belongs in a pre-eminent degree that retentiveness and modifiability which life and experience
everywhere imply—characters which we figuratively
express by reference to plasticity, as in such terms as
protoplasm, idioplasm, germ-plasm and the like. Plasticity, in a word, though most pronounced in the higher
organisms, where the physiological division of labour
has developed a distinct nervous system, is present in
all organisms: all alike, though in divers degrees, live
and learn. But now a multicellular organism, it is
generally allowed, originated in, and still consists of,
a colony of unicellular organisms—a colony that has
become more of a commonwealth the further its functional division of labour has advanced. It is important
then to insist on two points. First, every living cell,
whether living in isolation or as a member of a complex
organism, must be credited with that 'organic memory'
which all life implies. Next, we can set no limit to the
consentient interaction between such cells when they
have become 'members one of another.' "Even in
normal circumstances"—to quote Sir Clifford Allbutt
once more—"their play and counterplay, attractive
and repellent, must be manifold almost beyond conception."

Now the reactions of the body-plasm in the higher
organisms are, as said, guided mainly by the nervous
system; and there, we know, facility and familiarity become automatic, more or less 'unconscious' through

repetition. But in the germ-plasm the *rôle* of regu-
lating ontogeny, it is allowed, belongs mainly, if not
solely, to the cell-nuclei or chromatin, Weismann's
'germinal substance.' "May we not therefore consider
it probable that the nucleus plays in the cell the part
of a central nervous sytem?" was the question raised
by Dr Francis Darwin in his masterly Presidential
Address to the British Association in 1908. I am aware
of no smallest detail in which the analogy between the
two fails, and—in my opinion at all events—Dr Darwin
was amply justified in contending, as Hering in his
classic paper had done before him, "that ontogeny—
the building up of the embryo—is actually and literally
a habit."

Further, as Dr Darwin goes on to remark, this so-
called mnemic theory is "strongest precisely where
Weismann's views are weakest—namely in giving a
coherent theory of the rhythm of development." The
prodigious complication of Weismann's germ-plasm
with its idants, ids, determinants and biophores—a vast
army without a general—only spells confusion, when
we try to picture it in motion, a plight like that of the
builders of Babel after the confusion of tongues. According to the mnemic theory, on the other hand, the
germ-cell is a definite unity, the counterpart of the
structural alterations wrought by habit in the parental
organisms with which it has been in sympathetic *rapport* all along. It is potentially what Leibniz would
have called an *automate spirituel ou formel*, the latent
entelechy of a future organism. We may compare it
to a company of actors awaiting behind the scenes the
call to begin their play. Each one knows his part by
heart and also knows his cue. The routine or orderly
rhythm of the performance is thus ensured and the
play, though continually condensed at one end and
extended at the other, has been so often repeated as to

be acted without hitch or hesitation save perhaps in the cases of its latest amendments.

And now two or three last remarks by way of summary and conclusion.

No doubt when we try to ascertain the details of this process the difficulties in our way are, as Dr Francis Darwin candidly allows, 'of a terrifying magnitude.' But in all exploration the first thing is to secure, if possible, a general survey, a bird's eye view of the whole. If we are to see the wood, we cannot be among the trees. Now it is entirely with this preliminary problem that we have been concerned; and as befits such an inquiry we have tried—not to scrutinize the details of life—but to look at it as a real, concrete whole. Such a whole implies continuity: absolute breaks are impossible. Leibniz's maxim, *Natura non facit saltus*, is ours too. We find then no ground for separating organic life from psychical life: for us all life is experience. We cannot therefore assume that experience has no part in the building up of the organism, and only begins when a viable organism is already there. For us, ontogeny and heredity are aspects of a single process—a process that only experience will explain.

Again, the principle of continuity forbids us to assume that this process, by which an organism is built up, abruptly changes when we pass from unicellular organisms to multicellular. The way of trial and error and eventual success—function determining structure —followed in the earlier stages of the progress of life— in phylogeny, as it is technically termed—has equally been the way of its progress ever since. Every organism has proceeded from an organism; yet among unicellular organisms though there has been progress there has been no genealogy. Among multicellular organisms we find both: while the offspring is still unicellular at

the start, the parents from which it sprang are unicellular no more. The greater this difference in complexity between the offspring and its parents, the longer
the way its common ancestors will have traversed
phylogenetically or historically, and the longer too the
way that it will have to traverse ontogenetically or
automatically, before attaining to the parental level
and beginning a personal history of its own.

This pre-natal, so to say, prehistoric life, is called a
heritage. And why? Because, looking broadly at the
whole record of multicellular genealogies, there appears
to be everywhere more or less correspondence and
nowhere a positive deviation between the two itine-
raries—let us say—the historical and the automatic,
the route of the original struggle and the routine of its
recapitulation after many repetitions. But the more
repetitions the more fixity. In short, what habit is for
individual life that is heredity for racial life.

But the one lags enormously behind the other: the
repetitions that will suffice to make a habit automatic
for a lifetime are very far from sufficing to ensure
heredity for future generations. And the more advanced the race, the farther heredity lags behind acquisition. At the unicellular stage, they are on a par,
in other words there is as yet neither distinction nor
interval between body and germ. At the multicellular
stage there is both, and so, as the scale of life rises
farther, the greater becomes the disparity between the
still unicellular germ and the mature organism of ever
increasing complexity; the greater therefore is the
number of intermediaries through whose hands—so to
say—the acquisitions of the one have to pass before
they can be imparted to the other. And not only will
these engrams—as they are called—be fainter on this
account, and so require more repetitions to give them
any permanence; but also for the same reason they

will lose in definiteness and detail. Language, for example, will be inherited not as speech but as mere tongueiness and babble; art not as technical skill but as mere handiness or pure mischief; and so on. But if there is evidence of such inheritance of forms of behaviour impossible of acquisition at the unicellular stage, can we say that the continuity between body-plasm and germ-plasm ceased then? Can we at all understand such facts without recognizing this continuity still?

But what exactly is this continuity between body and germ, and how are new acquisitions passed on? The continuity is what it always was, the continuity of membership in a commonwealth, where the whole is for the parts and the parts for the whole[1]; where all are more or less *en rapport*. The key to all this is to be found, I believe, in social intercourse, not in physical transmission. Unhappily however—as it seems to me —most of those who uphold the mnemic theory of heredity seem to hanker unduly after a physical explanation of the *modus operandi*. Hering and Haeckel talked of peculiar vibrations: if they were writing to-day they would probably refer to wireless telegraphy, as Prof. Dendy has recently done[2]. But it is meaningless to talk of memory unless we are prepared to refer it to a subject that remembers. Records or memoranda alone are not memory, for they presuppose it. *They* may consist of physical traces; but memory, even when called 'unconscious,' suggests mind; for, as we have

[1] A Protozoan, we must remember, though unicellular, is far from simple, and an absolutely simple form of life is beyond our ken.

[2] *Outlines of Evolutional Psychology*, 1912. Signor E. Rignano, founder of the international review *Scientia*, in particular has developed a very elaborate theory of 'organic memory' to explain the inheritance of acquired characters, *Sur la transmissibilité des caractères acquis*, Paris, 1906.

seen, the automatic character implied by this term 'unconscious' presupposes foregone experience. But it is possible that a subject may impart his knowledge or dexterity to another without dragging his pupil through all the maze of blundering which his own acquisition cost. The mnemic theory then, if it is to be worth anything, seems to me clearly to require not merely physical records or 'engrams' but living experience or tradition. The mnemic theory will work for those who can accept a monadistic or pampsychist interpretation of the beings that make up the world, who believe with Spinoza and Leibniz that "all individual things are animated albeit in divers degrees." But quite apart from difficulties of detail, I do not see how in principle it will work otherwise.

IX

"IN THE BEGINNING..."

THE topic to which I would invite your attention is that of the method of philosophy. It is, I think, still an unsettled question what this method should be; though the question is one which was raised at the outset of what we call modern philosophy—and notably by Locke and by Kant. It is a question, too, which—till it is threshed out—seems seriously to bar the way to further progress: I doubt indeed if there is any "prolegomenon to every future metaphysic" which more urgently requires continuous discussion. The most I can hope to achieve now is, however, merely to make the issue as clear as I can; and I shall be amply rewarded if I should succeed in inducing any of you to follow it up further.

"Begin at the beginning" is a sound but common-place maxim; and if it should be respected anywhere, it should—many think—be respected by philosophers. They, it has been said, are bound to seek truth without making assumptions. In practical undertakings there is often no alternative: we must begin at the beginning. To build a house we must first lay the foundations; and we must first catch our hare before we can cook it. In philosophy, however, this practical maxim is one—as it seems to me—that we can never observe; and the failure of all the many attempts to conform to it that have hitherto been made is strong presumptive evidence against all methods in philosophy that purport to be primarily direct and constructive.

We must now try to be clear about our leading terms. When we say, begin at the beginning, the imperative refers to time, but the substantive does not necessarily do so, and, in fact, in the main does not. When we say: you must begin building by laying the foundations, the significance of these for the superstructure is not exhausted by their place in the temporal order of the process. When this is finished and the building stands complete, what we may call the logical priority of the foundations still remains. It is in this sense that—by a sort of metonymy—we come to talk of principles— *prima capienda*—or ἀρχαί as what epistemologically come first, and answer to what ontologically are their grounds, primary beings or *entia*, as Aristotle called them. But now in building a house, though we begin by laying *its* foundations, we do not provide the earth or ground on which these have to be laid, yet that is the first essential; but then it is already there. In keeping with this procedure in the practical arts, Aristotle found an analogous procedure in the theoretical sciences. These all rest on principles, take for granted grounds, which they do not examine; though some investigate further than others, mathematics further than physics, for example[1]. Aristotle, then, conceived the theoretical sciences as a sort of hierarchy, and thought it obvious that there must be a highest science, and this he called 'first philosophy.' But though first in the order of rank, it was as the highest the furthest removed from us.

   This is a point on which it will be well to enlarge. Speaking generally, *the problem that the universe sets us is an inverse problem*. George III's bewilderment as to how the apple got into the dumpling or the puzzle of bygone days as to which was first, the hen or the egg, are trivial instances of an inverse problem. George III had presumably never seen a dumpling made; and all that our forbears could say was that all the hens they knew of had been hatched from eggs and all the eggs they

[1] Cp. *Metaphysics*, IV, i–iii, VI, i.

knew of had been laid by hens. In some such quandary Goethe represents Faust on returning to his study after his Easter Day saunter with his colleague, Wagner. Wagner had lamented that life was not half long enough to reach the beginnings of things, and so Faust bethought himself of revelation. Taking up the New Testament, he sat down to render into his 'beloved German' the opening sentence of the fourth gospel: ἐν ἀρχῇ ἦν ὁ λόγος. *Im Anfang war das Wort* he found too literal: the meaning must be *Im Anfang war der Sinn.* Yet could it be merely *Sinn,* nothing but thought that moves in all things? Surely it should be *Im Anfang war die Kraft.* Still something warns him that he cannot stop at that. Then the inspiration comes and he boldly writes *Im Anfang war die That.* But what deed and whose deed; further, was there one doer or many?

Aristotle, as I have said, recognized at the outset that his problem was an inverse one, though unhappily before very long he forgot the fact. At any rate he did clearly recognize that, as he put it, the *ordo ad nos* is the inverse of the *ordo ad universum.* Goethe, too, recognized this inverse character of the philosopher's problem, and, moreover, suggested the only way towards its solution that seemed open:

> Willst du ins Unendliche schreiten
> Geh' nur im Endlichen nach allen Seiten.

And this is the way which, in fact, mankind has unconsciously followed. Partial advance from the more known, the *notiora nobis,* has secured partial knowledge of the less known, the *notiora natura.* From whatever side the unknown has been effectively explored, this, as I have said, has always been the method followed. A method implies definite direction, discursiveness, and implies, too, a definite starting-point, viz., from where we are, i.e., *in mediis rebus.* By induction from particulars we may advance to deduction; but such advance, though it may yield an exact science—as in mathematics—can never carry us beyond the restricted 'universe of discourse' to which such particulars belong. *A propos* of this, two or three remarks—though they must needs be more or less disjointed—may help us on. First, every special science, we say, represents a restricted universe of discourse. A satisfactory classification of these sciences, what Dr Bosanquet has happily called a morphology of them, is still a desideratum. But for our present purpose a single division will suffice, that into abstract and concrete. In the abstract sciences—logic, mathematics, and what is called rational dynamics, if it be conceded that this is truly an abstract science—we have universal propositions; in the special concrete sciences we never have. Their 'laws' are but generalizations and belong entirely to the region of what Hume called probability as distinct from exact knowledge. The knowledges furnished by the exact sciences are beyond cavil, true always and of all conceivable worlds, dependent on no other knowledges and implicated in all our concrete knowledge. So far as they go, we regard them as ideal knowledges, inasmuch as no other knowledges come up to their standard. For all that, they are not the ideal of knowledge, of that knowledge embracing the whole of things which is what philosophy seeks. They provide us, we are told, with our so-called 'laws of thought,' with all our theoretical axioms and 'archetypal' ideas: we *apply* them to the real world, but they do not belong there. The existence or non-existence of that is no affair of theirs.

And yet, we may next remark, they alone carry us on one side to *das an allen Seiten Unendliche* which Goethe talked of. We owe to them our precisest instances of the infinite, the absolute, the perfect, the simple. All the concrete sciences together, on the other hand, fall short of this. Moreover, at a time when these sciences were practically non-existent, the exact sciences were comparatively advanced. No wonder, then, that philosophy should have been started on a false track. It was, in fact, so started when Plato assumed that the exact sciences do furnish the ideal of knowledge, and therefore prescribe its method. From ideas as archetypes to things as but their ectypes or imperfect copies, seemed to be clearly the only way; and to be not only direct but unerring. Philosophy then for Plato began at the beginning. To be sure Aristotle protested, but in large measure he stultified his protest by forgetting it, as I have said, instead of holding to his first conviction. And so philosophy wandered in the wilderness for a couple of thousand years. How little the situation was changed is shewn by the attempt of Descartes and more especially of Spinoza to develope metaphysics *more geometrico*. The first effective protests were made by Bacon, Locke, and Hume; though Kant it was who formulated them independently with more completeness and more precision. He insisted on the strictly formal character of what is ordinarily called logic, and pointed out the radical difference between mathematics and philosophy; the difference being that mathematics can start from intuition and construct its concepts, whereas philosophy can do neither.

This is a point important enough to deserve special remark. Kant was fully alive to this difference quite early in his career. In an essay written for a Berlin Academy prize, *Concerning the Intelligibility of the Principles of Natural Theology and Morals*[1], he first of all examines how mathematics and philosophy respectively

[1] The prize was awarded to Kant's friend, Moses Mendelssohn, and his own essay, adjudged *proxime accessit*, was anonymously published as an appendix to Mendelssohn's in 1764. *Werke*, Hartenstein's ed., II, 281 ff.

obtain their definitions; for definitions are everywhere indispensable to permanent advance. Till these are laid down we are left with nothing better than temporary and tentative exploration by trial and error. Here, however, the mathematician is so far master of the situation that we may call his work almost creative; for he obtains his definitions directly in the very act of synthesizing the concepts they define. The philosopher, on the other hand, to obtain his definitions, has, as best he can, to analyse the more or less obscure concepts that are already there, thrust upon him by experience. As a matter of fact, in numberless cases, he finds his problem insoluble, or, like the old physicists, who resolved all matter into four or five elements, he goes off content with an analysis that turns out to be incomplete. The mathematician can begin at the beginning because he can define all the way through as he goes: pure intuition enables him at once to construct his most elementary concepts and to formulate axioms concerning them. But for the philosopher the elementary concepts that are first by nature are the last to be reached by his analytic method. When, then, he attempts by imitating the mathematician to begin at the beginning, he forgets that what is here first in the order of knowledge is not the easiest but the hardest to conceive, consists of *die allerabgezogenste Begriffe*, the most abstract concepts of all. Both psychology and the history of thought bear Kant out completely in maintaining that such concepts are therefore just those which are not reached historically till the last[1]. Accordingly he concludes, "that the right course for the philosopher is to start from what one certainly knows, *even though it be but little!*"[2] Albeit we may make attempts, setting out from such (avowedly) imperfect

[1] Cp. *Psychological Principles*, pp. 293, 231 ff.; Hegel, 'Phænomenology of Mind.'   [2] *Op. cit.*, p. 294.

knowledge, hoping that perchance we may come upon the trail of something more certain. But in any case we must not mix up the two[1].

In short, as everywhere in dealing with reality, so in philosophy, we proceed in Baconian fashion '*per scalam ascensoriam*,' through *axiomata media* towards the highest truth. But, if 'the sides,' as Goethe called them, are infinite, and if the steps along each are infinite too, obviously we can never accomplish our task. Aristotle bethought himself of this and maintained that the sides are finite, and that the steps must be finite too, or there would be no ἀρχή at all. I must content myself with saying that, so far as I know, his reasoning has failed to satisfy his commentators either of ancient or modern times[2]. As for Kant, he did not shrink from the consequences. We not only cannot begin at the beginning, the ultimate ground or ἀρχή of things, but theoretically we can never reach it. A *science* of metaphysics, that is a science transcending all science, is for us an impossibility. We cannot hope by intellectually searching to find out God[3]. But though philosophy must not try to imitate mathematics by beginning with exact definitions, it may, Kant maintained, make use of *provisional* definitions, as the concrete sciences do which it seeks to co-ordinate and systematize. This, in fact, is all that in spite of itself metaphysics has ever done: hence it comes that, unlike the formal sciences, philosophy, as he says, "swarms with faulty definitions, especially such as really contain some elements towards a definition though they are not complete."[4] So far, however, as these "relate to an object which we can

[1] Cp. Aristotle, *Metaphysics*, vii, iii *fin.*
[2] Cp. *Metaphysics*, bk i, ch. ii, *init. Post. anal.* ii, ch. xxv.
[3] *Critique*, on 'The Ideal of the Pure Reason,' § vii, A, pp. 635 ff., B, pp. 662 f.
[4] *Critique*, A, pp. 730 f.; B, pp. 758 f.

never reach in any experience," they are to be called speculative not scientific. Speculation, in fact, has been described as experimenting with ideas[1].

The proper function of speculation, according to Kant, is not to dogmatize beyond all we know, but—having criticized what knowledge we have—to organize in conformity with regulative ideas the further knowledge we may obtain. This is the main burden of his first *Critique*. Here, however, he proved to be anything but the ruthless iconoclast of dogmatic rationalism that he was at first supposed to be. On the contrary, his speculative ideas or 'ideas of reason,' as he himself called them, ushered in a new phase of philosophy which far outstripped in boldness and brilliancy the old dogmatic ventures of Descartes and Spinoza. Whereas the latter had taken mathematics as their paradigm, the new outburst sprang from logic; not, however, from the old Aristotelian logic that had reduced rationalism to the barren formalism of the Leibniz-Wolffians, but from the new 'transcendental logic,' which Kant himself had propounded[2]. This was not analytic but synthetic, and would effect, Kant claimed, a revolution in philosophy comparable with that effected in astronomy by Copernicus.

But—as often happens in revolutions—the immediate result was anything but what Kant expected; and it filled him with dismay, though he only lived to become acquainted with the first stage of it. The circumstances

---

[1] Cp. F. Harms, *Geschichte der Logik*, 1881, p. 24. Mr Bradley, in a specially interesting chapter (*Truth and Reality*, 1914) on 'Some Aspects of Truth,' describes his own speculation as experimenting. Here, however, Dr Bosanquet apparently does not follow him. Cp. his Presidential Address to this Society, *Proceedings*, 1914–15.

[2] On Kant's 'transcendental logic' as the fountain-head whence the 'metaphysical knowledge' of Fichte, Schelling, and Hegel sprang, cp. F. Harms, *op. cit.*, pp. 216 ff.

are one of the curiosities of literature, but I must resist the temptation to dwell on these at any length here. Suffice it to say that the young and struggling Fichte introduced himself to Kant in a gushing letter covering a manuscript entitled *Critique of Revelation*. This new critique claimed merely to fill a *lacuna* in Kant's own system; and Kant at first approved so far as to arrange for its publication; and when it appeared—as it chanced anonymously—it was actually hailed as a long expected work by Kant himself. I mention this as evidence of a certain continuity, such as that connecting an adventitious bud and its parent stem. It was as the bud developed that its divergencies—its sporting character —became alarming. Kant, compelled to disown Fichte, whom he called 'a clumsy friend,' described the *Wissenschaftslehre* as "like a sort of ghost; when you thought you had caught it, lo! there was nothing there but yourself, or rather just your hand vainly clutching." It was, in short, a case of hunting the snark and finding it a boojum. Such was all that, so far as he could see, Fichte's Absolute Ego and its *kleiner Anstoss* came to. Doubtless he would have said the same of Schelling's supplementation of Fichte's Absolute and of Hegel's development of Schelling's Absolute.

But the innovators themselves thought otherwise. In the first volume of his *Encyclopædia*, commonly spoken of as the *Smaller Logic*, published in 1817, nearly fourteen years after Kant's death, Hegel presumed to say: "People in the present day have got over Kant and his philosophy; everybody wants to get further." About fourteen years later Hegel died himself, and the collapse of the new movement at once began. A spell of rampant materialism, inaugurated in good part by Hegelians of the so-called 'left,' set in. A little over thirty years later still, a period of some sixty years after Kant's death—that of Hegel falling about half way—Otto

Liebmann, reviewing the collapse of each of the new idealisms in turn, raised the cry: *Also muss auf Kant zurückgegangen werden*[1]. (We must then, go back to Kant.) So neo-Kantianism began: Kant was revived, but Hegel slumbered on. Yet that is not altogether true; for have we not in England, at any rate, our neo-Hegelians too, and among them, in the opinion of most of us, the most distinguished of our contemporary philosophers? And so it comes that with us one still hears more about Hegel than about Kant.

From first to last in this whole movement, 'the Absolute' is the name for the dominant or first principle; this is the beginning, and with this the movement professes to begin. I do not propose to discuss the very different forms this Absolute assumed in the earlier systems—the Absolute Ego, the Absolute Identity of such polar opposites as Ego and non-Ego, the Absolute Idea. But the prior question, what in general is meant by the term itself—the Absolute—it may be worth while to raise. In what sense, can an Ego or an Idea, or anything else be called the Absolute? Now we are familiar in the works of Plato and Aristotle with such phrases as 'the true,' 'the beautiful,' 'the good'; and it seems to be on the analogy of these that modern philosophers talk of the Absolute. This terminology is peculiar, and perhaps it ought to strike us more than it does[2]. We can readily find particulars to which the adjectives true, beautiful, and good apply, and can more or less intelligently use the abstracts, truth,

---

[1] *Kant und die Epigonen*, 1865.

[2] Ficino in his celebrated translation of Plato published in 1482, *à propos* of τὸ καλόν, wrote, "Unumquodque e singulis pulchris, *pulchrum hoc* Plato vocat; formam in omnibus, *pulchritudinem*: speciem et ideam supra omnia, *pulchrum ipsum* [τὸ αὐτὸ καλόν]. Primum sensus attingit opinioque. Secundum ratio cogitat. Tertium mens intuetur." Quoted by Grote, *Plato*, ii, p. 210 n.

beauty, and goodness formed from those adjectives.
But when we come to the Absolute the case is by no
means so simple.

Absolute accordingly is often thus defined: it is unconditional or non-relative. But do we know of anything of which this can truly be said? At least, so we
are told, the relative or conditional *implies* the absolute
or unconditional. But is this so? Would it not be
more correct to say that what relative implies is some
correlative[1]—as father implies child or master implies
servant; and that what conditioned implies is its conditions—as effect implies a cause and means imply an
end? Further the term non-relative, like all so-called
'infinite terms,' unless the universe of discourse in
which they are applied is restricted, becomes meaningless. It is infinite in the old sense of ἄπειρον or indeterminate. The most we can say of the Absolute regarded
from this logical standpoint is that it is ambiguous. If
all things, *distributively* regarded, are correlative, then
the Absolute becomes nothing: hence perhaps Hegel's
favourite saying, "God without the world is not God."
If all things are *collectively* regarded, they as the whole
are all there is. The whole may be then called the
Absolute, for it is related to nothing. Hence perhaps
it is—such is the tendency of our intellect to cling to
relations—that we find the idea of the Absolute so
frequently associated with the idea of nothing; and
that not only by the Mystics and by Schelling, but even
by Hegel and the neo-Hegelians. The All, or as we
say the Universe, can, however, hardly be called an
ideal, save perhaps as the knowledge of it is an ideal,
since we can never attain to it. This, of course, was
the burden of Kant's cosmological antinomies.

[1] "The word absolute is put upon much too hard duty in
metaphysics not to be willingly spared where its services can be
dispensed with." J. S. Mill, *Logic*, i, ii, § 7.

But after all we reach an ideal if we go back to the meaning of absolute when it is applied to individuals. As ordinarily used, however, the word in this sense is always really comparative. The autocrat, as compared with the monarch limited by a constitution, is absolute; and similarly the decisions of a supreme court as compared with those of a court from which there can be an appeal. Still even the greatest autocrats live in 'fear of change' and have often been overthrown; and the highest judicial functions are liable to *ex post facto* legislation. But we can, or think we can, imagine an ideal individual free from all limitation. In this way, in fact, we attain our idea of God, which the very presence everywhere of limitation and dependence suggests—hence the argument *a contingentia mundi*[1]. Now between these two ideas of the Absolute, the Universe and God, there has been and still is more or less oscillation, even in philosophy, to say nothing of religion. We have theism, pantheism, often 'a polite atheism,' and panentheism[2]. Of course, when the two ideas of the Absolute are combined one must be subordinated, for there cannot really be two Absolutes. The alternatives are (1) Krause's panentheism, in some form the All in God, and (2) God in the All—for which I know of no name, unless we use *henism* in this sense. This seems to be the doctrine of our neo-Hegelians, with whom we are now chiefly concerned.

Let us see then what we can say about the Universe

---

[1] So Schleiermacher traced religion to *ein schlechthinniges Abhängigkeitsgefühl*—a feeling of absolute dependence.

[2] As to the last, see in J. E. Erdmann's *Geschichte der neueren Philosophie*, 1853, Bd. III, ii, 637–86, the account of an *allendliche Lösungsversuch*, by K. C. F. Krause, for a short time a junior colleague of Hegel. In consequence largely of the forbidding terminology which Krause invented, the high place which Erdmann assigns to him has only recently been at all generally recognized. Verily, a warning to us all!

so understood. First, we can deny that it had an origin in time and space; for they—however we explain them —must fall within it; since apart from it there is nothing. Secondly, we may deny that it had a cause and so is an effect; for again, all conditions must fall within it; since beside it there is nothing. To call it a first cause or *Causa sui* seems meaningless; for it only repeats the sort of mistake made by Locke's "poor Indian philosopher, who imagined that the earth [as well as everything in it] also wanted something to bear it up."[1] To apply to it the scholastic term 'aseity' is simply to say that it absolutely is. Obviously then we cannot call it phenomenal, for all appearance presupposes reality. Nor, thirdly, can we equate it with the entire sum of things as a plurality, regard it, that is to say, as merely what Wm James called a *multiverse*. It is the whole and therefore a unity. Regarding this one whole or Absolute, is there anything more which we are bound to say?

Indeed there is, we are told. It must be a self-consistent whole, for were it—even in its smallest part—contradictory, there would be no eliminating the contradiction. With one such 'little rift' within it, the universe could not be real. True as this is, it hardly seemed to need saying, since it is also trite. But have you realized all that it means, we may be asked? Apparently not; for, since the Absolute excludes contradiction, that implies, it is said, that it excludes discord. In other words the absence of logical opposition is identified with the absence of real opposition, Leibniz and Kant notwithstanding[2]. Not merely so: the

[1] *Essay*, II, xiii, § 19.
[2] I refer, of course, to the distinction drawn by Leibniz between our knowledge concerning possible existence and our ignorance concerning compossible existence (*De Veritatibus primis*, Erdmann's ed., p. 99); and especially to Kant's classic paper, *Versuch den Begriff der negativen Grössen in der Weltweisheit einzuführen* (*Werke*, Hartenstein's ed., II, pp. 71 ff.).

absence of discord—by no means the only form of real opposition—is forthwith equated with perfection; and finally the Absolute is declared to be 'Experience, individual and perfect.' These seem giant strides to accomplish by a principle 'so absurdly simple' to quote Mr Bradley—as "the law of contradiction which says no more than that sheer incompatibles must not be conjoined."[1]

Anyhow we may allow that the Absolute does not contradict itself, and with this negation as an absolute criterion the epistemological problem, the criticism of our knowledges is to begin. Now, in the tentative process of acquiring these, we are often pulled up by some logical opposition between two alternative possibilities. One or other must be false—so much the law of contradiction declares—but which? We may have to wait for long before we find some crucial instance that decides. Very different is the purely logical treatment of *propositions*. A proposition, without going beyond it, may by the mere explication of its content be shewn to contradict itself, and similarly two propositions to contradict each other. But no *thing*, I think we may confidently say, ever really contradicts itself, nor does one thing ever really contradict another. It is only on the strength of this conviction that we maintain that the universe is at least not self-contradictory. We may call this fact the ontological ground of the so-called 'law of contradiction,' and it was clearly announced in this form by Aristotle[2].

Yet the thinkers I have in view seem flatly to deny all this. According to them, Reality, i.e., the Absolute, being the one complete whole, must be the ultimate subject of every item of what we take for knowledge. But as they stand, and ignoring this implication, all

---

[1] *Principles of Logic*, 1883, p. 141.
[2] Cp. the author's article in *Mind*, October, 1919.

our knowledges are declared to be more or less self-contradictory—most so when the subject is merely designated as 'this,' least so when the subject is defined as Spirit or, if you will, as God. Instead of saying S is P, we ought, we are told, to say the Absolute as or in S is P^1. P is not strictly a predicate of S, for S itself is ultimately but a part, and, so far, but an adjective of the Absolute. Disregarding for the present this questionable identification of part and predicate, we may ask why it is contradictory to say S is P and yet not equally contradictory to say the Absolute is P. The logical definition of S or subject is that which cannot be a predicate but can only be predicated of: and taken strictly in this sense the Absolute alone is the ultimate subject, for whatever is, only is as a predicate of it. Suppose, taking a lump of sugar, I say this substance is white, is soluble, is sweet; I find, however, that it is only white in certain lights, only soluble in some liquids, only sweet to some tastes. What it would prove to be if it could be taken as an *ens per se subsistens* is more than any of us know. Some there are who like Hume maintain that it would be nothing, that it is but a bundle of relations; forgetting that relations imply fundamenta and that interactions imply agents. Others like J. S. Mill think it suffices to fall back on the notion of 'permanent possibility.' But obviously the 'bundles' of the one and the 'possibilities' of the other imply some actuality, and so our difficulties with the lump of sugar remain. We cannot deny that there is something there; for otherwise, treating all other things in the same fashion, there could be nothing anywhere. On the other hand, if I find that anything that I take up is what it seems to be *in itself*, solely in virtue of its relations to *other things*; and if all my attempts to determine

---

[1] Cp. Bosanquet, *Proceedings of the Aristotelian Society*, 1917–18, p. 484.

its own nature only lead me beyond it in a search that I can never complete; am I not driven to conclude that it is but a part, an element, or a member of a continuous whole, that is to say, of the Absolute?[1]

Let me say in parenthesis that I am not now objecting to this way of looking at things in itself, but only to the use that is made of it to resolve all finite things, along with their relations and interactions, into a tissue of contradictions; for it is just this tissue of finite things and their mutual appearances that constitute our real world. "Our procedure," it is allowed[2], "naturally makes its start from (these) common facts of our lives." Nevertheless, in almost the same breath we are told that "We should begin from above." This is the method I am venturing to question; and surely what we naturally do and have always done is 'a procedure' that should either be directly refuted at the outset or at any rate discredited by one that supersedes it by better results. Let us then briefly examine some of these results.

But first a word or two concerning the resolution of partition into predication which is offered, at one time as an epistemological ground, at another as an ontological consequence, of the doctrine of absolutism. I ventured just now to speak of such identification as 'questionable': to have said more then might have

---

[1] A long paragraph in Locke's *Essay* (IV, vi, § 11) is pertinently cited by Bosanquet (*Arist. Soc. Proc.* 1917–18, p. 483) in support of the affirmative. I may quote a sentence or two from the paragraph referred to: "This is certain: things, however absolute and entire they seem in themselves, are but retainers to other parts of nature for that which they are most taken notice of by us. Their observable qualities, actions, and powers are owing to something without them"—a something which he has previously described as "utterly beyond our view" and "impossible for us to determine." Then, of course, there is Tennyson's familiar apostrophe to the "flower in the crannied wall."

[2] Bosanquet, *Principle of Individuality and Value*, p. 383.

savoured of dogmatism. Now, however, I will go so far as to say that in my opinion the criticisms advanced from many sides against this logical innovation have completely disposed of it[1]. That the parts of any concrete whole are constitutive of its reality, not terms in its definition, is a truth recognized throughout the history of logic from Aristotle, who expressly rejected 'physical definition,' to Aldrich[2], and onwards to our own day[3]. The venerable doctrine of the five predicables is proof enough of this. A part as such is never predicated, though the possession of it may be. We may describe men as two-legged, dogs as four-legged, spiders as eight-legged, and so on; but we never say a man is *inter alia* two legs, or a dog four legs. Nor again, so far as I know, has this reality of a whole ever been maintained while at the same time the reality of its parts was denied. To be sure, the part may be called an appearance: it cannot be called a mere appearance. *Wie viel Schein so viel Hindeutung aufs Sein* was one of Herbart's trenchant phrases embodying the truth fully recognized by Kant, viz., that phenomenal reality is never mere illusion. If, however, the parts are to be called phenomenal, their whole must be called so too. To deny this is to ignore the difference between a partial whole which limits and is limited by other partial wholes, on the one hand, and the absolute whole which includes them all, on the other. Lastly, so far as I know, no logician has ever maintained that whatever is predicable of the part is predicable *simpliciter* of the whole, maintained, for example, that a cat with white paws must itself be white. *Secundum quid,*

---

[1] I refer especially to the criticisms of Prof. Stout, to be found in the *Proceedings of the Aristotelian Society*, 1917–18, pp. 530 ff.; as also to those of Prof. Pringle-Pattison and of Prof. A. E. Taylor.

[2] Whose laxity is censured by Mansel (*Rudimenta*, p. 41).

[3] Cp., e.g., Drobisch, *Neue Darstellung d. Logik*, §§ 17, 127.

viz., as to its paws, the cat may be said to be white. But what is this beyond the admission that perhaps, after all, the cat, which we may never have seen, is not white, though its paws are. We cannot, then, straightway apply to the Absolute as such what we can truly predicate of its parts as such.

Granted, it is said, not as such; for, though in the Absolute *all that is* is there, yet it is there so transformed and merged that its partial nature has vanished. In fact, much that we examine as appearance, in the hope of escaping its self-contradictions, is found on the way to the Absolute to be landed in the Castle of Despair, and there commits suicide. There are some seven or eight of such suicides on record. Well! this is one of the results of beginning from above, to which I would now invite your attention.

It is allowed that the Absolute *is* its appearances, for there is nothing it is not. But it is not its appearances *as such*, for they are a plurality. It is then its appearances, as utterly fused and transformed, i.e., as *Reality*. This is the new dialectic movement. Meanwhile the untransformed, unmediated discrepant appearances remain to perplex *us*—and to perplex us incomparably more, I will venture to add, if this is indeed the truth about them. Is the Absolute 'making a sport of us'? we ask. That can hardly be, since these appearances are said to be its revelation. Yet again we ask, But how is that possible since the two sides—if there are indeed two sides—are thus utterly different? Perhaps the way out of this difficulty is to treat the question not as ontological but as merely epistemological, not as concerning the being of what we simply 'feel' and do not differentiate, but as concerning what William James would have called the face-value of such differentiations, what for us they are known as. And, in fact, stress is laid on this 'aspect.' Comparing the knowledge and conduct of the grown man with that of the child he once was, we realize that many transformations and blendings have taken place. And a like contrast comes out when we compare the knowledge and conduct of savage races and of races that are civilized[1]. The unification and systematization of particular experiences is the principle underlying all human development, individual and social. Due reflection on this principle, imperfectly realized though it be with us, is yet sufficient, it is said, to remove any difficulty in conceiving what is, so to say, *fait accompli* in the Absolute—or rather 'never accomplished,' for it is always there. Such language ceases to be appropriate when what eternally is and never becomes is in question. Still we might pardon an expression so natural to our standpoint, if that were all. If, that is to say, the reality of the percipients to whom the so-called phenomenal world is 'given' or revealed was respected and retained. But even so, the progress of knowledge with us, though it involves both what Hegel called the *Aufhebung* or reconciliation of contradictions and also an ever-increasing coherence, yet shews no signs of reducing the leading categories of thought and the fundamental concepts of science to a number of mere adjectives.

When, however, those who know are also resolved into appearances destined to share the common lot of utter fusion and transformation, we begin to wonder what it all means[2]. For the principle illustrated from

[1] Cp. *Psychological Principles*, pp. 413, 467.

[2] I must confess it reminds me of the German legend of *Rübezahl*. With a stroke of his wand this gnome, it will be remembered, converted his carrots into companions for the princess he had carried off. They played their part so long as the juices of the carrots kept fresh, and thereafter were returned to the common earth from which they came, to be followed by others presently to be treated in like manner. All that was permanent

experience of this process of transformation and blending in its epistemological 'aspect' is now appealed to to shew that within experience a like process is discernable from the ontological standpoint. Persons are described as 'organizations of content'[1]—content which is essentially impersonal and objective—like 'the objective mind' of Hegel, we may assume. What we ordinarily call personality is but a formal distinction of a precarious and superficial nature, which is ever being transcended and impaired, as this identity of content within formally different selves preponderates more and more. In other words, selves in the truest sense tend ever more and more to coalesce, being, in fact, hindered only by the impotence which their formal distinctness entails. Nothing but our mortal coil with its partial outlets and their 'broken lights' stands in the way. In the absolute transparency all such division disappears.

So again, it is argued that our own experiences of the advance towards a higher unity should suffice to convince us that in the Absolute this unity is already complete. But the first question is: does our experience verily furnish the slightest evidence that with increasing understanding, sympathy, and co-operation, real personalities tend to disappear? It is a lamentable fact that in one respect it does; but that, unfortunately for the argument in question, is one that makes against the goal of our endeavours being reached. I mean, of course, the want of *character*, the absence of almost everything but formal distinctness, that makes so many people but *gens moutonniers*, as Ribot called them. On was just this common ground from which they sprang and with which they were once more blended. But anyhow the princess was not a carrot, and has still to be accounted for: without her the whole drama becomes meaningless. We shall fall in with her again under the *alias* of 'finite centre.'

[1] Bosanquet, *Individuality and Value*, pp. 173 ff., 323 ff.

the other hand, it is precisely the stability and originality of people of character that keep the world from stagnation. Nevertheless it is contended that all alike turn out in ultimate analysis to be but 'connexions of content,' within the Absolute. At all events we may at least maintain that our experience cannot fairly be appealed to in verification of any such contention.

Other results incident to the particular method of beginning from above that I am venturing to discuss follow from the identification of the Absolute with Reality. Reality, as Aristotle long ago remarked, is an ambiguous term. We owe the stress now laid on things to the Cartesian dualism of *res cogitans* and *res extensa*. Leibniz, for good and all, as I believe, started philosophy on a better track by making activity, not substantiality or reality, the fundamental idea. So Faust was right in yielding to the inspiration that led him to say: *Im Anfang war die That. Quod non agit non existit,* said Leibniz too. The main antithesis to 'real' is 'imaginary.' Appearances then are real or *actual*, that is to say they imply something active. But they are not active themselves. Appearances, therefore, cannot appear to other appearances, for so far there would be no activity at either end. But what experience implies is activity at both ends, i.e., reciprocal interaction, *commercium dynamicum*, as Kant called it. When, then, 'finite centres of experience' are mentioned, are we not entitled to understand this phrase as meaning individual agents *en rapport* together? We can give no explanation of this *rapport* which does not covertly imply it; for we come here to the bedrock of experience: it involves two agents, we know that, and that is all we can say in the beginning. But it requires also the Absolute, we shall be told, and that again perhaps now we should hardly think of denying altogether.

What comes first in our knowledge, however, and is the *basis* of all our speculations about the Absolute, is this interaction, this duality of subject knowing and object known. To reduce these finite centres to appearances means, I think, the '*Disappearance of Reality*' for us.

Again, is it not a mistake to speak of these finite centres as 'fragmentary'? To reduce the universe to fragments with 'ragged edges' comes perilously near to bringing back the chaos of older ways of thought. After all, 'Rags and Bones' is not the cry of science: what it finds everywhere, save *per accidens*, is form, unity, function, and organization. As Prof. Pringle-Pattison has said: it finds "that mind is organic to nature and nature organic to mind." From this, I repeat, we actually start. Our knowledge is acquired apart from any speculation about the Absolute, speculation that first becomes urgent as the limitations and difficulties of the pluralism from which we begin make themselves felt. This procedure our neo-Hegelians, as we have seen, are bent on reversing. Beginning with 'the concrete universal' which they denominate by the abstract term Reality, they are led by their logic to deny that the particular reals have any independence at all. They all fall somewhere in the rank of appearances, and have only less or more of such reality as may pertain to these. And so we seem back at the *bouleversement* just now indicated. The reality of our world, the major premiss from which we all start, is refuted by a conclusion which it could not yield—a conclusion based rather on a dialectic which has, I think, been shewn to be not entirely sound. And surely here we have a result which confirms this exposure. As another critic has said: "The unity with which the system concludes tends to abolish the plurality of centres from which it starts." I would rather say: the unity from which the system, as such, starts tends to abolish the plurality of centres which, in fact, it finds. But this leads on to a fresh point.

That experience takes place in finite centres, is admitted as a fact, but a fact that is felt to be inexplicable. Why or how the Absolute *divides* itself into centres and still remains one—this is beyond us. But to be inexplicable is by no means the same thing as to be incompatible. With this presumably we all agree. And if only the so-called 'divisions' of Reality into finite centres of experience were recognized as themselves real—real in a sense quite different from appearance, in short, as real in the sense in which the Absolute itself is real; if in other words, they were regarded as creatures who have their part in carrying on the work of creation, beings endowed with the 'main miracle' of will, to which one of our neo-Hegelians refers, a will that can accept as its own 'the immanent will of the Universe,' to quote a phrase of another—in that case, certainly, we should have less ground to dissent from their doctrine. We might still object to the so-called divisions of the Absolute being described as fragmentary, or as needing to be blended or 'cemented,' although the Absolute itself still remains one. Again, if the Absolute is the *Universe*, i.e., the totality of the interrelated plurality which we otherwise call the cosmos, then to speak of such diversity in unity as inexplicable is to utter either a paradox or a truism: a paradox in view of the admitted complexity of the Universe, a truism in view of the necessary inexplicability of what is all and ultimate. But if the Absolute is *Experience*, then why this should involve finite experiences is indeed inexplicable, especially experiences "in endless error hurled." Why such an Experience, like the νόησις νοήσεως of Aristotle's divine being, should not be absolutely self-sufficing, rendering, anything beside not only superfluous but even 'incompatible,' has been the common crux of absolutism from the first[1].

The two ideas of the Absolute, then, the Universe as the whole, and the Individual whose Experience is Reality, our neo-Hegelians, so far as I can discover, do not clearly distinguish. Both seem merged in a unity that has suggested henism as perhaps the most appropriate term by which to characterize their doctrine. But the two ideas cannot, I believe, be identified: 'predicates' seem more appropriate to the one, 'contents' in its psychological use, more appropriate to the other; and yet these terms are used almost interchangeably. So I think I find in the philosophy before us—what we find elsewhere—viz., more or less oscillation between two distinct ideas of the Absolute. The only solution of the difficulty open to us, as it seems to me, is the solution we naturally reach by beginning where we are, instead of attempting to begin with a 'One above' that is theoretically inaccessible. On this view the Absolute would consist of God and the World in which God is immanent, while yet transcending it. For this view we might, as I have suggested, adopt Krause's term, panentheism, if we concede to the agnostic that we cannot *prove* either by any logic or any science—any more than he can disprove—the existence of such a being as that which we call God. Such a concept is a rational ideal: it may be 'without a flaw,' as Kant maintained; but its use in theoretical philosophy can only be regulative, as he also maintained. Its value for religious faith is another matter; and it has there other grounds. This faith too we may contend is reasonable; but it is not science.

Only a word or two more must suffice by way of summary. Hegel compared Schelling to a painter who

[1] Cp. *The Realm of Ends*, pp. 30 ff.

had but two colours on his palette, suggesting that his work was ineffective through deficiency. I will venture to compare our neo-Hegelians to philosophers who work with two principles, which implies failure through redundancy. It is the sort of defect that Kant abhorred and stigmatized as philosophical rhapsodizing; it lacks continuity and so it lacks coherence. Ferrier too somewhat paradoxically maintained that it is more important that a philosophy should be continuously reasoned than that it should be true. I will content myself with saying that it is more important that philosophy should be systematic than that it should be complete. Complete, in fact, it cannot be. It seems, then, a hopeless attempt—one that, as I have said, is held by general consent to have hitherto always failed—to begin from the standpoint which only a completed philosophy would occupy (i.e., if it were not absorbed!). To advance continuously and to be coherent—that, it seems to me, should be our golden rule. The whole procedure will be tentative—that must always be the case with inverse problems. Crises will occur in the future as they have in the past: they are inevitable incidents in the development of concrete knowledge at any rate. But as the days of elemental cataclysms are over for our planet and merely superficial earthquakes are the worst that we need fear, so with philosophy. It has passed the nebulous stage and become at least an inchoate organism or system. What Poincaré has said of the present crisis in 'mathematical physics' would be true of philosophy: its crises would only be cases of 'sloughing an outgrown skin,' an incident of growth and enlargement rather than a real disease. Like knowledge generally, philosophy on the whole has progressed, growing from within, i.e., following the *ordo ad nos*; and so long as it abides by the method which nature herself observes, and makes no leaps, why should it not progress still?[1] But we cannot dismember philosophy and have two independent 'growing points.' Wolff tried to do this and failed[2].

But when we are offered two principles so disparate as, on the one hand, the self-contradiction that makes utter havoc of all our world, or at least 'infects' it in varying degrees; and as, on the other, the Absolute, in which it is reconstituted for ever beyond our ken; when, too, the result is such that, "forgetting other points of view, we might say:

> Thus every part is full of vice,
> Yet the whole mass is Paradise"[3];

when, finally, it is maintained "that it is through their imperfection (the 'infection' of the parts) that the Absolute is enabled to affirm itself,"[4] may we not exclaim with the *Geisterchor* in Goethe's *Faust*:

Weh! Weh!	Alas! alas!
Du hast sie zerstört	You've destroyed it
Die schöne Welt,	With violent hands;
Mit machtiger Faust;	The beautiful world
Sie stürzt, sie zerfällt!	Lo! it totters and crumbles!
. . . .	. . . .
Wir tragen	The ruins we bury
Die Trummern ins Nichts	In the outer void,
hinüber,	And bewail
Und klagen	The thing of beauty
Ueber die verlorne Schöne.	We've lost for ever.

---

[1] I trust I may be pardoned for referring here to an address (which I had the honour of giving just thirty years ago to another Philosophical Society) entitled 'The Progress of Philosophy.' It appeared in *Mind*, 1890, pp. 213 ff. See above, pp. 112 ff.

[2] Cp. Zeller, *Gesch. d. deutschen Philosophie*, pp. 217 f.

[3] Cp. Bradley, *Appearance and Reality*, p. 571.

[4] Bosanquet, *Value and Destiny of the Individual*, p. 67.

X

EINSTEIN AND EPISTEMOLOGY

SOME REMARKS ON THE RELATIVITY THEORY

SOME two or three years ago it was said: you cannot go to a ball without being asked by your partner in a dance what you thought of Einstein. I take it then that I may assume everyone here to be familiar with the gist of the new theory of relativity. Einstein himself expressed his approval of a saying of the distinguished physicist, Kirchhoff: "Every new truth of science must be such that...it may be communicated completely within the space of a quarter page." Well, in this spirit I will venture to say that the new theory of relativity consists in analysing out certain consequences of the Leibnizian doctrine that every percipient mirrors the universe from its own standpoint. But there is much more relativity among percipients than Einstein has taken into account; and so I will try first of all to give instances of relativity generally by way of impressing its very wide range. If, however, we pass from mere percipients to rational beings, it is a question whether there is any insurmountable relativity at all.

Though the standpoints of different percipients are always different; yet as standpoints they are all on a par as being particular, i.e., relating to an individual. Nevertheless, for each one his own standpoint is absolute: he calls it '*here*.' Here is where a percipient, if sufficiently intelligent, erects what the physicist calls his reference frame. Such frame, in fact, implies his body and not merely his mind—a point frequently overlooked. So far 'here' is not a point in space but a portion of space. Within his own body the percipient is ubiquitous. Standing on his feet he distinguishes up

and down, right and left, before and behind. So soon
as intellectual intercourse is possible, the fact of this
spatial relativity emerges, and may be something of a
surprise or the occasion of some ambiguity. Think for
example of the quondam inconceivability of antipodes,
or of your uncertainty when directed to turn to the
right, unless you know whether or not *your* right is
meant. Again, as we look out on our environment we
see it in perspective. To an observer at one end of a
long straight tunnel the other end suggests a needle's
eye; and so an ignorant but precocious child might
wonder how a camel could be made to pass through it;
but finding the thing could be done, the child might
conclude that the tunnel opened out in front as he
went along. The same child says "Twinkle, twinkle,
little star." Even Hegel so far failed to realize the vast
magnitudes involved as to talk of stars as just a light
rash on the sky, as if it had measles. In short, in this
projective space parallel lines meet in a vanishing point
different for different observers.

When we pass to metrical space, the relativity thereby
entailed becomes theoretically still more important.
Here again there is something absolute for each observer—viz., his *scale*; but the foot of a man is many feet
for a mouse. Unless then the observer is specified,
positive terms such as large or small become unmeaning. It is a matter of common remark that
grown-up persons removed at an early age from the
scenes of their childhood are surprised to find on re-
visiting them that everything appears so much smaller
than they had expected. A further relativity enters as
soon as we take motion into account: to an observer
in motion the length of an object lying parallel to the
direction of his motion seems shorter than it does to
an observer equally distant from it but at rest; and
this difference increases with the velocity of the motion.

The mention of motion brings us to time. Here it is to be remarked that our earliest perceptions are simply perceptions of events, that is to say they imply time-order or succession. And like '*here*' for spatial order, so '*now*' for temporal order, is an absolute datum for each individual percipient. There is however this important difference: he may be at rest when he is in space but he must move in time, and move too without any choice of direction such as spatial dimensions afford; he must move *on*, he cannot move *back*. But if his imagination get the better of him, he may find a possible relativity even here. So Plato described time as the moving image of eternity and Newton spoke of it as flowing at a constant rate. The mention of time-rate confronts us with a new relativity. It is the merest metaphor to picture *time* as moving equally; for we find this time-rate to vary with the percipient: as Shakespeare said, "Time travels in divers paces with divers persons." Each percipient has his own time-rate, and this—like his space-measure—affords an absolute unit for him. (This 'movement in time' as we call it is the most real thing we know: it is no mere extensity or dimension; it is for us intensity or life, the concrete duration of wearing on. Bergson, as everyone knows, has made much of this *durée*, as he calls it, but I may be pardoned for saying, as his own people have told him, that I had myself remarked it years before.) But 'now' is like 'here' in another respect: as *here* is for each percipient a portion, not a point, of space, so *now* is not an instant but a portion of time—what psychologists call the specious or psychical present. We do not journey through life on a knife-edge but—what is much more comfortable—on what William James called a saddle-back. Hence we have what I have termed time-perspective; for example we can take in a melody as a whole.

There is yet another matter worth noting: if we assume—as physiologists have done—that the natural *tempo* of a creature is determined by some organic rhythm, such as the heart-pulse of a man or the vibration of wings in a gnat, then the difference between the time-value of a minute as measured by the clock will be enormous. The result, if we picture it out, is somewhat surprising: if our *tempo* were increased sufficiently we might then see a bean-stalk grow: as it is we only infer it; on the other hand, if our *tempo* were diminished sufficiently, though we might infer that an express train moved, we could not then see it move. Thus without imagining the world itself to be magnified or diminished in respect of space and time we have only to compare the scales and *tempi* of different percipients to realize what relativity means.

Before attempting to proceed it will be well to make now a general remark with which it would perhaps have been better to begin. So far we have been talking of percipients merely and of the spatial and temporal order of the events which they severally perceive, that is to say we have been referring to the immediate experiences of diverse isolated individuals in what is sometimes called filled space and time. As they move about they have more or less inchoate perceptions of co-ordinated temporal and spatial relations connecting concrete events, but of what we call space and time as such, i.e., emptied space and time they have no inkling. For they have no means of recording and comparing their individual experiences. Such inter-subjective intercourse is possible to human beings alone and by this means mankind has gradually transcended the individual 'point of view' to which Leibniz referred: in this sense our common experience has become transubjective, and we have—if I may so express it—a certain amount of parallax in our outlook on a world[1]. From the naïve standpoint of the individual percipient, who is always 'here' and for whom it is always 'now,' all the changes in the *appearance* of his world are regarded as changes actually occurring in the world itself there and then and presumably for everyone. It is only at the intellectual level that we are confronted with alternatives which the bare percipient lacks—as for example, that between the Ptolemaic and the Copernican standpoints; in other words, that of an observer whose here is on the earth and that of one whose here is on the sun. Between these alternatives, however, though we have no sensible, we have intelligent, means of deciding.

Returning now to our main question—we may say that for a given intelligent individual A, space and time are not necessarily implicated. Remaining at rest in the same place—and this by the way it would be better to call a τόπος rather than a *locus*—he is still aware of events occurring there and of the lapse of time their succession entails. But for other observers, B and C situated elsewhere, though they too may distinguish time from space and each regard himself as at rest, yet A's τόπος may appear to them to be in motion. And *vice versa* for A's observation as regards them. Generalizing then we may say: though the separation of time and space suffices for individual observers—whether at rest or in motion—yet such observers, on comparing notes, find that time and space seem inseparable for the external world itself. Accordingly Minkowski proclaimed that this world is four-dimensional; relativity pertains to observers, not to the world. But now is there anything absolute in this four-dimensional world? It would seem that it is all absolute, if, as Prof. Eddington suggests, we define the absolute "as a relative which is always the same no matter what it is

---

[1] Cp. *Psychological Principles*, pp. 32 f.

relative to." Now, since as he begins by stating "there are two parties to every observation—the observed and the observer," and since for every specified observer time and space are distinct but in a four-dimensional world they are 'indissoluble,' it would seem that only by eliminating all observers could the knowledge of that world be obtained. But Prof. Eddington asks— and well he may—whether the idea of such knowledge conveys any intelligible meaning, and whether it could be of any conceivable interest to anybody even if it could be understood. However, though he raises these questions at the very outset of his exposition of relativity, he dismisses them with the remark: "these questions need not detain us now." Well, to me they seem vital and should they not be so to him? For he incidentally refers to the theory of relativity as a "search for an absolute world" and elsewhere speaks roundly of the four-dimensional world as absolute[1]. Similarly, de Sitter tells us that "the elimination of the relative is one of the things the theory of relativity has set out to do." Whether the said task is accomplished or not, one thing at least is certain, as Prof. Eddington says: "to gain an understanding of the absolute it is necessary to approach it through the relative," reminding one of Goethe's words:

Willst du ins Unendliche schreiten,
Geh' nur im Endliche nach allen Seiten.

There is, I think, no doubt about the method. Whether it is followed consistently, whether the relative is eliminated, whether an understanding of the absolute is eventually attained, are the epistemological questions I would invite you to consider. Newton, it is said, so far disregarded this method as to assume a superobserver aware of absolute time, absolute space, abso-

[1] *Mind*, 1920, p. 418.

lute motion. The relativists have decreed his abdica-
tion and set up what Prof. Eddington calls a dummy
observer in his place. The "confusing factor in our
present relative knowledge" is the motion of the actual
observer whose body is a part of the physical world
which he attempts to describe. Not so the dummy; he
is no part of the physical world or he would not be a
dummy. His world apparently lies behind ours, and
consists only of a "rudimentary objective differentiation of orderly relation" where as yet nothing is postulated, not even the number of dimensions. The statement that the world is four-dimensional contains an
implicit reference to some ordering relation. "The
result depends entirely on what this ordering relation
is." Time and space again, in the dummy's world are
not distinguished; our familiar terms, in which their
distinctness is implied, are derivative concepts. Their
premature introduction in this form was Newton's
mistake: "So far from being absolute, taken in themselves they sink to mere shadows," said Minkowski,
and his words are quoted by all writers on relativity
that I have come across. It might surprise some of
them to know that this master-stroke of Minkowski's
has long been a commonplace of philosophy. Motion
which combines space and time would be a meaningless non-entity if there were no moving things. Space
and time are not the real pre-supposition of things:
how can they be, for they are not real at all? To
suppose they were was the mistake of Newton, Locke
and Clarke. On the other hand, a world of things
without spatial and temporal relations is, for us at all
events, equally unmeaning. Still, things are the *fundamenta relationis*. So far Schlick has done better than
Minkowski by insisting that "the combination or oneness of space, time, and things is alone reality."[1]

[1] *Space and Time*, Eng. transl., p. 35.

But let us return to Prof. Eddington's dummy. What are we to make of him? His chief recommendation at first sight seems to be that we can do what we like with him. Why then can we not do without him? Because, apparently, he can be regarded as a mechanical automaton absorbing the impersonal points of view of all conceivable observers—that is to say, so far as physics is concerned—and so *pro tanto*, he transmutes physics into geometry[1]. In this respect he appears to be either a pure mathematician or the measuring appliances suggested by one. At any rate in this theory of relativity it is a pure mathematician with whom we have first of all to deal[2]. "Give me a world," he says, "a world in which there are relations—and I will construct matter and motion." Prof. Eddington quotes an eminent mathematician who defines his subject as one "in which we never know what we are talking about, nor whether what we are saying is true." So with this mathematician: "left to himself he 'never deviates into sense.'" But we give him a free hand and listen. "At first his symbols bring no picture of anything before our eyes...(But) we need not and do not form any idea of the meaning of each individual symbol"; for "the elementary concepts" answering to these symbols are "necessarily indefinable." I must here digress for a moment to remark on Prof. Eddington's use of this word *indefinable*. He refers to the objects of the every-day world which we see and feel around us as "our definables." The negative 'indefinable' then would seem to mean that which is not recognized or understood. *A propos* of this it occurred to me to consult the recent *Logic* of my old friend and former pupil, W. E. Johnson of King's. As I expected I find him saying: "so far from meaning the 'not understood,' the

[1] *Space, Time and Gravitation*, p. 183.
[2] *Ibid.*, p. 198 *fin.*

indefinable means that which *is* understood" and "because it is understood does not require a further process of definition." But lest it should be supposed that this view is peculiar to Cambridge logic, I will hasten to add that it is to be found in Descartes' classical *Discourse on Method*, and again in Leibniz who describes indefinable terms as the simple terms reached when analysis is carried to the uttermost. Thus the elementary concepts of mathematics are always definite though owing to their simplicity they cannot be defined. They can, however, be indicated and henceforth understood. Of course if we cannot complete our analysis we ought not to call what we don't understand elementary. Must we not then demur to Prof. Eddington's statement that we do not form any idea of the meaning of the pure mathematician's elementary concepts? In fact, if that were so, his further account of his *séance* with the mathematician would remind one only of the deciphering of the Rosetta stone. Prof. Eddington himself actually uses an analogy of this sort[1]. As there so here the individual symbols at first mean nothing to us; it is only "certain elaborate combinations of them that we recognize." Most of us, I suspect, have learnt by painful experience how little this analogy holds in the case of mathematics. Indeed, just because of this lack on our part of technical knowledge, Prof. Eddington confesses in his preface that he has had to content himself with a bowdlerized version, which misses "the perfect harmony of the geometry of relativity," the truth that can only be conveyed in the symbolism of mathematics.

Here at length we have a definite epistemological issue—as to the connexion between pure mathematics and experience generally, particularly what is called experimental physics, to which mathematics is said to

[1] Cp. *Space, Time and Gravitation*, p. 184.

be applied. What exactly is involved when we talk of
applying? Obviously two distinct things besides the
process of application; we may call them perhaps the
applicans and the *applicandum*. You cannot apply a
plaster to a disjoined limb that isn't there. But what
should we say, if when it was, the process ended in the
absorption of the limb? Yet this is the result towards
which the *theory* of relativity is said to tend—to our
surprise and apparently to that of its propounders.
"We did not consciously set out to construct a geometrical theory of the world," Prof. Eddington tells
us; "we were seeking physical reality by approved
methods, and this is what happened: as the geometry
became more· complex the physics became simpler."
In short, mathematics plays the vampire. "The exact
laws of gravitation, mechanics and electro-magnetism,
by which physics has won its high reputation...are
set aside as irrelevant," so that the physicist—as distinct I suppose from the mathematician—"is reduced
to very modest proportions."[1] "Length, duration,
mass, force, etc.," it turns out, "are not things having
an absolute significance in nature"[2]: in fact, "all the
more familiar terms of physics...denote not objective
characters, but relations to some observer or his ideal-
ized equivalent."[3] The applications of mathematics
in experience are manifold, but if they all ended in
the absorption of the *applicandum*, the result would be
strange. We may be excused, therefore, if in spite of
our ignorance of the complicated mathematical processes by which in this case such a result has been
achieved, we venture to demur.

Our misgivings are strengthened when we are told
that the mathematics in question were invented for

[1] *Mind*, 1920, p. 421.
[2] *Space, Time and Gravitation*, p. 155.
[3] *Mind*, 1920, p. 417 *fin*.

quite another purpose. "Poincaré has said that Mathematics is the art of giving the same name to different things. We have here in epigrammatic form the statement of a most fundamental characteristic of modern mathematics."[1] Perhaps the earliest, at any rate a very important example of such a mathematical *alias* was Descartes' discovery of analytical geometry. And to us this is specially interesting, for—if I am not mistaken—it is as analytical geometer that Prof. Eddington's mathematical oracle begins his cryptic discourse. Now analytical geometry, so-called, presupposes spatial intuitions: spatial relations can then be *represented* by symbols, but they cannot be *defined* by this means without logical fallacy. Riemann—who has, I believe, contributed largely to the complicated mathematics as to which I am airing my ignorance—begins his dissertation as follows: Geometry, as is well known, presupposes not only the concept of space but also the fundamental concepts required for constructions in it. The famous Pythagorean proposition (Eucl. 1, 47) seems in fact to have been the corner-stone of his investigation. But our spatial intuition gives out at space of three dimensions: not so, however, that of analytical geometry. Prof. Eddington, for example, tells us that "for an exact representation of his geometry of the world, Euclidian space of *ten* dimensions is required." The comment on this, which people less enlightened and convinced than himself would almost certainly make, is very different from his own. "We may well ask," he says, "whether there is merit in Euclidian geometry sufficient to justify going to such extremes."[2] But as a matter of fact we have no sort of intuition of space of even four dimensions. There is, however, no necessity about matters of fact, Riemann remarks.

[1] Hobson, *Mathematics: Address to Math. and Phys. Soc.* 1912, p. 15.
[2] *Space, Time and Gravitation*, p. 84.

That may be, for when we talk of necessity we are in the domain of logic; but in *applying* pure mathematics, though, as pure, it is limited only by the possible, we are confined to matters of fact. And for science what is actual is more important than what is possible, though the converse may be true for mathematics. In disregarding the Baconian maxim here implied, the *theory* of relativity, it seems to me, is false to the methodology it professes to follow. This is the first point I would ask you to consider. For my own part I will for the present only say I am not objecting either to the special or to the general principle of relativity, but merely to the mathematical theory by which they are said to be proved[1]. To me they appear to be just matters of fact. Minkowski, I suspect, has been the evil genius of the whole movement[2].

Then comes the second question I mentioned: what about 'the elimination of the relative'? Has it been successful? In one sense it may be truly said that the progress of thought has always consisted in the elimination of the relative. Contrary positions, the theses and antitheses of Hegel's dialectic, have been continually reconciled or removed through a synthesis which the wider horizon attained by a higher standpoint opened out—as for instance in the case of Locke's poor Indian philosopher. The identification of inertia and gravity which Einstein has shewn is no doubt an instance of progress of this sort. But in this *theory* of relativity we have found the relative not transcended but only transferred from physics to a so-called world geometry. Space has become heterogeneous; and a complex

---

[1] It has been objected that it is incorrect to speak here of 'proof.' But compare the language of Minkowski (quoted by Eddington, *Space, Time and Gravitation*, p. 30): "The views of time and space, which I have set forth, have their foundation in experimental physics. Therein is their strength," etc.

[2] Cp. *Space, Time and Gravitation*, chap. III, pp. 47 f.

kinematics, in which time and space become indissoluble dimensions, takes the place of the physicist's dynamics. Length, duration and mass, the three fundamentals in this, are declared, as we have already seen, to have "no absolute significance here."[1] "As the result of long algebraic calculations" matter or mass turns out to be a pucker or "hummock" in space or rather in the indissoluble time-space[2]. After all, this heterogeneous space-time with its puckers and hummocks—which puckers if straightened out in one direction only re-appear in another—is but a complex of relations. "The relativity theory of physics," says Prof. Eddington, "reduces everything to relations."[3] But they appear to be final relations: for, "steered by mathematics," i.e., "keeping entirely to tensors, we contrive that there shall be behind our formulæ an undercurrent of information having reference to the intrinsic state of the world."[4] It is moreover claimed for this theory that it is the simplest since it "contains a minimum number of *arbitrary* factors, whereas the more complicated views necessarily contain superfluous conceptions," whilst "in the case of the simplest theory...the *rôle* of each particular conception is made imperative by the facts: such a theory forms a system of symbols, all of them indispensable." So Moritz Schlick[5]. Well, we shall see: for my part I cannot tell, the mathematics of tensors being beyond my grasp. Anyhow, a system of symbols that can give us information concerning the intrinsic state of the world reminds me of the closing sentence of Whitehead's Tarner Lectures: "the guiding motto in the life of every natural philosopher should be, Seek simplicity—and distrust it."

We come now to the last question which I suggested

---

[1] *Space, Time and Gravitation*, p. 155. [2] *Ibid.*, p. 97.
[3] *Ibid.*, p. 197. [4] *Ibid.*, p. 189.
[5] *Space and Time*, Eng. transl., p. 87.

might be raised—what about this information concerning the intrinsic (or absolute) state of the world,
which the theory of relativity has 'contrived' to
furnish? Of course only the physical world is meant,
but even so, the result is bewildering and disappointing.
Still, I will try to give an outline of it by stringing together various passages of Prof. Eddington's. "In the
relativity theory of nature," we are told, "the most
elementary concept is the *point-event*."[1] Regarded as
simply a "given instant at a given place" it may be
said to belong to the world-frame, but if we include
"the physical happening which occurs at and identifies
a particular place and time,"[2] this concrete event is
part of the world fabric; it concerns a particle. (This
particular distinction is implied but not stated by
Prof. Eddington.) "The track of a particle through
four-dimensional space-time is called its world-line."[3]
It is this track that the new mathematics enables us
to trace by providing us with the means of measuring
the interval between two adjacent events. "A world
of point-events with their primary interval relations"—
this sort of knowledge then we have. "Now, the
world-lines of two particles either intersect or they do
not intersect. . . . Insofar as our knowledge of nature
is a knowledge of the intersections of world-lines, it is
absolute knowledge independent of the observer. . . .
It seems clear that *if* [a large *if*, where we did not
expect any ifs] we could draw all the world-lines so
as to shew all the intersections in *their proper order* . . .
this [drawing] would contain a complete history of
the world and nothing *within reach of observation* would
be omitted."[4] Many difficulties at once suggest themselves. I can only refer to a few. First, how do we
know that the particle remains numerically the same

---

[1] *Space, Time and Gravitation*, p. 186.   [2] *Ibid.*, p. 145.
[3] *Ibid.*, p. 87.   [4] *Ibid.*, p. 87.

while its track continues? Prof. Eddington has in fact described actual motion as the disappearance of a body from one point of space and the appearance of an apparently identical body at a neighbouring point[1]. This does not prove identity; and indeed he scouts "the permanent identity of particular particles of matter" as "an abusive idea." Again, what is the significance of the intersection of two world-lines for the world-fabric itself? It is likely to be very different in different cases—the intersection say of two rays of light or of a ray of light with an atom which explodes—to take two cases Prof. Eddington mentions. This mention of atoms leads to another question which he raises himself. Point-events suggest continuity: atoms imply discontinuity. Whence arises this discontinuity? Prof. Eddington asks. The question seems to have given him pause, for he presently remarks: "probably our analysis into point-events is not final"![2] Can this be called gaining an understanding of the absolute through the relative?

Prof. Eddington concludes his last chapter entitled "On the Nature of Things" by two brief paragraphs, part of which I will quote: "The theory of relativity has passed in review the whole subject-matter of physics.... And yet, in regard to the nature of things this knowledge (which it has attained) is only an empty shell—a form of symbols. It is knowledge of structural form, and not knowledge of content. All through the physical world runs that unknown content, which must surely be the stuff of our consciousness. Here is a hint of aspects deep within the world of physics, and yet unattainable by the methods of physics. And moreover, we have found that when science has progressed the farthest, the mind has but regained from nature that which the mind has put into nature. We have

[1] *Mind*, 1920, p. 153.   [2] *Space, Time and Gravitation*, p. 199.

found a strange foot-print on the shores of the unknown. We have devised profound theories, one after another, to account for its origin. At last, we have succeeded in reconstructing the creature that made the foot-print and lo! it (the foot-print) is our own." A singular climax and on the whole an unexpected one. It smacks of Kant and yet Prof. Eddington never refers to him. And there is here more of the anthropomorphic and less of the absolute than we find in Kant. However, I must leave this without further comment. Perhaps it may interest some of you. From his second paper in *Mind*, however, I should also like to quote a few cognate passages: "The difference between space occupied by matter and space which is empty is simply a difference in its geometry. There seems no reason to postulate that there is an entity of foreign nature which causes the difference of geometry....But the distinction of substance and emptiness is the mind's own contribution, depending on the kind of pattern which it is interested in recognizing....There is no obligation in Nature to provide explicitly anything permanent; the permanence is introduced by the geometrical quality of the configuration which the mind looks out for in whatever Nature provides." Referring to "a great number of the well-known laws of physics, mechanics and geometry" (whatever this last may mean here), he says "these laws do not govern the course of events in the objective world, but are automatically imposed by the mind in selecting what it considers to be substance." If that were all, then we should know no laws which have not their origin in the human mind. "But I am not as yet prepared to admit that," Prof. Eddington adds. "I think that we do, more especially in modern physics, encounter the genuine laws governing the external world, and are attempting—perhaps rather unsuccessfully—to grapple with them."[1]

[1] *Mind*, 1920, pp. 420 f.

On these somewhat cryptic passages I should like to make a concluding remark. For the last twenty years or so there has existed what Poincaré called a crisis in physics. This he discusses in his little book, *La Valeur de la Science*: he deals with five different lines of attack on the old classical or mathematical physics; and that of relativity is one. He foresaw that a new physics was coming and that the old rational dynamics no longer sufficed, that is to say, the physics of the future would be more inductive and lack a formal mathematical basis such as the Newtonian doctrine of central forces afforded. Is it not possible that the theory of relativity is the result of this transitional stage? For, on the one hand, it strives to provide a new mathematical scaffolding; on the other, it makes principles out of empirical facts—such as the velocity of light and the connexion between velocity and mass. It is the mathematical scaffolding and the employment of such real categories as substance and cause that Prof. Eddington would trace wholly to the human mind. It is the empirical "laws, which have not their origin in the mind and may," he hints[1], "be irrational," that are what he calls "genuine laws of the external world." "The task of formulating these," he concludes, we may expect to be far harder than anything yet accomplished by physics." In connexion with these, the quantum theory and allied topics, will, I expect, overshadow the theory of relativity which has grown up round certain empirical facts, which, as Poincaré suggests, the old dynamics is elastic enough to include.

[1] *Space, Time and Gravitation*, p. 200.

XI

IMMANUEL KANT

ASSUREDLY Kant has found a place among the
world's master-minds. He shewed his originality
as a thinker before he was twenty-five years of
age, and before he was fifty he inaugurated (or at least,
adumbrated) what has proved to be a revolution in
philosophy. He was one of those great minds, who, as
Goethe said, "will not let the world go till it understands them."

But the best of men are but men, at the best. And
in view of the numberless defects and inconsistencies of
his philosophy that for more than a century and a half
foes and friends alike have been exposing, one cannot
but wonder, in the first place, how it was that Kant so
speedily attained, and, in the second, how it is that he
is still accorded, the unique place he unquestionably
holds among the great philosophers. For as an ad-
miring commentator not long ago said: "*The Critique
of Pure Reason* is the work which is at once the fullest of
genius and of contradictions in the whole range of
philosophical literature."[1]

As to Kant's early eminence—though there are, I
think, several philosophers who would be ranked as
superior to him in native genius, there is probably not
one who towered so much above a dead level of un-
relieved mediocrity such as prevailed in his time.
Leibniz, more than Kant's compeer for pure genius,
was near enough in time to challenge comparison, had
he not been levelled down too drastically by his so-
called systematizer, Chr. Wolff. But, as it was, this

[1] H. Vaihinger, *Strasburger Abhandlungen zur Philosophie*, 1884,
p. 126.

conceited pedant alone dominated the philosophy of Germany in Kant's early days. And even his influence was already on the wane, leaving little beyond a shallow and incoherent eclecticism in its place. In the general philosophical chaos which then prevailed it was natural that some abler minds, not content with disposing of Wolff, should also be casting about to bring in unity and order, some by treatises on method, others by essays on psychology on English lines. Here then in all were three distinct but compatible movements in progress at once; and Kant took part in them all. In his first philosophical work he may perhaps be said to have driven a nail into the coffin of the Leibniz-Wolffian rationalism. We find him later reading Locke's *Essay* (translated into French, 1700; into German, 1757), *Hume's Enquiry* (translated in 1755) and Rousseau's *Émile* (1762). We also find him competing for a prize on method (one of the many offered about this time) in his so-called *Prize Essay* (1764); and finally, in an announcement of his lectures for 1765, stating his intention of inverting the customary order in which Metaphysics had been treated, by beginning with Empirical Psychology[1]. I mention these facts simply to shew that so far Kant was just the child of his time —the time of the so-called Enlightenment (*Aufklärung*).

Two other of his contemporaries were then similarly occupied: Lambert, who brought out a *Neues Organon* in 1764 and an *Architectonik* in 1771, and Tetens, who in 1760 wrote an essay entitled: *Why there are so few established truths in Metaphysics*, and who in 1777 published *Philosophical Essays on Human Nature and its Development*. With Lambert Kant corresponded for years, and it was his intention to dedicate to him the *Tractate on Method* which gradually expanded into the *Critique*; but Lambert had died in the meantime. As to Tetens

[1] *Werke*, Hartenstein's ed., 1867, II, 316.

—it is reported that his *Essays on Human Nature* lay always open on Kant's desk, as he toiled at the problems of the said *Critique*. If at this time the question of 'placing' had been raised, it is more than likely that not Kant but Lambert would have headed the list.

In 1781, however, the *Critique* appeared. At first—that is as soon as it was noticed at all—it was either denounced as untrue or depreciated as not new; but as time went on, slowly at first, but presently by almost universal acclamation, it was hailed as both new and true. Yet probably what was chiefly appreciated was its novelty. We might infer this from the *furore* for Kant which for a while took possession of all sorts and conditions of men, and even women too[1]. It reminds one of the similar, though milder, outburst in our day of public interest in Bergson and Einstein, when not one in a hundred of the people who loved to talk and even to write about them understood what they really meant.

On a superficial glance what is striking in the *Critique of Pure Reason* is its so-called 'architectonic': on this Kant specially prided himself, although—as is now generally acknowledged—it is as artificial as it is ingenious. Still it was likely to amaze a casual reader as a revelation of the unsuspected *a priori* antinomy on which the very possibility of experience and its limits were said to depend. We find there:

(1) Two forms of sensory intuition, in which the 'Manifold' of the external and internal senses respectively is arranged;

(2) Twelve categories of the Understanding, involved in the logical table of judgments, which are systematically distributed into four classes of three members each—seemingly contrary to the funda-

---

[1] Ample details as to this, almost incredible were they not well authenticated, will be found in Stuckenberg's *Life of Immanuel Kant*, 1882, pp. 365 ff.

mental law of dichotomy; but then the third proves to be always the synthesis of the other two;

(3) A Schematism of sensory form and of categories rendering the *application* of the latter to experience possible.

(4) Four classes of Synthetic Principles determining this application, the first two being intuitive, constitutive, and mathematical, the last two discursive, regulative, and dynamical;

(5) Four pairs of concepts of Reflection; dealing with the relation of being and knowing,

and finally

(6) Three Ideas of Reason, involved in the logical forms of syllogism, which point beyond experience to the Unconditioned which it implies.

Novel detail of this sort could be read, marked, and learned without much reflection, and would tend rather to repress than to arouse any further question as to what it was about. In confirmation of this surmise I may cite the *Elucidations* (*Erläuterungen*) *of the Critique* published by Kant's friend and colleague, Johann Schulze, in 1784. The book is clearly written—comparing favourably in this respect with the *Critique* itself —and Kant stood sponsor for it in words of warm approval quoted by the author in his preface. On these and other grounds the book at once 'caught on,' as we say, and did much to popularize the new philosophy. But it begins by referring to this as a *Lehrgebäude* that is thought out down to its minutest fragments (*Bruchstücke*)[1]. And the greater part of the book is

[1] How impressive the *Lehrgebäude* of Kant's at first proved to be is still more strikingly shewn in a rare book on *Kant's Works* by one Thomas Wirgman, consisting in a collection of articles contributed by him to the *Encyclopaedia Londinensis* (24 vols., 4to, 1810–29). Here there are some fifteen steel plates (to say nothing of others in the letterpress) in which Kant's architectonic is plotted out for the better exhibition of its *Bruchstücke*.

occupied with these, which, as I have said, any commonplace intellect could apprehend. As to Kant's main purpose—this, it is stated, was to refute Hume and establish the truth of the Christian religion—these being the further grounds of the book's popularity to which I referred just now. Of the cardinal problem of Kant's *Analytik*, the writer had hardly an inkling: it is handled very briefly, and yet is misrepresented[1].

In short, what I am venturing to maintain is that the transcendental philosophy rose to fame without being understood: for that, as Kant himself said later on, a hundred years would be required. His philosophy, in fact, first became famous through its vigorous iconoclasm—Mendelssohn, it will be remembered, called Kant *der Alles Zermalmende*—and through its rigorous 'Systematic'—artificial though it was[2]—which replaced the loose eclecticism then in vogue. How little its central theme was understood is shewn by the disputes which soon arose as to what was and what was not '*echt Kantisch*,' as the phrase went. As to this, opponents and partisans alike differed not only from each other but among themselves. For all sorts of reasons Kant's philosophy was attacked on the one hand and accepted on the other; but what it essentially was nobody seemed to know[3]. All the same, as the eighteenth century wore on, ideas about Kant were

---

[1] Thus not apperception but imagination seems to be regarded as the highest principle. For this, however, it is only fair to say Schulze was not alone to blame. He had only Kant's first edition to go upon; and how inadequate that was is evident from the changes Kant found it needful to make in the second.

[2] As to this Adickes, *Kant's Systematik als systembildender Factor* (1887), is well worth consulting.

[3] And in fact this was still the case a whole century later, despite Kant's forecast. Cp. B. Erdmann, *Kant's Kriticismus u.s.w.*, 1878, pp. 245–247, where six different formulations of Kant's philosophy extant since 1865 are given; and the review of the book, *Philosophische Monatshefte*, 1879, xv, pp. 170 f.

more and more widely diffused and at the same time more or less profoundly modified. On the one side it was realized that the new views propounded by him were not entirely false, and on the other that he himself was certainly not infallible[1]. So it was that before the century closed the entire philosophical atmosphere of Germany was pervaded with Kantianism, and lectures on the new philosophy—mostly expository but occasionally polemical—were delivered in every university in the land[2].

Still in all this ferment the question grew more and more pressing whether anybody had yet succeeded in distilling out the pure spirit of it all. So in 1797 a plot was laid to draw forth an answer from Kant himself. He was publicly called upon to name the man "who in the main understood him as he wished to be understood." Kant named Schulze, but with the caution that he was to be taken literally (*nach Buchstaben*), not according "to some imagined underlying spirit (*Geist*)."[3] Why did Kant answer thus: why stress the *letter* when what was asked for was surely the *spirit*? Because, as I think, he had no better answer to give. Shocked, as he had been, by the interpretation Fichte had recently put upon his work, he was anxious to repudiate in advance any future attempts to *explain*

---

[1] As he himself plainly shewed, for he never formulated an important doctrine twice in the same way, as Edward Caird once pointed out to me.

[2] It is perhaps worth remarking by the way that in 1786 a rescript was issued by the Landgraf of Hesse forbidding such lectures, which, however, was rescinded a year later at the instance of Tiedemann, one of Kant's opponents. As a pendant to this piece of intolerance I cannot forbear mentioning another on the other side, viz., the persecution of Feder, the Göttingen professor who was the first to make an onslaught on Kant, a persecution which led him to resign his professorship, though still vigorous, and to leave Göttingen.

[3] Cp. *Werke*, Hartenstein's ed., VIII, 599.

what he had said. All the same, though the true inwardness of his work may, as he foretold, appear at length, it was certainly not then clearly apparent even to him. It possessed him, no doubt, but more or less unconsciously. He did not himself fully realize the goal of the inspiration—the *Zeitgeist*, as Hegel called it—by which he was led. He was, I must repeat, the child of his time: philosophical orientation was what the *Aufklärung* wanted and he succeeded at least in pointing the way. It was this which, in spite of his many defects and inconsistencies, made him the master-mind that he is still held to be. And this is, I think, the answer to our second question.

But it is time to attempt a brief account of Kant's philosophical development, and this, I trust, will incidentally exemplify what I have said and justify my characterization of Kant's position as a philosopher. But first a word as to his starting-point. As a student Kant was at first chiefly interested in astronomy and physics; and he had produced a number of ambitious works and articles on these subjects before he attempted—not till his thirty-first year—to handle any philosophical problem. It was this double interest that gave to his philosophy its peculiar character and value, and also helps to explain its seemingly erratic course. The philosophy which he had been taught and had assimilated only too thoroughly, the Leibniz-Wolffian rationalism, concerned itself not with what is but with what could be, not with the actually real but with the absolutely possible. The former, experience could apprehend, but to the latter only pure thought could attain. Had Kant known nothing but this he might never have been heard of: as it was, his early study of Newton gave him an external standpoint from which what he would have called the πρῶτον ψεῦδος of the old rationalism became apparent, and from which it could be effectively assailed. The *vera causa* of Newton will not rhyme with the *vernünftige Gedanken* of Wolff. Existence is not a predicate and cannot be reached by mere thought. *Causa* is not to be identified with *ratio*, and to conjure *ratio* into *actio* no reasoning will 'suffice.' Here were two truths Kant had reached once for all. Following upon this—in the *Prize Essay* already referred to—Kant disposed of the ancient prejudice that mathematics furnished the true paradigm for the philosopher—a prejudice which in modern times was still shared by Descartes and Spinoza. He then went on to contend, like a confirmed empiricist, that the true method for metaphysics was the method of Newton—in a word, that philosophy must be 'zetetic,' must feel its way. In philosophy definitions must needs come, not first as in mathematics, but last; if happily the analysis of what is given can at length be adequately performed. Here then was a third *Buchstabe* or *Bruchstück* to be wrought into Kant's *Lehrgebäude*. Like Newton he had been picking shells on the shores of the Unknown, and with the finding of these what has been called his empirical phase came to an end: that was in 1766[1].

Then, after bidding a sad farewell to his beloved *Metaphysica*, and lapsing for four years into a profound silence, interrupted only by a short paper of some seven pages, Kant—having been appointed a full professor (1770)—was forced to speak. He then delivered his famous *Inaugural Dissertation*; and lo! he seems to be a dogmatic rationalist once more! How was this? "The year 1769," he noted later, "brought me great light." His *Aufklärung* had well begun. This nearing dawn appears in the short paper just mentioned. It was written in 1768 and dealt with what he called "the difference of regions in space"—the fact that we

[1] Cp. my *Study of Kant*, § 4.

orientate our position in space first of all from our own
body as 'origin.' This led him finally to abandon the
Newtonian doctrine of the objective existence of absolute space, and by parity of reasoning, that of absolute
time. Both space and time he now concluded, in agreement with Leibniz, were merely phenomenal. This
conclusion was established beyond question by a further
insight which 'the great light' of 1769 revealed, viz.,
the antinomy between the position of the pure understanding that the world is a *whole* of *simple* substances
in mutuo commercio, and the inability of sense either to
advance to the totality or to regress to the simple. So
there emerged a radical difference in kind between the
sensible and the intelligible where Leibniz had recognized only a difference in degree of clearness and
distinctness[1].

On this fundamental difference of faculties—a fourth
Bruchstück of Kant's *Lehrgebäude*—the argument of the
Inaugural Dissertation is based. Here Kant had found
an answer to Tetens's question why metaphysics had
hitherto explained so little: it was because from lack
of method these two domains of knowledge had not
been kept distinct. So soon as the truth of this distinctness is realized, a striking parallel is apparent between
the sensible and the intelligible world. Each has its
form and its principles and each can yield an *a priori*
science—mathematics in the sensible or phenomenal
world, and metaphysics in the world of the intelligible
or noumenal. Well, but we have been long in possession
of the one science, why is the other still to seek? For
want of method, Kant repeats. The all-important
desideratum then is to make clear what this method is.
In dealing with this problem Kant falls back on his
old distinction between mathematics and metaphysics.
The former starts from intuition; and though, no doubt,

[1] Cp. *Study*, § 5, pp. 29 f.; § 6, pp. 36 ff.

there is and must be an intellectual intuition, yet it is not the sort of intuition which is vouchsafed to us. Here then was an *impasse* that might lead Kant to pause, as indeed it eventually did. Meanwhile, however, he continues as if he knew at any rate the matter and form of the intelligible as well as he did those of the sensible world. Accordingly he gives an account of the intelligible world which is essentially that of Leibniz's *Monadology*, save that he rejects *pre-established* harmony and recognizes *occasionalism*. It is then only the principles of that world which he is not prepared to state[1]. Before this could be done it was needful first of all to clear away the errors by which those principles had till then been hidden. To this preliminary task, a *Propaedeutic to Metaphysics*, it was fitting to call attention at his first public recognition as professor; and it was with this task that what he afterwards declared to be the only *important* parts of his *Dissertation* were concerned. It was his intention to revise and extend these, and to publish the whole immediately under some such title as *The Boundaries (Grenzen) of Sense and Reason.*

It is, I think, greatly to be regretted that Kant never carried this intention through; and in so thinking I am by no means singular. He imagined such a *Tractate on Method* (as he also called it) would not occupy him long, would be only a matter of a few sheets. Here he was, then, under the influence of an inspiration—the great light of '69—with one part at any rate of his new philosophy secure[2]. If he had now set about rounding

[1] But obviously his monadology involves more than mere form; and in fact he incidentally enumerates, by way simply of example, all the real principles afterwards given, *as applicable to phenomena*, in the *Critique*.

[2] In sending a copy of the *Dissertation* to Lambert, within a fortnight of its delivery, Kant wrote: "Since about a year (ago) I have reached that idea (*Begriff*) which I flatter myself I shall never need to alter, but only to enlarge." *Werke*, VIII, 662

off this part and making it in itself complete while it was in full possession of his mind, he could hardly have failed to raise one question essential to such completeness, viz., the question as to the ground or source of this difference between sense-knowledge and thought-knowledge. This question, so close to him then, he lost sight of later. Otherwise he might have saved himself much of the useless labour of the next ten years, as perhaps in the end we may come to see. However, this is anticipating. But in place of expounding his new idea as it was, Kant decided at once to enlarge it. This proved to be a more arduous task than that which he had at first proposed, and in consequence the projected tractate never appeared. But after a yet longer interval of complete silence as regards philosophical topics—this time lasting more than ten years—the *Critique of Pure Reason* appeared instead.

Here we come upon another of Kant's characteristic oscillations—*Umkippungen* as he called them, and it is the last. It ensued as soon as he paused to reflect on the fact that while we have intuitions of the objects of sense, *phenomena*, we have no intuitions of the objects of understanding or reason, *noumena*. There, objects of sense imply things; for sensations, as to which we are passive, cannot arise from nothing: on the other hand, here we have only thoughts, and thoughts in our case do not create things. How then and with what reservation can we say that our thoughts correspond to things and even prescribe universal and necessary laws to which they are subject?[1] As a first step in pursuance of this inquiry Kant supposed it to be indispensable to investigate the fundamental forms of thought, the categories, not, however, after the empirical fashion with which Aristotle was content. It was essential, Kant supposed, "to ascertain the precise number of

[1] Cp. *Study*, § 7, pp. 42 f.

these categories and how they arrange themselves in classes according to some few principles of the understanding." Here Kant's evil genius, the craving for 'Systematik' which he inherited from Wolff, began to mislead him. I make bold to say that this entire enterprise, over which he seems to have wasted years, was worse than useless, and that its futility has hardly yet been sufficiently exposed[1]. One odd thing about it is worth mention. Kant rejected Aristotle's list of categories, which, if incomplete, has yet found general acceptance so far as it goes. But he was content to take the table of judgments—supposed to be based on Aristotle—as the certain clue to the discovery of the categories, though no such table has ever found any general recognition at all, and Kant himself found 'a few defects' in it which he must first correct!

In what he called the 'objective deduction' Kant raised the really fundamental question, which he could quite as well, and indeed far better, have raised independently—the question as to the meaning and the source of this term 'category.' It means, he tells us, "the function of synthesizing into a definite unity the manifold items of a given intuition"—*given*, and therefore sensory. Such function, since it involves not only form but content, is beyond the range of formal logic; for that ignores content altogether. So he came to distinguish what he called 'transcendental logic' from 'general logic'—a distinction which unfortunately he often forgot. Now comes the question as to the source of this function. It is due to the subject of experience as self-conscious, is his answer: in his own terminology to "the original synthetic unity of apperception" involved in all judgments when we say 'I think.' At the

---

[1] On this point the excellent remarks of Lotze (*Metaphysik* (1879), *Einleitung*, § xii) are to be commended, little heeded though they have been.

self-conscious level, to the Self or Subject that *thinks*
there is a correlative not-Self which is the Object of
its *thought*. Hence the term '*objective* deduction.' In
this 'critical analysis' it is till assumed, as in the *Dissertation*, that the sensible and the intelligible are fundamentally distinct. But whereas this distinction seemed
then to reopen the way to the dogmatic realism of the
Leibniz-Wolffians, that way was closed for Kant by
further reflection as soon as he began the revision of
the *Dissertation*. He now calls his philosophy *Transcendental Idealism*, since he was at length convinced that
we have no knowledge of things in themselves at all,
but only of the presentations[1] to which they give rise.

It is on the basis of this 'transcendental idealism'
that Kant framed his main critical inquiry, and he did
so in a thoroughly Wolffian fashion. How, he asks, is
Experience *possible*? Volumes have been written on
Kant's different formulations of this question and their
implications. Yet on the whole its meaning is fairly
plain, provided we remember that the kind of experience Kant had in view is Experience involving
universal and necessary laws, and further, that he made
the quite unwarrantable assumption that we have in
fact any experience of this sort. The question, *as a
question*, then becomes simple enough: *How is this fact
intelligible?* And from the standpoint of Kant's transcendental idealism—supposing *that to be granted*—the
answer is also simple. Things *per se* have provided us
with nothing but the stuff, yet here we are with an
a priori science of nature. This, *ex hypothesi*, things *per se*
have not given us. But if those *a priori* laws were not
given to us, we must then conclude that they were
imposed by us. It was in putting forward this new
answer to the problem which those, he contended, who
failed to distinguish between phenomena and noumena

[1] *Study*, § 8, pp. 49 ff.

could not solve, that Kant compared himself to Copernicus. As Copernicus had simplified the description of
celestial motions by relating them to the sun instead
of to the earth, so Kant claimed to have simplified the
epistemological problem by substituting the understanding as the lawgiver to nature as we know it, in
place of things *per se* which we do not know at all.

But after all Copernicus was mistaken if he supposed
that the whole problem of the celestial motions was to
decide between the two alternatives, viz., that either
the sun or the earth was at rest. It was soon discovered
that both were in motion. And so too Kant was certainly mistaken, when he assumed, as he did assume,
that the epistemological problem was an antithetic one.
Fairly obvious considerations suffice to shew that this
standpoint could not be maintained; and in fact Kant
did not sustain it[1]. None the less this position is founded
on the great truth which he was himself the first effectively to enounce as the supreme principle in the development of all knowledge, the activity of the experient subject itself. This we may mark down as the
fifth and central *Lehrstück* in his philosophy.

Such activity, however, is present not only at the
self-conscious level; it is present even at the lower level
of mere perception. But Kant ignored this fact in the
first part of the *Critique*, the so-called *Aesthetik*, on which
his transcendental idealism is based. He did so, he
said, to simplify his exposition: anyhow he admitted it
fully later on, and that is enough. But one important
point Kant altogether overlooked, in consequence of
his piecemeal fashion of regarding experience. Experience is not merely cognitive: it is always conative
as well. As I have said elsewhere, "in our intercourse
with the external world we have limbs which the Ego
controls as well as senses which the non-Ego affects."[2]

[1] Cp. *Study*, §§ 9–11. [2] *Study*, p. 83.

The fundamental fact of experience, in a word, is the interest taken in, and not merely the bare presence of, this non-Ego. An adequate statement of Kant's central truth must then include both these facts, if the full meaning of experience and its development is ever to be understood. But the non-Ego has no interest in us: it faces all alike with a sublime indifference. The relation of the two is then not symmetrical in any respect[1]. Further, no experient is interested in all that confronts him, and no two experients therefore react in precisely the same way. What I have called 'subjective selection' seems, then, to be also implied in Kant's central truth. This, I may observe, was clearly recognized by Leibniz in assigning to every monad a unique standpoint from which "it mirrored the universe." All these points were as yet ignored by Kant, though all seem to be involved in his central truth, and moreover all came gradually to light in a more or less fragmentary fashion, in *Bruchstücke*, as his critical enterprise moved on. And we shall have to deal with them very soon.

Meanwhile let us look back to see where Kant—more or less unbeknown to himself—has already brought us: very much nearer, I think it is, to the dogmatic position of his *Inaugural Dissertation* than he himself supposed. The most concrete of his real categories is the third, interaction (*Wechselwirkung*); for according to his own teaching it is the synthesis of the other two, substance and cause. Now the most fundamental interaction is that of subject and object, which we have just considered. Recalling Kant's distinction between formal and transcendental logic, we can now see that in talking of categories as denoting *functions* that pertain to the experient subject, he is thinking of

[1] Though Kant assumed that in one important respect it was; but the consequences for his philosophy were disastrous, as we may presently see. Cp. below, pp. 342 f.

what they really *mean*. To realize this is to realize that they cannot have their source in formal logic. We may abstract the form from the meaning, but we cannot derive the meaning from the form. This is again clear from Kant's admission—referred to just now—that at the perceptual level there is subjective synthesis, though all *knowledge* of categories is then lacking.

Therein is involved another fundamental distinction of Kant's, which it will repay us to consider for a moment. In the *Critique* it appears as the distinction between empirical and transcendental apperception. The former implies only subjective or individual experience, which varies from one experient to another; whereas the latter implies the objective or universal Experience *par excellence*, which is the same for all. In the *Prolegomena* this distinction appears as that between what are called 'judgments of perception' and 'judgments of Experience.' But there is experience in some sense in both: in the first it is subjective, individual, and perceptual; in the second it is objective, universal, and categorical. Plainly, however, though there may be this so-called subjective experience without the objective, the converse is impossible. Kant's central truth, then, is alike fundamental in both. We have only to interpret Kant's *Ich denke* as Descartes did his *Cogito* (= *Co-agito*) and we then see at once that this is the case[1].

This distinction interests us in yet another way. It leads us to inquire how this higher level of experience was attained—a question which Kant, with the want of historical sense characteristic of his time, never

[1] The example that Kant used in the *Prolegomena* is instructive. Here the very same objective situation, the sunlight and warmth which prompt a lizard to come out of his hole, leads a physicist *after experimenting* to infer that the sun is the cause of the warmth. But he, when he began life, started with the lizard. Cp. *Study*, pp. 72 f.

raised at all[1]. He was content with the hard and fast
line that Plato had already drawn between sensibility
and intelligence; and this plainly was an effectual bar
to such an inquiry. Had Kant but sought for the
source of the distinction between sensible and individual, intelligible and universal, another 'great light'
might have dawned upon him, as in fact it was actually
dawning on his former pupil, Herder, about this time.
He might have seen that transcendental apperception
is bound up with trans-subjective intercourse, and again
that in this discourse of mind with mind, 'winged words'
were the medium, so that at length λόγος came meto-
nymically to mean *that* pure reason which Kant was
essaying to criticize as the basis of experience[2].

This leads us finally to inquire what exactly the relation is between Kant's central truth and this pure
reason, which constitutes the *a priori* factor indispensable if universal and necessary laws are to be
found in Experience. His answer is on the whole, I
think, clear. A single sentence from the preface to the
second edition of the *Critique* may now suffice to shew
this. "We assume," he there says[3], "that we know
a priori of things only what we ourselves put into them
(*in sie legen*)." Keeping to this we attain to what he
called 'immanent metaphysics.' The counterpart of
this, 'transcendent metaphysics,' in which the attempt
is made to treat of things *per se*, is what he is intent on
refuting. It will be thought, I fear, somewhat rash to
say so, but I must confess that to me an immanent
metaphysics limited to the projection on to the Object
of attributes pertaining to the Subject—more exactly,

[1] It is true that he did attempt in what he called 'the subjective deduction' of the categories to analyse it from the standpoint of the current individualistic psychology; and he was aware
that his attempt was unsatisfactory, but he did not see why. Cp.
Study, p. 59.
[2] Cp. *Study*, pp. 187 f.   [3] *Critique*, 1787, p. xviii.

the interpretation of the World in terms of the Self—
is just anthropomorphism. Yet what other construction can we put on Kant's Copernican hypothesis?
Moreover—as I have just tried to shew—Kant himself
more or less unconsciously furnishes ample justification
for deriving the real categories from what the Subject
knows of itself at the social or self-conscious level.

In passing from the categories of the understanding
to what he called the Ideas of the reason, we find Kant
is avowedly anthropomorphic[1]. These Ideas correspond to the three divisions of the Wolffian ontology,
known as rational psychology, rational cosmology, and
rational theology. An anthropomorphic interpretation
of the Self would be meaningless tautology. In the case
of the World which confronts us as an interacting
plurality, the only anthropomorphism possible is to
interpret that plurality as consisting of experients,
i.e., of objects which are also 'ejects'—to employ a
useful term that has at last found its way into our
language. And this is just what the primitive mind
does. To this primitive ejectification or personification
Leibniz's monadology is clearly akin; and this doctrine
Kant shared, as a 'private opinion' at all events,
throughout his many *Umkippungen*, and in the end he
openly espoused it. As to his Idea of God—this was
as anthropomorphic as it is possible to be in view of
our finitude and the Supreme Being's infinite perfection. In other words God for him was what Lotze
called a perfect person; this perfection being for us a
pure Ideal, altogether surpassing all the limitations of
finite beings.

In the *Critique* of *Reason as practical*, we come upon
new categories, categories of value or axiological categories as they are now technically termed. Here moral
obligation with its categorical imperative or absolute

[1] Cp. *Study*, § 13, pp. 88 ff.

'ought,' not only puts the reality of freedom beyond question, but also—in Kant's opinion—justifies us in postulating the existence of God, the Supreme Reality that, for theoretical reason, was only 'a flawless Ideal.' But, as I have said elsewhere, "a postulate essential to the realization of what we ought to be, yet based not on what we know but on what we are, is surely nothing if it is not anthropomorphic."[1] There are other points in this *Critique* to which we must return presently. Meanwhile the last *Critique* is the more important in respect of the anthropomorphic tenor of Kant's philosophy: so I propose now to pass on to that.

This *Critique* treats of the function of what Kant calls the faculty of judgment as distinct from the understanding. Logically regarded, the function of the judgment is to provide appropriate minor premisses for a given major; and in the transcendental philosophy all the major premisses are those of the fundamental principles of the understanding. Now an appalling problem arises when we reflect that those principles as universal and ultimate afford no guidance when the judgment comes to deal with the bewildering multiplicity of contingent particulars that actually confront us. How are these to be subsumed continuously and systematically in accordance with those principles? They themselves afford no help: subsumption is not their business. The problem is one for the judgment alone to solve, and random ventures will be no better than playing blind-man's-buff. The judgment then must have some clue or it could never venture on what is else obviously a hopeless task. An assumption is therefore made, and it is this—that just as *our* understanding has prescribed universal *a priori* laws to Nature, so an understanding *not* ours has prescribed that Nature

[1] *Study*, § 13, p. 93.

shall specify its general laws in accordance with the
forms of a logical system (or classification) for the
benefit of the judgment—tempering Nature to it as
the wind is tempered to the shorn lamb, as we might
say. Criticism of this arbitrary and inconsistent attempt
to bring induction within the range of the *a priori* is
not my concern now. I refer to it only as an instance
of what seems to me to be anthropomorphism. Kant
calls this assumption which the judgment is driven to
make a principle of purposiveness (*Zweckmässigkeit*),
but urges that after all, though *a priori*, it is only regulative for the reflecting judgment, and does not pre-
tend to be constitutive of things. But surely that is
only to emphasize its anthropomorphic character.

But it is with judgment about judgments (*Beur-
theilung*) in a more restricted sense that the two loosely
connected parts of this *Critique* are occupied. Some
reference to its origin will then be here in place. In
1788, having his two earlier *Critiques* lying before him,
Kant realized that a link was wanting to connect them.
In the one he had ascertained the *a priori* principles of
cognition, in the other those of conduct: in the one
the concept of Nature was supreme, in the other the
concept of Freedom. But as such they had nothing
in common; and though so far he had not sought for
a principle to connect them, yet he was sure that such
a principle there must be. Now Tetens, in his *Philosophical Essays*, had recently formulated the trichotomy
of the mental powers, placing feeling as independent,
yet intermediate, between cognition and conation. This
new doctrine Kant had accepted as true in fact. He
recognized that to feeling our interest in what we know
is due, and that it is this interest which moves us to act.
The empirical fact, however, was not enough for Kant;
but if he could find an *a priori* feeling, a feeling, that
is to say, which is necessary and universal, therein

might lie the principle which he had missed. Such a feeling he believed the 'sense of the beautiful' to be.

He proceeded accordingly to analyse the state of mind when an object is appreciated as beautiful. He found the essential feature consisted always in a certain 'form': beauty, in short, was just 'unity in variety,' as Francis Hutcheson, for instance, had already said. This form gives rise to a free play of the imagination which the understanding can control, and the *effect* of this facile interplay of both faculties as quickened by their mutual accord is æsthetic pleasure. Being formal, it is the same for all; and in this respect it is *a priori*, though what calls it forth is objectively contingent. It is solely because of this adaptation to us that we talk of the beauties of natural objects—crystals, flowers, and the like. Here again a kindred spirit greeting our own suggests itself; and this again I take to be anthropomorphic[1]. The connexion with the reflective judgment was an afterthought of Kant's which filled him with delight, and it led to what is perhaps the most wonderful, and not the least fanciful, of his many systematic diagrams[2].

In the second part of this *Critique*, however, the reflective judgment as teleological is fundamental, and it is in this part that Kant completes his philosophical *Lehrgebäude*. But I can deal with it here only very summarily. Final causes are now the problem. They force Kant to take into account a wider view of Nature than the rigidly mechanical view which dominated his first *Critique*: they lead him to distinguish from the 'external causes' to which that was confined, other 'internal causes,' which—so far as we can see—mechanism will not explain. We require '*at least one principle more*' to make these intelligible. Hitherto, in

[1] Cp. *Study*, § 15, pp. 105 f.
[2] Cp. his Introduction, § ix *fin.*, and *Study*, pp. 106 ff.

dealing with external causes, Newton had been a sufficient guide, but now Kant sets out by declaring that
the Newton of a blade of grass will never appear. If
at the outset Kant had been as familiar with biology
as he was with physics, if he had known Aristotle as
well as he knew Newton, he would have included
teleology as well as ætiology among his fundamental
principles. As it was, that very resourceful faculty, the
judgment, had somehow to obtain the new principle
required. Purposiveness (*Zweckmässigkeit*) is still its
stand-by. But this now means more than the 'subjective purposiveness,' as Kant termed it, which was
all that the sense of the beautiful implied: it now means
"causes working in a purposelike way," i.e., objective
ends (*Zwecke*). But how did the reflective judgment
come by this very different concept? The judgment,
it seems, works conformably to two maxims. The
understanding determines it so long as external causes
are concerned; but the understanding fails it when
internal causes have to be dealt with; reason then comes
to the rescue and prescribes a new maxim. This
maxim, as is appropriate where reason is concerned,
involves not concepts or categories, but an Idea. Now
what exactly is this Idea?

The start, it must be remembered, is from the empirical plane, to which the judgment, as dealing with
particulars, is confined. We observe, say, a caterpillar,
to take Kant's earliest instance of such particulars,
mentioned and then forgotten for thirty years[1]. Its
behaviour leads us anthropomorphically to regard it
as not merely an object but as also an eject. Then—to
quote the substance of Kant's own words—"prompted
by the infinity of such instances we are led on to assume
that design in the combination of natural causes is *the
universal principle* of the world." It is the Idea under-

[1] Cp. *Study*, p. 8.

lying this inductive assumption which converts it into an *a priori*, though only regulative, principle. Precisely in this way the teleological argument for the existence of God has arisen. That argument, however, *taken alone*, Kant rightly argues is really circular. The evidence of design in Nature points, it may be, towards, but it does not justify, the Idea of a Supreme Intelligence. But apart from all teleology reason, as we have seen, finds in human freedom a practical justification for postulating a realm of ends in which such a Supreme Being is sovereign. Consequently, by means of this "remarkable fact of human freedom," as Kant calls it, "reason can extend beyond the bounds within which every theoretical concept of nature must remain hopelessly confined." Hence reason alone can provide the judgment with the new maxim required. With those words, without indicating more precisely the Idea we have been seeking, Kant concluded this, his last *Critique*, last in the order of time but second in logical order, as he himself had said[1]. In returning presently to what was actually his second *Critique* we may there see more fully what this fact of human freedom means. But already in this, which now I must needs leave, the anthropomorphic vein running through Kant's philosophy is to me again apparent. It is in general to interpret the world in terms of ourselves, and here more especially to orientate the natural from the standpoint of the spiritual. But it all turns on the one cardinal truth contained in the transcendental unity of self-consciousness and what that involves. This was the inner core that gave his philosophy what coherence it had and made it the germ of the brilliant outburst of German culture in science and literature, as well as in philosophy, which followed upon it. I will cite only two witnesses out of many, and I will not

[1] Cp. his Introduction, § iii *fin.*

weaken their words by translation. Goethe, talking with Eckermann in 1827, said: "Kant ist der vorzüglichste, ohne allen Zweifel. Er ist auch derjenige, dessen Lehre sich fortwirkend erwiesen hat, und die in unsere deutsche Kultur am tiefsten eingedrungen ist."[1] And Jean Paul Richter: "Kant ist kein Licht der Welt, sondern ein ganzes strahlendes Sonnensystem auf einmal."

But alas! there was in Kant's system one *great* rift, a fatal one indeed, had he not himself been inconsistent enough incidentally and half unconsciously to heal it. I refer, of course, to his transcendental idealism, coupled as that was with the dualism which he strove to maintain between phenomena and things *per se.* That he had transcended it is evident from his doctrine of freedom (to which we may now return), and he transcended it in dropping by implication the sensationalism from which he started in his first *Critique.* On this ground I leave aside any discussion of this topic here, though I have tried to treat of it at some length elsewhere[2].

Returning then to the problem of Freedom, we find Kant treating of this in all three *Critiques.* In a general survey, the salient feature of the whole is the three different dualisms we meet with. I call them dualisms, because they are neither satisfactorily unified in themselves nor clearly connected with each other. They are the distinction (1) of *homo phaenomenon* and *homo noumenon*, (2) of sensible and intelligible character, and (3) of theoretical and practical reason. The first

---

[1] Cp. also E. Zeller, *Geschichte der deutschen Philosophie seit Leibniz,* 1873, pp. 515 ff.; F. Harms, *Die Philosophie seit Kant,* 1876, p. 282; Caird, *The Critical Philosophy of Immanuel Kant,* 1889, II, pp. 645 f.; W. Windelband, *Die Blütezeit der deutschen Philosophie,* 1907, p. 181.

[2] Cp. *Study,* §§ 21–24, pp. 139 ff.

emerges in the solution of the third antinomy of
rational cosmology—the antinomy supposed to arise
between the causality of nature and the causality of
freedom. The range of the understanding is limited to
occasional causes, causes which are in turn effects:
hence the naturalistic view of the world which finds
no place for freedom. And if the phenomenal world
were all, there could be, Kant allows, no place for
freedom. But reason, not content with an indefinite
regress of conditions, but insisting on the necessity for
an Unconditioned, recognizes the Idea of primary or
efficient causes; and as these imply freedom, freedom
is a legitimate Idea. This antinomy, it should be noted,
is cosmological, and the solution directly concerns the
world as a whole. Kant, however, did not hesitate—
as he ought to have done—to regard human freedom
as the main problem here. So we come upon this distinction of Man as phenomenal and as noumenal.

Whether Man is noumenal or not, he is certainly
phenomenal. Assuming that he is both we come upon
the second distinction, that of his sensible from his
intelligible character. The latter clearly will then
belong to him as an efficient cause outside the temporal series of the phenomenal—as *homo noumenon*, that
is to say. What of the former? Sometimes it seems to
be the effect which he produces in the phenomenal
series—the *operari* which discloses his *esse*, as Schopenhauer said. But for us in dealing with the world as a
whole there is theoretically according to Kant an impassable boundary separating phenomena from things
per se. But that boundary is crossed in the case of the
homo noumenon, if he is aware of his acts and intended
their overt effects. Obviously if he were not aware,
there would be an end of ethics. There is then here
no dualism, but there is a question as to how the two
are related. Sometimes, however, this distinction of

characters seems to refer to man's nature as both sentient and intelligent. But in that sense it cannot be said that a man's sentient nature is the effect of his intelligent nature. And yet Kant does seem to assume this; for, starting from the intelligent character, he maintains it to be impossible in any particular case to explain why the intelligible character should give the empirical character which it does. But, as already said, in a particular case they cannot be sharply resolved into two, and when we consider individuals historically, as Kant never does, it is past question that the sensible precedes the intelligible character, which is in fact only possible at the trans-subjective level, and then not till the man comes to realize his human personality.

As to the dualism of theoretical and practical reason —whereas the theoretical reason shews that *transcendental* freedom is legitimate as an Idea, practical reason is content to abide by *practical* freedom as actual fact. In that case, according to Kant's use of 'pure' as equivalent to 'independent of everything empirical,' there should be no talk of pure *practical* reason, and no call for a *Critique of reason* in this sense. This is the dualism we have now very briefly to consider. The disparity between the two is obscured by Kant's puerile attempt to force the exposition of his ethical principles into the Procrustean bed of his '*architectonic*': thereby the semblance of criticizing pure reason in both cases is kept up. The source of this dualism is just the bad psychology responsible for so many of Kant's mistakes. According to that Understanding (which as a generic term includes reason) is one faculty, and Will is another with which it has nothing in common[1]. If the 'domains' of the two, to use his own terms, were

---

[1] Hence in fact the gap that he discovered later on and found Feeling to bridge over. Cf. above, p. 339.

'co-ordinate' and in no way connected, each would be simply foreign to the other. However, Kant maintains that they are not co-ordinate; that practical reason has the primacy. What Kant, in asserting this primacy, has in mind—though more or less obscurely, at the back of his mind, as we say—is a great truth of the very first importance, a truth which, by the way, Fichte realized as Kant never did. What exactly is this truth? It is just his own central truth, the unity of the complete self at the level of social intercourse, when conscience emerges and the experient subject becomes a person and autonomous.

And now I must attempt in a few words to make a final summary. Kant belonged to the *Aufklärung*, and, moreover, put an end to it for others; but he failed even to the last to get altogether beyond it himself. In his efforts to get more light from any quarter, his early interest in science brought him into contact with empiricism, although he began to study philosophy in the school of the rationalist, Christian Wolff. Having thus a foothold in each of these one-sided extremes, the outcome of his philosophy, and a great one too, was a successful synthesis embracing what was true in both. "All our knowledge begins with experience: about that there can be no doubt." In this, the first sentence of his *Critique*, the truth there is in empiricism is recognized. But he continues: "It does not therefore follow that all our knowledge springs entirely from experience: it may be a complex to which the mind has contributed something from itself." Something; but not as much as rationalism assumed in basing all philosophy on the so-called logical laws of thought. Unhappily, however, Kant never completely emancipated himself from the bias which this rationalism had imparted, though at one time he got very near it; but devotion to his '*architectonic*' foreclosed this possibility for ever. Again, for

some reason or other—possibly in consequence of his
familiarity with physical science—Kant had a very
mean opinion of psychology. Instead of trying to make
it better, he was content to take what he found ready
to his hand, the old faculty psychology. Here again
he only made bad worse by inventing new faculties
as often as he thought one necessary. What was worst
of all, he accepted without examination the doctrine
of an 'inner sense,' current in the psychology of his
time.

In spite of these drawbacks, he made it clear once
for all, I think, that the method of mathematics, its
formal exactness notwithstanding, cannot be the
method of philosophy. Further, he made it clear that
mathematics derives this exactness primarily from intuition and not from thought. Finally, he also made
it clear, as a consequence of his central truth, that
valid metaphysics must be immanent, not transcendent.
But he erred in sundering the real from the phenomenal—this as a consequence of his transcendental
idealism and that Achilles' heel of his philosophy, the
thing *per se.* Another defect in Kant's entire *Weltanschauung* was his want of what we call 'historical sense.'
In spite of occasional speculations on evolutionary lines,
he tended to regard the whole world as ready-made,
and Man as created in full possession of the powers
which it took ages to attain. Like Milton's Adam,
Kant's *homo noumenon* started capable of discussing with
an archangel the problem of "fixed fate, free-will,
fore-knowledge absolute."

But the great motive of Kant's endeavour was to
establish 'immutable morality.' "The origin of the
Critical Philosophy is in Morality—responsibility for
actions" was found written on one of his 'loose leaves.'
Even his theology is an '*ethico*-theology.' Of that side
of theology which Schleiermacher, for instance, de-

veloped, Kant had little or nothing to say. He was not an emotionally religious man. He apostrophizes Duty in sublime words as the mainspring of action even for God. Over his tomb in the cathedral of Königsberg are appropriately inscribed the two things which filled his mind with awe—"the starry heavens above me, the moral law within me."

XII

THE CHRISTIAN IDEAS OF FAITH
AND ETERNAL LIFE

THESE are two fundamental ideas of Christianity which, in my opinion, are very commonly misconceived: Faith being regarded as something essentially intellectual and Eternal Life as something to be realized only beyond the grave. Now in the currency of thought, as in that of commerce, we find 'bad money driving out good,' concepts—in which only the letter survives—being tendered as if they still retained the spirit which 'giveth life.' That a debasement of this sort has befallen these two connected verities in Jesus Christ's teaching is what I shall now try to shew.

1. Let us begin by asking what it is, strictly speaking, that is ordinarily meant by faith. First and foremost, faith is not regarded as cognitive; but rather, primarily as just conative and eventually volitional. So much, I think, psychology warrants us to affirm, and we have no need here to enter into details; but it may be worth while to state dogmatically the main facts. Life from beginning to end is a striving for self-conservation and betterment. At first there is only the venture of a primitive trustfulness in trying open possibilities—an instinct which precedes knowledge and is the chief means of acquiring and increasing it. Such is faith at the very outset of life. But gradually, as knowledge advances, this instinctive trustfulness is supplemented by intelligent prevision till at length, when the 'age of reason' is reached, definite ideals become ends, not peradventure but through deliberate resolve.

The highest of these ends, I think we may say, is that which possesses[1] the man who has a Christian's faith; for it is an 'enthusiasm' involving the greatest transformation—a transvaluation of all his values—that a human being can undergo. To estimate it, if we know nothing of it by direct experience, we ought—if we are open-minded—to judge of it by the lives and the language of those who, for themselves, do know the peace and strength which this 'new birth,' as they well call it, has brought to them[2]. Impressive pictures might be drawn of what such men and women were in themselves and of what they accomplished for the world. In contemplating such facts we ought not to forget that it was 'the full assurance of their faith' in the indwelling presence and power of the Divine Spirit, to which both were unanimously ascribed. There are honest men among us to whom the ideas about God in the Christian creeds are as truly anthropomorphic fictions as were the graven images of Him made by our heathen forefathers. Anthropomorphic doubtless they both are—idols and ideals alike—though the former are merely childish while the latter have been held to embody the flawless ideal of reason. But the lives and works of the saints who 'walked by faith not by sight' are not ideas but facts historically of the same order as those inspired by other noble yet less sublime

[1] I use this expression advisedly, having in mind the Christian doctrine of grace, with which, however, it is beside my purpose here to deal.

[2] To them, we must remember, this 'regeneration' is not a metaphor but a veritable fact. "Old things are passed away . . . all things are become new." Like the metamorphosis of the crawling caterpillar into the perfect insect with wings, "behold! it is a new creation"—the highest phase of creative evolution that we know. I have dwelt at length on this point elsewhere, and would now only urge that nothing less is an adequate description of what this 'new birth' means and the position it has in the scale of life.

ideals, facts such as nobody questions. The motives in the two cases are indeed very different: those of the one we may all understand, for they concern the seen and temporal; whereas those of the other do not; and so are beyond belief to many, who remain without the pale in which they spring. We may, indeed, reasonably discredit certain secondary, and—possibly, abnormal —accompaniments of religious faith in the past and even now: such are called over-beliefs or *Aberglaube*, and are incidental to our inevitable anthropomorphism. But these are not the one thing essential, nor the source whence the new life is derived. Ignorance of that source is not a reason for denying this, the life which flows from it. An analogy may perhaps here be helpful. Those born blind do not doubt what vision enables us to know and to do; nor, though they are themselves unable to conceive *what* this sense they lack can be, do they for a moment question *that* we have it. Such in regard to Christian faith, I think, should be the position of the agnostic. He does not know what it is, and cannot account for what it enables those whom it possesses to do; and yet their lives in fact are there as its fruit. And, though this is not the time to urge it, those lives are perhaps the chief among the evidences for Christianity. It was, however, one that Paley ignored altogether.

2. We come now to the Christian idea of eternal life. We cannot here set out from facts: the question we have to consider is largely one of documentary evidence. It is beset, no doubt, with collateral difficulties and to these we shall have to refer presently; but in dealing with the main question we may be brief. If we start from the sayings of Jesus in the Synoptic Gospels, the words 'eternal life,' which occur but five times, may seem to refer to a life to come which may be gained or lost. The phrase 'Kingdom of heaven' or

'Kingdom of God,' however, is frequent; and this Kingdom is continually described as present now, wherever the new life of faith has begun; though it is present only as the seed and promise of what 'the full corn in the ear' will be; and this Kingdom is identified with eternal life (cp. Mark x, 17–25). When, however, we turn to the fourth gospel and to the Pauline and Johannine epistles it is the *present possession* of this life by all who love God, far more than its future fruition, that is asserted and reiterated in the plainest terms. There is, however, no need for me to refer now in detail to this evidence: it has been already exhibited fully by recent writers[1]: one or two citations then will here suffice. According to the Evangelist, personal acquaintance with God (γνῶσις)—called in later times, 'God-consciousness'—is already eternal life (Jn. xvii, 3); and hereafter, according to John the Apostle, when we shall see Him as He is, we know that we shall be like Him (1 Jn. iii, 2). As to St Paul—the contrast which he draws, in his epistle to the Romans, between the old life and the new would lose all its point, if both alike did not belong to persons living in the present world; and it is this new life that he calls 'eternal' (Rom. vi, 22, 23). St Paul too recognized that this eternal life is one of development and progress. "For now we see in a mirror, darkly; but then face to face; now I know in part, but then shall I know fully" (1 Cor. xiii, 12). In short we miss the meaning of 'eternal' in the New Testament, if we associate it with time at all, and especially if we interpret it as referring simply to a future life everlasting. The one sure way to have eternal life 'more abundantly' hereafter is to

[1] Cp. E. Caird, *The Evolution of Religion*, 1893, ii, 146, 169 ff., 241 ff.; F. von Hügel, *Eternal Life, a Study*, 1912, ch. v; Dean Inge, *Outspoken Essays* (2nd series), 1922, pp. 38 ff.; and especially J. Oman, *Grace and Personality*, 2nd ed., 1919, pt. iii, ch. viii.

have it actually now; and the Christian view—whether it be true or not—is and always has been that, as Jesus taught, the soul possessed by Christian faith already has eternal life and is a member of the Kingdom of God— a realm of ends higher than that of Nature or of Mind as the natural sciences and psychology describe them.

3. But is there verily any such Kingdom of God: is that not a purely mystical idea, lacking altogether in objectivity? In that case it would be idle to talk further about Christian ideas at all. This question, then, is one which we cannot entirely ignore; yet to attempt a full discussion of it now is impossible. I must try to put a few main points briefly, though it will be hard to be concise and at the same time clear. The difficulty lies here. When we trust and love our fellow man we know him as a person distinct from ourselves: we are individuated from each other by our bodies. But how when we talk of trusting and loving God? "The long-standing inability to distinguish between the characters of an experience as a temporal inner state and the characters of its object has cost religion much," a recent writer has said[1]. It has certainly cost the philosophy of religion much. Volumes have been written in our time on the psychology of religious experience, but few, if any of them, have held fast to what, as I think, is fundamental to any experience at all—the duality of subject and object. It is from this that we must start. Whenever we talk of experience we imply (1) a subject aware of an object then and there present and confronting it, whereby (2) it is affected, and to which (3) it actively responds. In no case can such immediate experience be shared by another; and as to the experient himself, all he can say is that the object is 'given' to him, and does not

[1] W. E. Hocking, *The Meaning of God in Human Experience*, 1912, p. 353.

emanate from him. On the other hand, he never confounds it either with the feeling it has occasioned or with the reaction to which this feeling leads. In a word, subject and object, though always related in every experience, are also always distinct.

Our experience, however, does not stop at this private, immediate, or sensory level. It advances to some acquaintance and intercourse with our fellowmen, as soon as we begin to interpret their behaviour in terms of our own. In this way mankind has attained to a certain steadily increasing sympathetic *rapport* between one man and another. But this mutual understanding and co-operation, though it is physically mediated, cannot be physically explained; and the further our advance on this higher or intellectual level, the more obvious its physical inexplicability becomes[1]. And, in fact, instruments or means never explain the ends which they subserve. This new level of experience has also been called trans-subjective, since it is no longer exclusively private and immediate, but enables the individual subject to participate in a *common* intellectual world. Of this world the lowest or sensory level of experience gives no hint and the lower animals never get so far. *And yet it is there.* Then, may there not also be a yet higher—we may call it a spiritual world —which mere intelligence cannot discern? Nevertheless, we may have hints of it from other sides of our being, for intellect is neither the only nor the highest of human 'faculties.' And surely we find such hints —truths that wake to perish never, noble deeds long done that never die, things of beauty that are a joy for ever! All these have a meaning and value for us, which are quite beyond the purview of science[2]. Yet

---

[1] This is a point of vital importance, which naturalistic thinkers constantly overlook.

[2] Cp. W. R. Sorley, *Moral Values and the Idea of God*, 1918, pp. 286 ff.

none the less they too are there; and we have come to
call them 'the true, the beautiful and the good'—
eternal values; for they are not temporal events. And
again the intelligence which enables us to express this
appreciation does not explain it, and is not its source.

And now what are we to say of religion, for it also
belongs to this domain? At first, merely a vague sense
of a 'something beyond' and a feeling of helpless dependence—and this much is found among men everywhere[1]—at length religion culminates in the Christian's
faith in an indwelling presence as the source of a new
life of peace and power—an experience without any
sense of vagueness or isolation. The 'something beyond,' the 'not ourselves' has become for him a divine
Personality, anthropomorphically so regarded indeed;
for we can none of us understand what a person neither
finite nor changeable can be. But a personality appre-
ciative of the eternal values is the highest that we
know; and we can hardly suppose that the divine
Personality of whose presence the genuine Christian is
assured—if it is anything at all—is not something higher
(not something lower) than this. But that it must
be something and a something beyond himself is evi-
denced already by the childish anthropomorphisms of
the savage which the Christian has outgrown. It is
the *object* of his faith, and of its supreme reality he is
convinced by the love which it awakens and the new
life which it imparts. At the same time it is not an
object mediated by the senses or by thought. As to the
senses, he may say with Tennyson: It is "closer to us
than breathing and nearer than hands and feet." As
to thought, he may say with Kant that reason leaves
room for faith and postulates the Idea of God; though
it cannot prove that he exists. On the whole we are

[1] Cp. J. B. Pratt on 'Mana' in *The Religious Consciousness*, 1918,
pp. 286 ff.

led even as psychologists to the Graeco-Pauline doctrine of the threefold nature of man as body, soul and spirit. It is at the last or highest level that we all find the eternal values, and that the Christian's faith finds God, and enjoys already "the peace which passeth all understanding," the beginning of eternal life. It is true that all this is beyond the reach of the 'natural man.' But that no more proves its unreality than the inability of the brute to reach to our common intellectual world is any argument for denying the reality of that.

I may now pass to my contention that in the course of time these inspiring ideas of primitive Christianity have been supplanted or overlaid by others altogether lacking in their religious value or their power to 'overcome the world.'

4. First, as to Christian faith—wherein lay this power to overcome the world? In that 'enthusiasm of humanity,' it is replied, that love for mankind which animated Jesus and was by his example so conspicuously quickened and deepened in his immediate followers. It was a matter of character and life, i.e., of the whole personality, not merely of cognition or intellectual belief. Unhappily it soon became only too easy to attack the over-beliefs which gathered round it and to ignore the living faith even when it was there. This line the agnostic has adopted and, as I have said, it was an easy one. It was provided for him by the course of events in the history of Christianity, by the development of its doctrines, and by its ritual and its ecclesiastical polity. Compare Christendom as we see it to-day with what Christianity was when its founder surrounded by a little band of disciples was followed by crowds who adored his presence and heard him gladly: must we not confess that the living spring of new life in its purest and simplest form—the noumenal reality, if I may so say—is now obscured, nay, half-

smothered, by what we may call phenomenal accretions? The evolution of Christendom, as of all things
with which men have to do, has not been orthogenetic.
Though I am at present proposing to discuss its deviations and back-slidings, I do not forget that it has
nevertheless advanced civilization on the whole far
beyond its level at the beginning of our era. But
merely to enumerate the many untoward circumstances
which have delayed its progress or the many conflicting
doctrines that have perturbed its peace is beyond my
competence and our present limits. Still, to help in
establishing my case, I should like to refer to one or
two points under the several heads just mentioned.

It will be best to begin with the 'winds of doctrine.'
Already before the New Testament canon was closed,
philosophical ideas were mingled with the simple
teaching of Jesus as recorded in the Synoptic gospels.
There is, for example, nothing in these of the Pauline
antitheses between the first and the last Adam or of
an incarnate Logos akin to that of the Alexandrian
Jew, Philo, a contemporary of Jesus himself. In these
there were doubtless elements of genuine development.
But through the same channels came also the so-called
heresies and consequent schisms associated with such
terms as Gnosticism, Manichaeism, Arianism, Pela-
gianism, etc.—some eighty were enumerated by Augustine. Whereas Jesus had simply bidden his disciples
to go into all the world and preach his gospel to the
whole creation, so letting their light shine before men,
that seeing their good works, they might glorify their
Father in heaven—what do we find as the salient
characteristic of the history of doctrine during the first
four centuries of our so-called Christian era? As one
Church historian relates: "Under the sons of Constantine, Christian bishops in numberless synods cursed
one another, turn by turn," "denying to each other,"

23-2

as another has said, "the name of Christian, and even the hope of salvation." Even in our day the so-called creed of Athanasius consigning Arians to everlasting perdition is still ordered to be said or sung in the Established Church. But it will be convenient at this point to turn for a while to the course of events in the world outside, which enables us to account further for the debasement of religious faith.

The decline and fall of the Roman Empire brought the invading barbarian hordes within the pale of Christendom. Unlike the Greek and Latin converts, they were intellectual babes without ideas to amalgamate with, and perhaps to obscure, the new Light presented to them. And if we may judge, for example, by what is known of the character of Ulfilas, the great missionary to the Goths, it was that '*light*' which converted them, not his Arian creed which then and for centuries after was rending the Churches. And we may say too that it was not the controversial zeal of St Athanasius, but his personal piety and Christian life which secured for him in his many exiles the unshaken devotion of all classes, even when a high price was set upon his head. For, as I have said, in those dark ages the conflicting dogmas of Greek and Roman Christianity were too unintelligible to give rise to "diversity of opinion on curious points"—to use the language of the Prayer Book: all such dogmas alike were then mysteries beyond the laity's concern. They could feel the superiority to their uncouth deities of war and thunder, not of a god whose unique attribute was omnipotence—that alone is far from an alluring attribute[1]

[1] The phrase Almighty God, so frequent in the Old Testament, never occurs in the New save once in a quotation from the Old (1 Cor. xi, 18) and in the Apocalypse. In the English Prayer Book it is almost invariable. References to such 'worship' as mere power evokes again are never applied to the Christian's spiritual devotion to the Heavenly Father.

—but of One who was their heavenly Father, who out of love sent his Son to save the world. They could appreciate the parables of Jesus about the prodigal son and the good Samaritan; and in the life and works of the messengers he sent to them they saw the manifestation of his spirit and came to put their trust in him. If, however, as time went on, here and there one did chance to inquire, he would be told, as he is often told still, that "the intellectual duty of a Christian is to resist the natural tendency of his reason and believe what he is told."[1]

But things did not stop here. Initiatory rites and sacrificial offerings conducted by priests specially ordained for the purpose were features common to most forms of religion, and Christianity was not altogether an exception. The observance of two 'sacraments' Jesus enjoined upon his followers. How far he intended that these should be administered by persons specially 'consecrated' is a question on which commentators still differ. One thing, I think, is certain: there was nothing strictly sacerdotal in primitive Christianity, and the Apostles were never called priests. Some organization there must be in every community: the appointment of deacons as described in the Acts of the Apostles was due to this. But the rise which occurred later of a so-called 'hierarchy,' i.e., orders of men ceremoniously set apart and therefore to be revered as holy, men who were entitled as his vicars on earth to intervene between their one heavenly Father and the rest of their brethren, from whom, as mere laymen, they differentiated themselves—this, I cannot refrain from saying, has always struck me as the first and most serious rift that befell the Christian ideal of the Kingdom of God on earth. No doubt these *soi-disant* priests

[1] Father Knox as quoted in an article, 'Spiritual Evolution,' *Hibbert Journal*, Jan. 1924, p. 322.

in the early days of persecution were for the most part sincere, devout and earnest men, who helped rather than hindered their brethren in leading Christlike lives. But it was far otherwise when persecutions ceased. For the decline did not stop with the rise of sacerdotalism either.

A further lapse from the ideal of Jesus very soon followed. In the fourth century the civil power exchanged ineffectual persecution for political alliance, when that worldly but wily despot Constantine the Great professed to have been suddenly converted by the miraculous vision of a flaming cross. Thus it came about that, in place of rendering unto Caesar only the things that were Caesar's, things that were God's were likewise rendered to Caesar as well. And it was as Emperor that Constantine, who was not yet even baptized, summoned and largely controlled the great Council of Nicaea[1]. This second great lapse would have been impossible but for the first. An alliance between two merely human polities might well be to the advantage of both. But if such a proposal to serve two masters—as if to make the best of both worlds—had been made to the primitive church, it would have been met by the admonition of St Paul to the Corinthians: "Be not unequally yoked with unbelievers, for what fellowship hath righteousness with iniquity? or what communion hath light with darkness? And what concord hath Christ with Belial (or Antichrist)?" These very words were, in fact, afterwards appealed to—when the mischief was done—by the reformers who were striving to remedy it.

Owing to one or other of these two defections from the Christian ideal some of the earliest schisms had

---

[1] And according to the Articles of Religion of our Established Church, it is still enacted that "General Councils may not be gathered together without the commandment and will of Princes," Art. XXI.

arisen, the Novatian and Donatist, for instance: in this connexion Tertullian's question, *Quid est imperatori cum ecclesia?* will occur to many. And almost all the schisms after the fourth century might be characterized as revolts against this secularization of the church, and as such were persecuted by ecclesiastical authority as ruthlessly as the primitive Christians had been persecuted by the pagan emperors, Decius and Diocletian —to say nothing of the addition of excommunication —the most terrible weapon of oppression ever devised. Among these so-called 'heretics' were the Albigenses, known as *bons chrétiens*, a title still more deserved by the Waldenses, who shared some of their tenets and the same heartless persecution. Following these were the Lollards, the Hussites and the Moravian brethren, to whom John Wesley attributed his conversion—all alike striving to revive the living faith of the primitive church, their very persecutions testifying how completely it had been lost. Last of all—unless we take account of our own Nonconformists and the disabilities to which they were long subject—there came the great protest of Martin Luther and the happy, though still imperfect, Reformation, embracing half of Europe, which followed in its train. I do not propose to enlarge on 'the luxury, simony, and cruelty,' that put the name of Christ to open shame during all this time, nor to describe in detail what 'the plain man's religion in the middle ages' came to be[1]. The central defect of that was the debased idea of the eternal life which Jesus and his apostles had preached. To this defect then we may now pass.

5. This eternal life, as I have already said, came to be regarded as a state that only begins after death; and it is too commonly so regarded still. Accordingly

[1] Cp. G. G. Coulton's *Mediaeval Studies*, No. 13, 1916, and *Hibbert Journal*, xiv, 592 ff.

repentance even *in articulo mortis* was, and is, held sufficient to secure it. Hence perhaps the supplication in the Anglican litany to be delivered from sudden death. Hence, at any rate, the practice said to prevail among Sicilian peasants of praying in the name of 'the holy gallows-birds[1], i.e., criminals who, having confessed their crime and being absolved by a priest, were nevertheless forthwith launched into the next world by the public executioner on account of it. And surely such a practice was logical enough, if we are to believe that baptized persons, whatever their lives may have been, who on their deathbed make "a special confession of their sins" are to be "absolved from all their sins" by the priest in virtue of "the authority committed to him."[2] Not how a man lived but how he died thus naturally came to be the supremely important thing: so far, all was well that ended well[3]. But *poenitentia sera raro vera*; and in fact the worthlessness of such tardy repentance has long been a by-word: "When the devil is sick the devil a monk would be, when the devil gets well, the devil a monk is he."[4] Even with those who believe themselves to have repented by times, who regularly '*say* their prayers,' go to church and keep the ten commandments, their main religious concern is the *safety* of their own souls. So they sing:

> When I can read my title clear
> To mansions in the skies,
> I'll bid farewell to every fear, etc.

[1] Cp. G. G. Coulton, *op. cit.*
[2] Cp. the Anglican 'Order for the Visitation of the Sick.'
[3] To be sure, according to the Church of Rome there must be some halt in purgatory, but this could be shortened, if the saying of masses on their behalf were paid for by their friends.
[4] In the middle ages to become a monk was to be converted and to lead the *vita religiosa*.

or:

> 'Tis a point I long to know,
> Oft it causes anxious doubt,
> Do I love the Lord or no?
> Am I his or am I not?

'Anxious inquirers' of this self-centred sort are never found among those truly regenerated by Christian faith and animated throughout their daily lives by the Christian Spirit. It was neither the hope of heaven nor the fear of hell that led them to love their heavenly Father. Love does not, nay cannot, spring from prudential motives, let them be what they may. Moreover, faith and love here go together, and no one can trust God and not love him or love him and not trust him.

6. But the profession of a creed is a poor substitute for the living faith of the New Testament; and a baptismal certificate to start with and priestly absolution on your death-bed are anything but a clear title to the fruition of eternal life as there understood. Yet, I ask again, are there not thousands of professing Christians who are content with this? Can we then say that religiously we have emerged from the dark ages? In fact, though we have had one religious reformation, many earnest men of our time have felt or are feeling that there is a crying need of another, and one more thorough. I can now refer only to very few. Even John Morley, discussing religious conformity, spoke of "some prophet to come who should unite sublime depth of feeling and lofty purity of life with strong intellectual grasp"; but whose gospel, he thought, could "hardly be other than an expansion, a development, a re-adaptation of all the moral and spiritual truth that lay hidden under the worn-out forms."[1] Again F. H. Bradley—acclaimed, till his lamented death a few

---

[1] *On Compromise*, 2nd ed., 1877, pp. 124 ff.

weeks ago, as the doyen of British philosophy—has said: "There is a need, and there is even a certain demand, for a new religion. We want a creed to recognize and justify in due proportion all human interests, and at the same time to supply the intellect with what it can hold with confidence. Whether we shall get this new religion, and if so, how, whether by modification of what exists or in some other way, I am unable," he says, "to surmise."[1] And a brave thinker still among us has said: "The future will shew whether civilization, as we know it, can be mended or must be ended. The times seem ripe for a new birth of religion and spiritual life, which may remould society as no less potent force would have the strength to do."[2] But what is wanted, I think, is not a new religion. "Let the human mind expand as much as it will," Goethe has somewhere said, "beyond the grandeur and moral elevation of Christianity, as it sparkles and shines in the Gospels, beyond that, the human mind will not advance."[3] I would say, need not advance; agreeing here with Martineau, "that Christianity, understood as the personal religion of Jesus Christ, stands clear of all perishable elements and realizes the true relation between man and God."[4] But, speaking as one whom you must regard as an outsider, I am amazed at the growing disparity between that Christianity and the Christendom of to-day. This seems to me, I confess, too much like salt that has lost its savour or leaven that has no longer the power to raise. I can see no hope of amendment without more earnest courage and more intellectual honesty than

---

[1] *Truth and Reality*, 1914, p. 446.

[2] Dean Inge, *Outspoken Essays*, 2nd series, 1922, p. 253.

[3] Quoted without a reference by Harnack in *What is Christianity?*, Eng. transl., 1904, p. 4.

[4] *The Seat of Authority in Religion*, 1890, p. 651.

the leaders of religious thought in our day for the most part display. "The Christian religion," as Harnack has said, "is a sublime and simple thing; it means one thing and one thing only: Eternal life in the midst of time, by the strength and under the eyes of God."[1] But nowadays it appears bedecked 'with gold, silver and costly stones,' the venal offerings of the worldly wise, or fenced in by 'wood, hay and stubble,' the erections of centuries of misguided dogmatism and superstition. By such various accretions its own inherent simplicity, sublimity and power are eclipsed till now large numbers, instead of being attracted to it, are either indifferent or perplexed, and some are even repelled.

Yet never, I believe, has a Christlike life failed to attract the unsophisticated and open-minded. This is the light the world still wants; and there is no substitute for it, be it dogma or hierarchy or state patronage. More than twenty years ago I ventured to say in a society consisting of bishops and statesmen, philosophers and men of science: "In so far as he lets his light shine and men see his good works, the religious man affords practical evidence of the worth of his faith. With enough of such light the survival of faith would be sure." And before writing this paper I came across a letter in the *Times* of Sept. 13, 1924, from which I cannot forbear to quote. "We cannot too often remind ourselves," the writer says, "that the force by which Christianity is most surely propagated is an individual life. When we have seen with our own eyes the loveliness of but one life guided by Christian values, we know what is meant by 'the beauty and winsomeness of Christ.'" This is the practical outcome of all I have now been trying to say.

Postscript. I am told I shall be expected to say some-

[1] *Op. cit.* p. 8.

thing positive concerning a future life. I have deliberately refrained from so doing. The one experience which we all lack is that of passing through the valley of the shadow of death. Vague analogies and dim surmises as to what may lie beyond it are then surely worthless so long as we have no empirical *evidence* that there is anything beyond at all. But an assurance—absolutely abolishing death and bringing life and incorruption to light—Christian *faith* is said to give to those who love God, those who live and work that his will may be done on earth as it is in heaven. This assurance, however, does not lift the veil dividing these two states of the divine kingdom: "it is not yet manifest what we shall be" is and always has been the confession of Christian faith. And this lack of knowledge has its advantage in confining our practical interests to this present world in which alone we are able to work[1]. For all that the true Christian has no misgivings. Eternal life in God is, as I have urged, two-sided; and, as Saint Augustine has somewhere said: "What does not perish for God cannot perish for itself." To regard this life, then, not as intrinsically valuable in itself, but as merely a means to some final perfection ever beyond and yet ceaselessly to be pursued, would, it seems to me, reduce eternal life for God and man alike to nothing better than an endless mirage[2].

[1] Cp. further on this important point, Kant's *Critique of Practical Reason*, II, ii, § 9, Abbott's transl., pp. 244–246.
[2] Cp. *The Realm of Ends*, 1911, pp. 475 f.; F. H. Bradley, *Truth and Reality*, 1914, p. 439.

INDEX TO THE ESSAYS

CAMBRIDGE: PRINTED BY W. LEWIS, M.A., AT THE UNIVERSITY PRESS

CPSIA information can be obtained at www.ICGtesting.com
Printed in the USA
LVOW080937180812

294893LV00004B/38/P

9 781163 193266